Houghton Mifflin
Mathematics

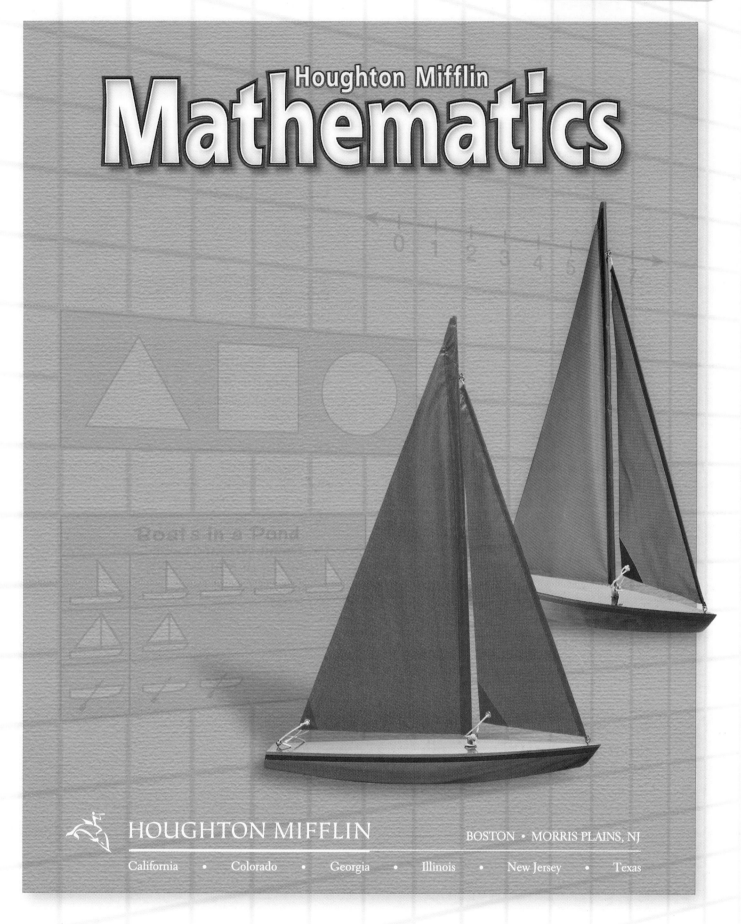

HOUGHTON MIFFLIN

BOSTON · MORRIS PLAINS, NJ

California · Colorado · Georgia · Illinois · New Jersey · Texas

ISBN-13: 978-0-618-08175-2
ISBN-10: 0-618-08175-5

16 17 18 19 20 -WC- 11 10 09 08 07

Authors

Senior Authors

Dr. Carole Greenes
Professor of Mathematics Education
Boston University
Boston, MA

Dr. Miriam A. Leiva
Distinguished Professor of
Mathematics, Emerita
University of North Carolina
Charlotte, NC

Dr. Bruce R. Vogeli
Clifford Brewster Upton Professor
of Mathematics
Teachers College, Columbia University
New York, NY

Program Authors

Dr. Matt Larson
Curriculum Specialist for Mathematics
Lincoln Public Schools
Lincoln, NE

Dr. Jean M. Shaw
Professor of Elementary Education
University of Mississippi
Oxford, MS

Dr. Lee Stiff
Professor of Mathematics Education
North Carolina State University
Raleigh, NC

Content Reviewers

Lawrence Braden (Grades 5–6)
Mathematics Teacher
St. Paul's School
Concord, NH

Dr. Don Chakerian (Grades 3–4)
Emeritus Professor of Mathematics
University of California
Davis, CA

Dr. Kurt Kreith (Grades 3–4)
Emeritus Professor of Mathematics
University of California
Davis, CA

Dr. Liping Ma (Grades K–2)
Visiting Scholar
Carnegie Foundation for the
Advancement of Teaching
Menlo Park, CA

Dr. David Wright (Grades 5–6)
Professor of Mathematics
Brigham Young University
Provo, UT

Reviewers

California Math Teacher Advisory Board

Doug Hedin
Park Oaks Elementary
  School
Thousand Oaks, CA

Vicky Holman
Mount Pleasant Elementary
  School
San Jose, CA

Jennifer Rader
Desert Trails Elementary
  School
Adelanto, CA

Fran Range-Long
Alice Birney Elementary
  School
Fresno, CA

Sylvia Kyle
Chester Nimitz Elementary
  School
Cupertino, CA

Karlene Seitz
Citrus Glen Elementary
  School
Ventura, CA

Grade 4
Beth Holguin
Graystone Elementary
  School
San Jose, CA

Marilyn Higbie
Jane Addams Elementary
  School
Long Beach, CA

Tarie Lewis
Melrose Elementary School
Oakland, CA

Sandra Jo McIntee
Haynes Street School
West Hills, CA

Mike Tokmakoff
Hoover Street Elementary
  School
Los Angeles, CA

Nancy Yee
Valhalla Elementary School
Pleasant Hill, CA

Grade 5
Patty Jernigan
Santa Susana
Simi Valley, CA

Joe Koski
Nu-View Elementary
  School
Nuevo, CA

Bill Laraway
Silver Oak Elementary
San Jose, CA

Steve Monson
Castro Elementary School
El Cerrito, CA

Sherri Qualls
Weibel Elementary School
Fremont, CA

Arlene Sackman
Earlimart Middle School
Earlimart, CA

Robyn Suskin
Sierra Madre School
Sierra Madre, CA

Grade 6
Herb Brown
Lake Gregory Elementary
  School
Crestline, CA

German Palabyab
Harding Elementary School
El Cerrito, CA

Carole Patty
West Riverside Elementary
  School
Riverside, CA

Maureen Smith
Patterson Elementary
  School
Fremont, CA

Jeff Varn
Sierra Madre Elementary
  School
Sierra Madre, CA

Family Letter

Dear Family,

Every parent hopes his or her child will be confident and successful in school. *Houghton Mifflin Mathematics* is designed to provide children with a solid foundation in mathematics that will help lead to such success.

This program is based on the Mathematics Content Standards for California. The goals of this program are

- Providing a curriculum that balances skills, conceptual understanding, and problem solving

- Providing instruction and practice to help children become proficient in computational skills

- Helping children become good mathematical problem solvers

- Enabling children to use correct mathematical terms to communicate their understanding of math concepts

Look for the standards box in each lesson.

Standards
NS **1.1**

The notation in this box represents the following standard.

Number Sense 1.1   **Count, read, and write whole numbers to 100.**

On pages vi–viii you will find a full listing of all the Mathematics Content Standards for California for Grade 1.

As you work with your child throughout the year, the listing of these standards will help you understand what he or she is learning in each lesson.

We trust your child will have a successful year!

Sincerely,
Houghton Mifflin Company

California
MATH STANDARDS

By the end of grade one, students understand and use the concept of ones and tens in the place value number system. Students add and subtract small numbers with ease. They measure with simple units and locate objects in space. They describe data and analyze and solve simple problems.

Number Sense (NS)

1.0 Students understand and use numbers up to 100:

   1.1 Count, read, and write whole numbers to 100.

   1.2 Compare and order whole numbers to 100 by using the symbols for less than, equal to, or greater than (<, =, >).

   1.3 Represent equivalent forms of the same number through the use of physical models, diagrams, and number expressions (to 20) (e.g., 8 may be represented as $4 + 4$, $5 + 3$, $2 + 2 + 2 + 2$, $10 - 2$, $11 - 3$).

   1.4 Count and group object in ones and tens (e.g., three groups of 10 and 4 equals 34, or $30 + 4$).

   1.5 Identify and know the value of coins and show different combinations of coins that equal the same value.

2.0 Students demonstrate the meaning of addition and subtraction and use these operations to solve problems:

   2.1 Know the addition facts (sums to 20) and the corresponding subtraction facts and commit them to memory.

   2.2 Use the inverse relationship between addition and subtraction to solve problems.

   2.3 Identify one more than, one less than, 10 more than, and 10 less than a given number.

   2.4 Count by 2s, 5s, and 10s to 100.

   2.5 Show the meaning of addition (putting together, increasing) and subtraction (taking away, comparing, finding the difference).

   2.6 Solve addition and subtraction problems with one- and two-digit numbers (e.g., $5 + 58 = \underline{}$).

   2.7 Find the sum of three one-digit numbers.

3.0 Students use estimation strategies in computation and problem solving that involve numbers that use the ones, tens, and hundreds places:

   3.1 Make reasonable estimates when comparing larger or smaller numbers.

Algebra and Functions (AF)

1.0 Students use number sentences with operational symbols and expressions to solve problems:

1.1 Write and solve number sentences from problem situations that express relationships involving addition and subtraction.

1.2 Understand the meaning of the symbols +, −, =.

1.3 Create problem situations that might lead to given number sentences involving addition and subtraction.

Measurement and Geometry (MG)

1.0 Students use direct comparison and nonstandard units to describe the measurements of objects:

1.1 Compare the length, weight, and volume of two or more objects by using direct comparison or a nonstandard unit.

1.2 Tell time to the nearest half hour and relate time to events (e.g., before/ after, shorter/longer).

2.0 Students identify common geometric figures, classify them by common attributes, and describe their relative position or their location in space:

2.1 Identify, describe, and compare triangles, rectangles, squares, and circles, including the faces of three-dimensional objects.

2.2 Classify familiar plane and solid objects by common attributes, such as color, position, shape, size, roundness, or number of corners, and explain which attributes are being used for classification.

2.3 Give and follow directions about location.

2.4 Arrange and describe objects in space by proximity, position, and direction (e.g., near, far, below, above, up, down, behind, in front of, next to, left or right of).

Statistics, Data Analysis, and Probability (SDP)

1.0 Students organize, represent, and compare data by category on simple graphs and charts:

1.1 Sort objects and data by common attributes and describe the categories.

1.2 Represent and compare data (e.g., largest, smallest, most often, least often) by using pictures, bar graphs, tally charts, and picture graphs.

2.0 Students sort objects and create and describe patterns by numbers, shapes, sizes, rhythms, or colors:

2.1 Describe, extend, and explain ways to get to a next element in simple repeating patterns (e.g., rhythmic, numeric, color, and shape).

Mathematical Reasoning (MR)

1.0 Students make decisions about how to set up a problem:

1.1 Determine the approach, materials, and strategies to be used.

1.2 Use tools, such as manipulatives or sketches, to model problems.

2.0 Students solve problems and justify their reasoning:

2.1 Explain the reasoning used and justify the procedures selected.

2.2 Make precise calculations and check the validity of the results from the context of the problem.

3.0 Students note connections between one problem and another.

Contents

CHAPTER 1 Addition Concepts

Subtraction Concepts

CHAPTER 3 Addition and Subtraction Facts to 10

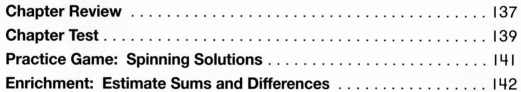

Data and Graphing

CHAPTER 5

Numbers and Patterns to 100

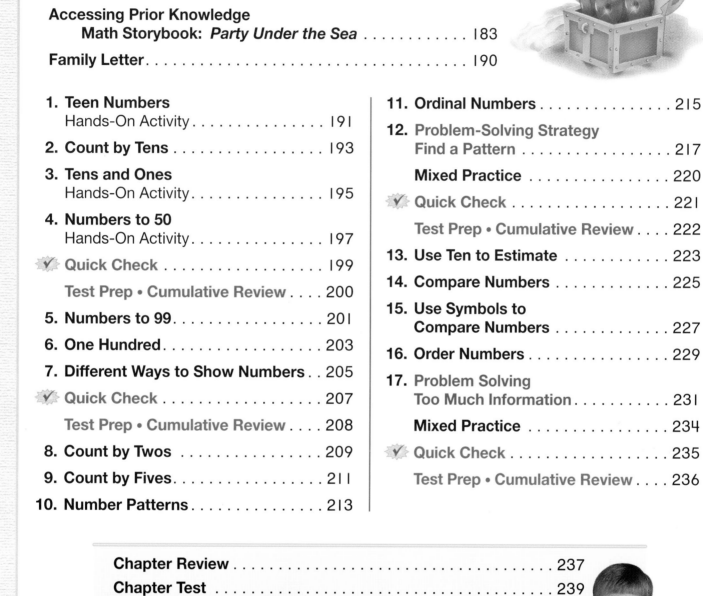

Addition and Subtraction Facts to 12

CHAPTER 7 Money

80¢

Geometry, Fractions, and Probability

Addition and Subtraction Facts to 20

Measurement

heavy   **heavier**   **heaviest**

Time and Calendar

CHAPTER 12 Two-Digit Addition and Subtraction

Book Resources

Name _____

What Comes Just After?

1. Write the missing numbers in order.

			September			
Sunday	Monday	Tuesday	Wednesday	Thursday	Friday	Saturday
						1
2	3					
	10	11				
					21	22
23	24	25	26	27	28	29
30						

Write the number that comes just after.
Use the calendar to help.

2. 8 | 9

3. 6 |

4. 4 |

5. 7 |

6. 3 |

7. 9 |

A

Write the number that comes just after.
Use the number line to help.

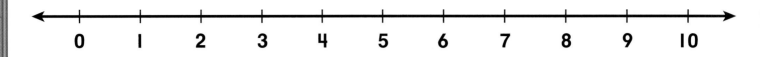

0   1   2   3   4   5   6   7   8   9   10

1. | 1 | 2 |

2. | 9 | |

3. | 3 | |

4. | 7 | |

5. | 4 | |

6. | 6 | |

7. | 5 | |

8. | 2 | |

9. | 8 | |

Circle the word name for the
number that comes just after.

10. two, _____

   one   (three)

11. four, _____

   five   three

12. seven, _____

   six   eight

13. three, _____

   four   two

14. six, _____

   five   seven

15. nine, _____

   eight   ten

16. one, _____

   zero   two

17. five, _____

   six   four

18. eight, _____

   nine   ten

B

Name _____

What Comes Just Before?

1. Write the missing numbers in order.

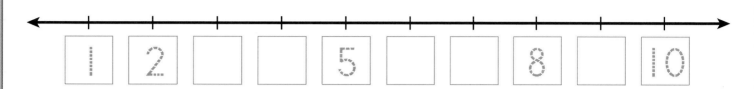

Write the number that comes just before.
Use the number line to help.

2. | 8 | 9 |

3. | | 6 |

4. | | 3 |

5. | | 7 |

6. | | 2 |

7. | | 4 |

8. | | 8 |

9. | | 5 |

10. | | 10 |

11. Write the missing numbers.

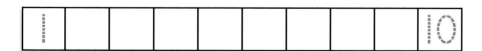

12. Count backward.
Write the missing numbers.

c

Write the number that comes just before.
Use the number line to help.

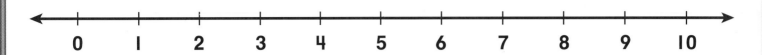

0 1 2 3 4 5 6 7 8 9 10

1. | 7 | 8 |

2. | | 5 |

3. | | 10 |

4. | | 6 |

5. | | 3 |

6. | | 7 |

7. | | 4 |

8. | | 9 |

9. | | 2 |

Circle the word name for the
number that comes just before.

10. _____, four

    five   (three)

11. _____, ten

    eight   nine

12. _____, six

    five   seven

13. _____, eight

    seven   nine

14. _____, three

    two   four

15. _____, five

    six   four

16. _____, nine

    eight   ten

17. _____, two

    one   three

18. _____, seven

    eight   six

D

Accessing Prior Knowledge

This story will
help you review
• Counting

Off to School

A Read-Aloud Story

written by Rob Arego
illustrated by Karen Stormer Brooks

A Math Storybook for

_____

First day of school
And all through the town
The school bus drives
Around and around.

"Here comes the bus!" we all call.
How many children wait in all? _____

First day of school
And all through the town
The school bus drives
Around and around.

Here comes the bus—find a seat!
How many lunchboxes hold things to eat? _____

First day of school
And all through the town
The school bus drives
Around and around.

Here comes the bus with its blinking light!
How many books are there in sight? _____

4

First day of school
And all through the town
The school bus drives
Around and around.

Here comes the bus—happy are we!
How many hats do you see? _____

5

First day of school
And all through the town
The school bus drives
Around and around.

Here comes the bus—shout hurray!
How many backpacks can you count today? _____

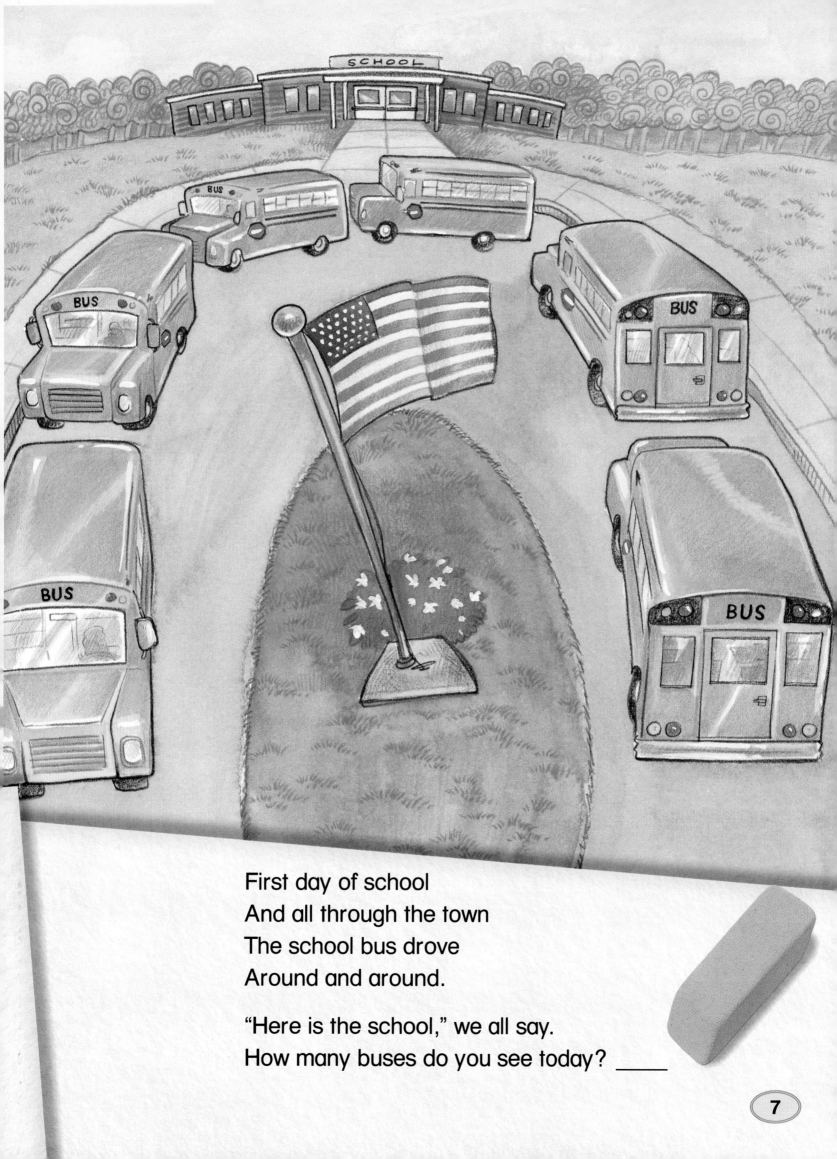

First day of school
And all through the town
The school bus drove
Around and around.

"Here is the school," we all say.
How many buses do you see today? ____

Family Letter

Dear Family,

During the next few weeks, our math class will be learning addition facts with sums through 8.

You can expect to see work that provides practice with these addition facts. As we learn addition facts with sums through 8, you may wish to use the following sample as a guide.

Sums Through 8

$1 + 1 = 2$ ← sum

↑ plus sign   ↑ equals sign

Knowing that addition is joining two or more groups to find how many in all, or the sum, can help children identify addition situations in their lives.

Sincerely,
Your child's teacher

Name _____

Standards
NS **2.0, 2.5,** MR **1.2**

Addition Concepts

Learn About It

Listen to the stories.
Show each story with counters.

Explain Your Thinking When you put groups together,
what can you find?

Try It Out

Show each story with counters.
Write the numbers.

1.

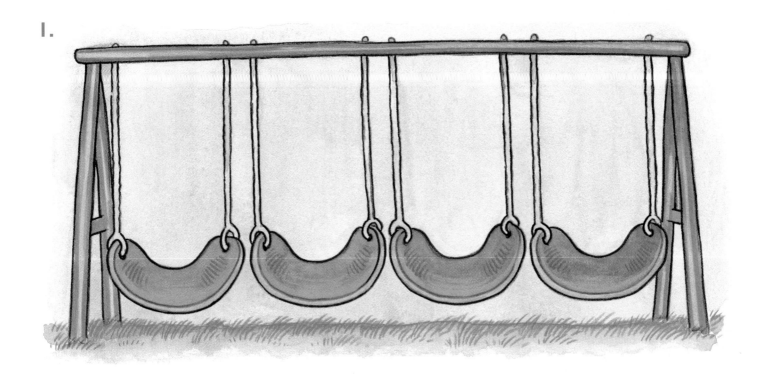

_____ girls   _____ boys   _____ in all

2.

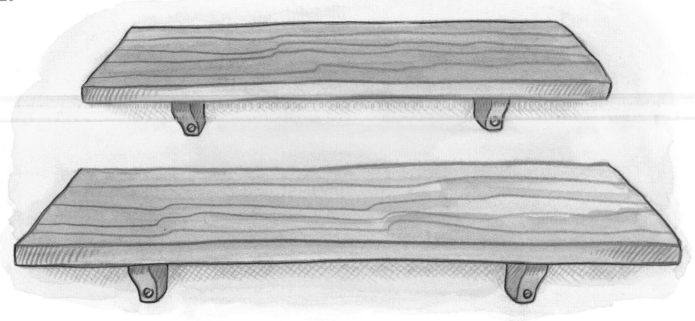

_____ cars   _____ trucks   _____ in all

At Home Place a group of 2 objects and a group of 3 objects on a table. Ask your child how many objects there are in all.

Hands-On **Activity**

LESSON **2**

Name _____

Model Addition

Learn About It

You **add** by putting groups together.

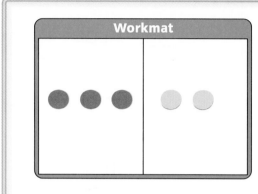

3 ● and 2 ○   _5_ in all

Guided Practice

Use Workmat 2 and counters to add.
Write how many in all.

1. 1 ● and 3 ○   _4_ in all

2. 2 ● and 2 ○   ____ in all

3. 2 ● and 3 ○   ____ in all

4. 4 ● and 1 ○   ____ in all

5. 3 ● and 1 ○   ____ in all

Explain Your Thinking What does the word **add** mean?

Independent Practice

Use Workmat 2 and counters to add.
Write how many in all.

	Show	Add	How many in all?
I.	1 ⬤	1 ⬤	_2_ in all
2.	2 ⬤	3 ⬤	____ in all
3.	1 ⬤	3 ⬤	____ in all
4.	2 ⬤	1 ⬤	____ in all
5.	2 ⬤	2 ⬤	____ in all
6.	3 ⬤	2 ⬤	____ in all
7.	1 ⬤	4 ⬤	____ in all

Problem Solving • Reasoning

8. Draw dots to show each number. Write how many in all.

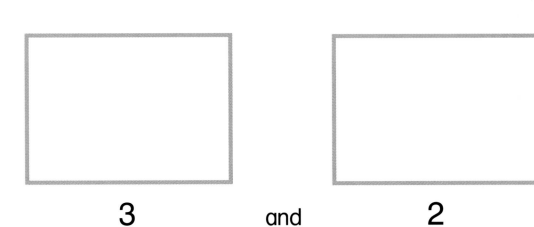

3   and   2   ____ in all

At Home Use dried beans or other objects to help your child model different ways to make 5.

LESSON 3

Use Symbols to Add

Learn About It

Use the **plus sign** and **equals sign**
to write about addition.

2   +   2   =   _4_ ← **sum**

↑   ↑
plus sign   equals sign

The sum tells
how many in all.

Guided Practice

Write how many in all.

1.

2   +   4   =   _6_

2.

1   +   5   =   ___

3.

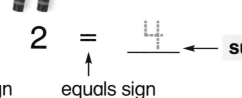

3   +   2   =   ___

4.

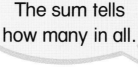

3   +   3   =   ___

5.

1   +   3   =   ___

6.

1   +   4   =   ___

Explain Your Thinking What does the plus sign mean?

Independent Practice

Write how many in all.

1.

    5 + 1 = _6_

2.

    2 + 1 = ___

3.

    3 + 1 = ___

4.

    2 + 3 = ___

5.

    4 + 2 = ___

6.

    4 + 1 = ___

7.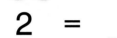

    1 + 1 = ___

8.

    1 + 2 = ___

Problem Solving • Reasoning

Visual Thinking

9. Circle the group that shows 1 + 4 = 5.

At Home Have your child use pictures in books or magazines to create addition stories showing sums of 5 or less.

Standards
NS **1.1, 2.5**
AF **1.0, 1.1, 1.2**

LESSON 4

Write Addition Sentences

Learn About It

Write an **addition sentence** to show how many in all.

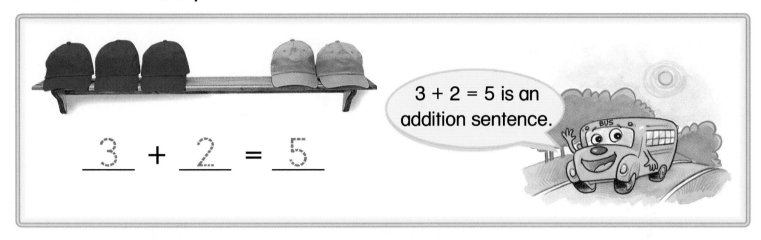

_3_ + _2_ = _5_

3 + 2 = 5 is an addition sentence.

Guided Practice

Write each addition sentence.

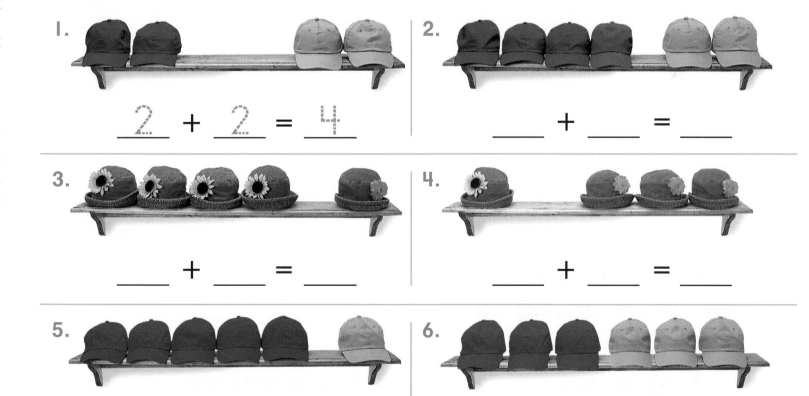

1. _2_ + _2_ = _4_

2. ___ + ___ = ___

3. ___ + ___ = ___

4. ___ + ___ = ___

5. ___ + ___ = ___

6. ___ + ___ = ___

Explain Your Thinking What does the word **sum** mean?

Independent Practice

Write each addition sentence.

1.

   ___ + ___ = ___
   1   5   6

2.

   ___ + ___ = ___

3.

   ___ + ___ = ___

4.

   ___ + ___ = ___

Write each sum.

5. 2 + 4 = ___

6. 5 + 1 = ___

7. 2 + 1 = ___

8. 1 + 1 = ___

9. 3 + 1 = ___

10. 2 + 3 = ___

11. 3 + 2 = ___

12. 3 + 3 = ___

13. 1 + 3 = ___

14. 1 + 2 = ___

15. 1 + 4 = ___

16. 4 + 2 = ___

Problem Solving•Reasoning

Number Sense

17. Write how many in each group.
    Circle the group that has more.

   ____

   ____

At Home Use objects to model one of the addition sentences on this page. Have your child add the objects and then write an addition sentence to match.

LESSON 5 Add With Zero

Learn About It

New Vocabulary
zero

Sometimes you add **zero** .

Sometimes you add a number to zero.

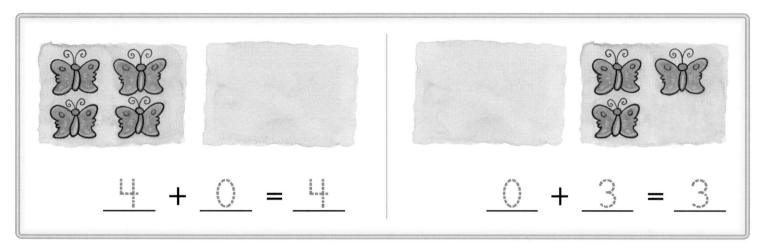

$$4 + 0 = 4$$

$$0 + 3 = 3$$

Guided Practice

Write each addition sentence.

1.

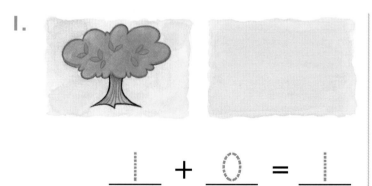

$$1 + 0 = 1$$

2.

$$\_\_ + \_\_ = \_\_$$

3.

$$\_\_ + \_\_ = \_\_$$

4.

$$\_\_ + \_\_ = \_\_$$

Explain Your Thinking When you add 6 and 0, why is the sum 6?

Independent Practice

Write each sum.

1.

$$4 + 0 = \underline{4}$$

2.

$$0 + 2 = \underline{}$$

3. $3 + 0 = \underline{}$ 4. $2 + 3 = \underline{}$ 5. $0 + 4 = \underline{}$

6. $2 + 1 = \underline{}$ 7. $5 + 0 = \underline{}$ 8. $3 + 3 = \underline{}$

9. $2 + 4 = \underline{}$ 10. $6 + 0 = \underline{}$ 11. $1 + 4 = \underline{}$

12. $0 + 1 = \underline{}$ 13. $2 + 2 = \underline{}$ 14. $5 + 1 = \underline{}$

15. $3 + 1 = \underline{}$ 16. $4 + 2 = \underline{}$ 17. $0 + 0 = \underline{}$

18. $1 + 1 = \underline{}$ 19. $2 + 0 = \underline{}$ 20. $3 + 2 = \underline{}$

Problem Solving • Reasoning

Using Vocabulary

Write each addition sentence.

21. Four plus two equals six.

_____

22. Three plus zero equals three.

_____

At Home Ask your child to explain what happens when you add zero to a number.

18 eighteen

Name_____

Standards
NS **2.0**
MR **1.0, 1.1, 1.2, 2.2**

LESSON 6 Problem Solving: Use Models to Act It Out

You can use models to act out problems.

2 children are feeding the fish.
2 more come to watch.
How many children are there now?

Understand

What do you already know?

_____ children feeding fish

_____ more children come

Plan

Circle what you would use to act out this problem.

counters

paper and pencil

Solve

Show 2.
Show 2 more.

Now there are _____ children.

Look Back

Count to check.

Guided Practice

Solve.

Use counters.

Remember:
► Understand
► Plan
► Solve
► Look Back

Remember to use the 4 steps.

① You see 4 toys.
You see 2 more.
How many toys do
you see in all?

___6___ toys

Think. What do I need to find out?

Draw or write to explain.

② Mike read 2 books.
Sara read 2 books.
How many books
did they read in all?

_____ books

Think: How can I show how many books?

③ My picture shows 1 tree.
Your picture shows 3 trees.
How many trees
do our pictures show?

_____ trees

Think: How can I solve the problem?

④ Tom used 4 blocks.
I used 1 block.
How many blocks
did we use?

_____ blocks

Think: What do I already know?

At Home Make two groups of items totaling 5 or less. Ask your child to add the groups.

Name_____

Choose a Strategy

Solve. Use models to act it out or draw a picture.

1. Beth has 3 turtles.
   Ted has 3 turtles.
   How many turtles do they
   have in all?

   _____ turtles

   Draw or write to explain.

   turtle

2. The teacher has 4 lizards.
   He gets 1 more. How many
   lizards does he have now?

   _____ lizards

   lizard

3. There is 1 hamster in the cage.
   Lin puts in 3 more. Now
   how many hamsters are in
   the cage?

   _____ hamsters

   hamster

4. 3 rabbits are eating.
   Then 2 more join them.
   How many rabbits are
   eating now?

   _____ rabbits

   rabbit

Name_____

Mixed Practice

Write how many in all.

1. $2 + 2 = $ ____

2. $3 + 2 = $ ____

3. $1 + 2 = $ ____

4. $2 + 4 = $ ____

5. $5 + 1 = $ ____

6. $2 + 3 = $ ____

Write each addition sentence.

7.

____ + ____ = ____

8.

____ + ____ = ____

9.

____ + ____ = ____

10.

____ + ____ = ____

❓ Brain Teaser In the Bag

There are 6 rocks in all. Some are in the bag. How many rocks are in the bag?

____ rocks

 Safe Site

Internet Brain Teasers
Visit **www.eduplace.com/kids/mhm**
for more *Brain Teasers*.

Name _____

Quick ✓ Check

Check Your Understanding of Lessons 1–6

Write the numbers.

1.

   ____   ____   ____ in all

2.

   ____   ____   ____ in all

Write how many in all.

3.

   $1 + 2 =$ ____

4.

   $4 + 1 =$ ____

Write each addition sentence.

5.

   ____ + ____ = ____

6.

   ____ + ____ = ____

Solve.

Use counters if you want.

7. Blair read 3 books.
   Bob read 2 books.
   How many books did
   they read in all?

   ____ books

Draw or write to explain.

Name_____

Test Prep • Cumulative Review
Maintaining the Standards

Fill in the ○ for the correct answer.

1 Which is the number four?

3   4   5   6
○   ○   ○   ○

2 How many stars are there?

○ 2 stars

○ 3 stars

○ 4 stars

○ 5 stars

3 How many are there in all?

6   5   4   3
○   ○   ○   ○

4 Which is the number six?

3   4   5   6
○   ○   ○   ○

5 Add.

$3 + 0 = $ ▦

0   3   4   5
○   ○   ○   ○

6 Dora has 1 red hat and 3 blue hats. How many hats does she have in all?

5   4   3   2
○   ○   ○   ○

7 Dave has 3 red trucks and 2 blue trucks.

Explain how you can find how many trucks he has in all.

_____

_____

_____

_____

Safe Site

Internet Test Prep
Visit **www.eduplace.com/kids/mhm**
for more *Test Prep Practice*.

Name _____

LESSON 7 Add in Any Order

Learn About It

You can change the order of the
numbers when you add them.

Make a cube train.

I can turn this train around and write another fact.

$$\underline{4} + \underline{1} = \underline{5}$$

$$\underline{1} + \underline{4} = \underline{5}$$

Guided Practice

Use cubes in two colors.
Write two addition sentences for each train.

1. Make a **4** train.

   $$\underline{1} + \underline{3} = \underline{4}$$

   $$\underline{3} + \underline{1} = \underline{4}$$

2. Make a **5** train.

   $$\underline{} + \underline{} = \underline{}$$

   $$\underline{} + \underline{} = \underline{}$$

3. Make a **6** train.

   $$\underline{} + \underline{} = \underline{}$$

   $$\underline{} + \underline{} = \underline{}$$

4. Make a **3** train.

   $$\underline{} + \underline{} = \underline{}$$

   $$\underline{} + \underline{} = \underline{}$$

Explain Your Thinking Why is the sum of 5 + 1
the same as the sum of 1 + 5?

Write each addition fact.

1.  $\begin{array}{r} \square \\ +\ \square \\ \hline \square \end{array}$

2. 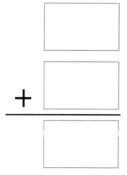 $\begin{array}{r} \square \\ +\ \square \\ \hline \square \end{array}$

Write each sum.

3. $\begin{array}{r} 5 \\ +3 \\ \hline \end{array}$
4. $\begin{array}{r} 3 \\ +4 \\ \hline \end{array}$
5. $\begin{array}{r} 8 \\ +0 \\ \hline \end{array}$
6. $\begin{array}{r} 2 \\ +5 \\ \hline \end{array}$
7. $\begin{array}{r} 0 \\ +6 \\ \hline \end{array}$
8. $\begin{array}{r} 2 \\ +4 \\ \hline \end{array}$

Add. Then write each fact another way.

9. $5 + 3 = $ ___

___ + ___ = ___

10. $7 + 0 = $ ___

___ + ___ = ___

Solve.

11. Ali read 4 books. Then he read 3 books. How many books did he read in all?

____ books

Draw or write to explain.

12. Alma has 4 pencils. Cory has 2 pencils. How many pencils do they have in all?

____ pencils

Chapter Test

Write how many there are in all.

1.

   3 + 4 = ___

2.

   1 + 3 = ___

Write an addition sentence for each train.

3.

   ___ + ___ = ___

4.

   ___ + ___ = ___

Add. Then write each fact another way.

5. 0 + 3 = ___

   ___ + ___ = ___

6. 2 + 5 = ___

   ___ + ___ = ___

Write each sum.

7. 6 + 2 = ___

8. 5 + 1 = ___

9. ___ = 4 + 2

10. 2 + 0 = ___

11. 3 + 4 = ___

12. ___ = 3 + 5

Write each sum.

13. 5
   +3
   ―――

14. 4
   +3
   ―――

15. 1
   +7
   ―――

16. 3
   +3
   ―――

17. 0
   +6
   ―――

18. 2
   +6
   ―――

19. There are 3 cows under a tree. Then 2 more cows join them. How many cows are under the tree in all?

____ cows

Draw or write to explain.

20. One mother cat has 3 kittens. Another mother cat has 4 kittens. How many kittens are there in all?

____ kittens

Write About It

Think of an addition story.
Draw a picture to show it.
Write the addition sentence.

____ + ____ = ____

Explain why your story shows addition.

_____

_____

_____

Name _____

3 in a Row

Players
2

What You Need

2 number cubes

counters

How to Play

① Choose ● or ○ .

② Take turns. Toss the
and place one of the counters
on the correct sum below.
If the box is taken, lose a turn.

③ The first player to have 3 counters
in a row wins.

7	6	8
3	7	5
1	2	6

Mama puts carrots on a plate.
It's time for lunch, and Papa's late.
Randy and Rita are ready to dine.

Count the carrots. There are _____ .

48

Randy takes one and starts to munch.
The sound of the carrot is crunch, crunch, crunch!
Since Papa is late, they did not wait.

How many carrots are on the plate? _____

Family Letter

Vocabulary

subtract To take away to find out how many are left.

minus sign The symbol for subtraction.

difference The answer to a subtraction problem.

subtraction sentence An equation such as $6 - 2 = 4$.

Dear Family,

During the next few weeks, our math class will be learning subtraction facts with differences from 8.

You can expect to see work that provides practice with these subtraction facts.

You may wish to use the following sample as a guide.

Differences From 8

$$8 \underset{\substack{\uparrow \\ \text{minus} \\ \text{sign}}}{-} 2 \underset{\substack{\uparrow \\ \text{equals} \\ \text{sign}}}{=} 6 \leftarrow \text{difference}$$

Knowing that subtraction is taking away part of a group to find the difference, or what is left, can help children identify subtraction situations in their lives.

Sincerely,

Your child's teacher

Hands-On Activity LESSON 1

Subtraction Concepts

Learn About It

Listen to the stories.

Show each story with counters.

Explain Your Thinking When you take away, are you putting together or separating groups?

Try It Out

Show each story with counters.
Write the numbers.

1.

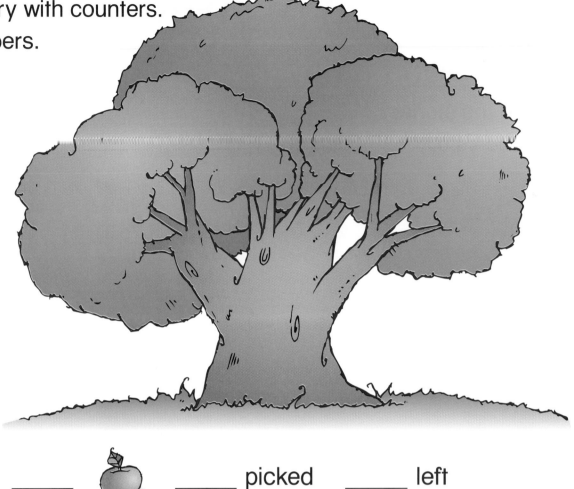

_____ <img: apple> _____ picked _____ left

2.

_____ <img: pear> _____ eaten _____ left

56 fifty-six

At Home Ask your child to create a subtraction story. Have him or her use objects to show the story.

Hands-On Activity — LESSON 2

Model Subtraction

New Vocabulary
subtract

Learn About It

When you **subtract**, you find how many are left.

Show 4 ●.

Take away 1 ●.

How many are left?

3 ● left

Guided Practice

Use Workmat 1 and counters to subtract.
Write how many are left.

1. 3 ● take away 1 ● ___2___ left

2. 5 ● take away 2 ● _____ left

3. 2 ● take away 1 ● _____ left

4. 4 ● take away 2 ● _____ left

5. 5 ● take away 4 ● _____ left

Explain Your Thinking If you start with 4 and take away 3, can you have more than 1 left? Why or why not?

Independent Practice

Use Workmat 1 and counters to subtract.
Write how many are left.

	Show	Take away	How many are left?
1.	5 ●	1 ●	___4___ left
2.	3 ●	2 ●	_____ left
3.	4 ●	1 ●	_____ left
4.	5 ●	4 ●	_____ left
5.	2 ●	1 ●	_____ left
6.	4 ●	3 ●	_____ left
7.	5 ●	3 ●	_____ left

Problem Solving • Reasoning

Number Sense

Draw each group with 1 less.

8.

9.

Explain how you know there is 1 less.

At Home Start with 5 objects. Take away some.
Ask your child how many are left.

Standards
NS **2.5**, AF **1.2**

LESSON 3 Use Symbols to Subtract

Learn About It

Use the **minus sign** and equals sign
to write about subtraction.

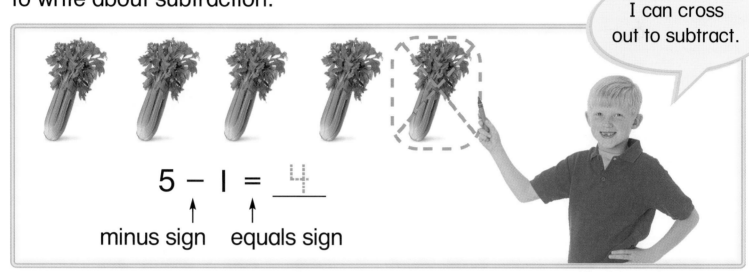

I can cross
out to subtract.

$$5 - 1 = \underline{4}$$

↑ minus sign   ↑ equals sign

Guided Practice

Cross out to subtract.
Write how many are left.

1.

$$6 - 2 = \underline{4}$$

2.

$$5 - 3 = \underline{}$$

3.

$$4 - 1 = \underline{}$$

4.

$$6 - 5 = \underline{}$$

5.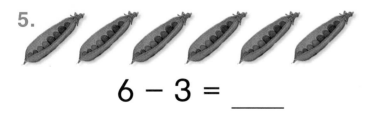

$$6 - 3 = \underline{}$$

6.

$$5 - 2 = \underline{}$$

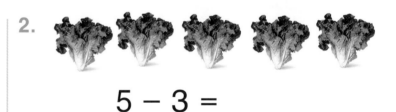

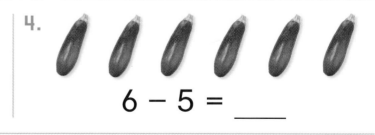

Explain Your Thinking What does the minus sign mean?

Independent Practice

Cross out to subtract.
Write how many are left.

1.

    $6 - 1 = \underline{5}$

2.

    $5 - 2 = \underline{}$

3.

    $4 - 3 = \underline{}$

4.

    $3 - 1 = \underline{}$

5.

    $6 - 3 = \underline{}$

6.

    $4 - 2 = \underline{}$

7.

    $3 - 2 = \underline{}$

8.

    $6 - 4 = \underline{}$

Problem Solving•Reasoning

Visual Thinking

9. Circle the picture that shows $5 - 4 = 1$.

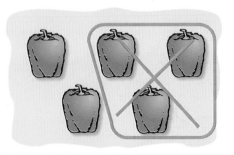  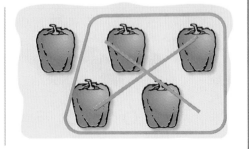

 At Home Have your child draw 5 or 6 objects. Then have your child cross out some and write how many are left.

LESSON 4 Write Subtraction Sentences

Learn About It

Write a **subtraction sentence** to show the **difference**.

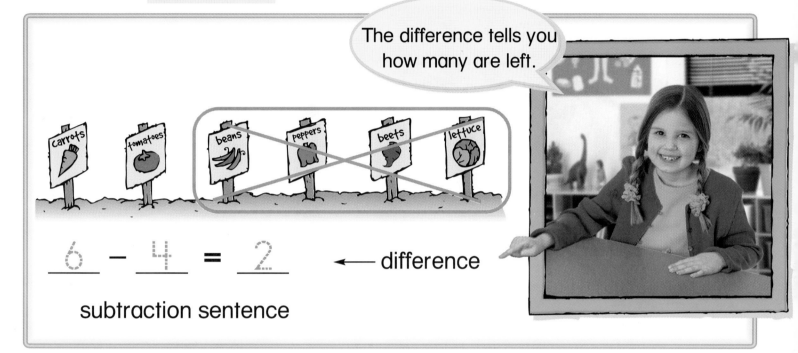

The difference tells you how many are left.

$\underline{6} - \underline{4} = \underline{2}$ ← difference

subtraction sentence

Guided Practice

Tell a story. Write each subtraction sentence.

1. $\underline{5} - \underline{2} = \underline{3}$

2. _____ − _____ = _____

3. _____ − _____ = _____

4. _____ − _____ = _____

Explain Your Thinking What math word tells you how many are left?

Independent Practice

Write each subtraction sentence.

1.

$$\underline{\ \ 3\ \ } - \underline{\ \ 1\ \ } = \underline{\ \ 2\ \ }$$

2.

$$\underline{\ \ \ \ } - \underline{\ \ \ \ } = \underline{\ \ \ \ }$$

3.

$$\underline{\ \ \ \ } - \underline{\ \ \ \ } = \underline{\ \ \ \ }$$

4.

$$\underline{\ \ \ \ } - \underline{\ \ \ \ } = \underline{\ \ \ \ }$$

Write each difference.

5. $5 - 3 = \underline{\ \ \ }$ 6. $2 - 1 = \underline{\ \ \ }$ 7. $4 - 3 = \underline{\ \ \ }$

8. $3 - 2 = \underline{\ \ \ }$ 9. $6 - 1 = \underline{\ \ \ }$ 10. $5 - 4 = \underline{\ \ \ }$

11. $4 - 1 = \underline{\ \ \ }$ 12. $6 - 5 = \underline{\ \ \ }$ 13. $5 - 2 = \underline{\ \ \ }$

Problem Solving·Reasoning

Logical Thinking

14. I am greater than 4.
    I am less than 7.
    I am not 5.
    What number am I? _____

Draw or write to explain.

At Home Use objects to act out subtraction stories.
Have your child write a subtraction sentence for each story.

LESSON 5 Zero in Subtraction

Learn About It

Review
Vocabulary
zero

When you subtract, sometimes you take away **zero.**

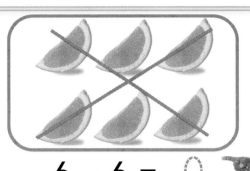

Sometimes the difference is zero.

$6 - 0 = \underline{6}$ $6 - 6 = \underline{0}$

Guided Practice

Write each difference.

1.

$5 - 0 = \underline{5}$

2.

$5 - 5 = \underline{}$

3.

$4 - 4 = \underline{}$

4.

$4 - 0 = \underline{}$

5.

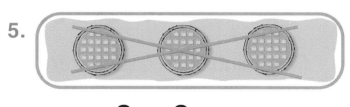

$3 - 3 = \underline{}$

6.

$3 - 0 = \underline{}$

Explain Your Thinking When you subtract, when is the difference zero?

Independent Practice

Find each difference.

1.

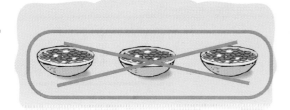

$3 - 3 =$ ____ 0

2.

$4 - 0 =$ ____

3.

$2 - 0 =$ ____

4.

$6 - 6 =$ ____

5. $6 - 0 =$ ____   6. $1 - 1 =$ ____   7. $5 - 5 =$ ____

8. $2 - 0 =$ ____   9. $4 - 4 =$ ____   10. $3 - 0 =$ ____

11. $2 - 2 =$ ____   12. $5 - 0 =$ ____   13. $1 - 0 =$ ____

Problem Solving•Reasoning

Using Vocabulary
Write each subtraction sentence.

14. Six minus four equals two.

____ – ____ = ____

15. Five minus five equals zero.

____ – ____ = ____

At Home Ask your child to show how $4 - 4$ and $4 - 0$ are different.

Name_____

LESSON 6

Problem Solving: Draw a Picture

Standards
NS 2.0
MR 1.0, 1.1, 1.2, 2.2

You can draw pictures to help you solve problems.

There are 6 carrots in the garden. Rob picks 2 of them. How many are left?

Understand

Circle what you need to find out.

How many in all

How many left

Plan

Write the numbers you will use to draw a picture.

Carrots in the garden ____

Rob picks ____ .

Solve

Draw a picture.

____ carrots left

Look Back

Count to check your answer.

Guided Practice

Draw a picture to
solve each problem.

Remember to
use the 4 steps.

① There are 5 apples.
Nina picks 3.
How many are left?

Think:
What do I
need to find out?

Draw or write to explain.

__2__ apples

② There are 6 peppers.
Mark takes 3.
How many are
there now?

Think:
How many
peppers
do I draw?

_____ peppers

③ There are 8 potatoes
in a bowl. Pam
takes out 2.
How many are left?

Think:
What do I do
to solve the
problem?

_____ potatoes

④ There are 3 beans.
Lex eats 2.
Now how many
are there?

Think:
How many beans
do I cross out?

_____ bean

At Home Tell subtraction stories, such as *3 rabbits were playing. One went home. How many are left?* Have your child draw a picture to show the problem.

Choose a Strategy

Solve. Draw a picture or use models to act it out.

1 Ron sees 4 pumpkins.
He buys 2. How many
pumpkins are left?

_____ pumpkins

Draw or write to explain.

pumpkin

2 There are 5 bunches of broccoli.
Lou takes 4. How many
are there now?

_____ bunch of broccoli

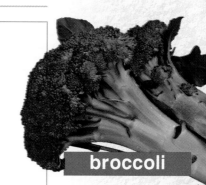

broccoli

3 Teri sees 6 carrots.
She buys 5. How many
carrots are left?

_____ carrot

carrot

4 There are 8 red peppers.
Dana picks 3.
Now how many are there?

_____ red peppers

red pepper

Name _____

Mixed Practice

Write each difference.

1. 5 − 2 = ___   2. 6 − 2 = ___   3. 2 − 1 = ___

4. 3 − 0 = ___   5. 4 − 4 = ___   6. 5 − 3 = ___

7. 4 − 2 = ___   8. 5 − 4 = ___   9. 3 − 3 = ___

Write each sum.

10. 4
    +3

11. 6
    +2

12. 3
    +0

13. 5
    +1

14. 4
    +4

15. 5
    +2

16. 3
    +1

17. 2
    +0

18. 5
    +3

19. 6
    +1

20. 2
    +3

21. 4
    +2

 Brain Teaser Seat Number

I am 2 seats away from Seat 4.
I am 3 seats away from Seat 3.
What is my seat number?

seat number ____

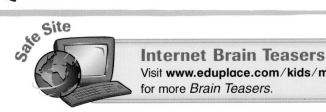
Safe Site

Internet Brain Teasers
Visit **www.eduplace.com/kids/mhm**
for more *Brain Teasers*.

Name _____

Check Your Understanding of Lessons 1–6

Use counters.

Write how many are left.

	Show	Take away	How many are left?
1.	5 ●	1 ●	____ left
2.	4 ●	2 ●	____ left
3.	3 ●	1 ●	____ left

Cross out to subtract.

Write how many are left.

4.

$$6 - 4 = \underline{\quad}$$

5.

$$5 - 3 = \underline{\quad}$$

Write each subtraction sentence.

6.

$$\underline{\quad} - \underline{\quad} = \underline{\quad}$$

7.

$$\underline{\quad} - \underline{\quad} = \underline{\quad}$$

Write each difference.

8. $4 - 0 = \underline{\quad}$ 9. $6 - 5 = \underline{\quad}$ 10. $5 - 5 = \underline{\quad}$

Solve.

11. Flora has 6 carrots. She gives 2 to Sean. How many carrots does Flora have left?

_____ carrots

Draw or write to explain.

Name _____

Test Prep • Cumulative Review

Maintaining the Standards

Fill in the ○ for the correct answer.

1 Add. 2 + 1 = ⬛

1	2	3	4
○	○	○	○

5 Subtract. 4 − 3 = ⬛

1	2	4	7
○	○	○	○

2 Subtract. 5 − 2 = ⬛

7	6	3	2
○	○	○	○

6 Add. 3 + 4 = ⬛

8	7	6	5
○	○	○	○

3 Chen has 3 green blocks and 2 red blocks. How many blocks does Chen have in all?

1	3	4	5
○	○	○	○

7 How many pears are there?

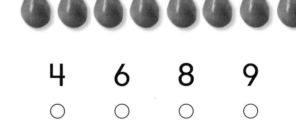

4	6	8	9
○	○	○	○

4 How many cubes are there altogether?

8	7	6	4
○	○	○	○

8 Danielle made 4 pies. She gave 1 away. How many pies does she have left?

Explain why you subtract to find the answer.

_____

_____

Safe Site

Internet Test Prep
Visit **www.eduplace.com/kids/mhm**
for more *Test Prep Practice.*

Hands-On Activity
LESSON 7

Subtract From 7 or Less

Learn About It

You can find ways to subtract from 7.

Use 7 cubes. Snap off one.

$$ 7 - 1 = 6 $$

subtraction sentence

The subtraction sentence shows that the difference is 6.

Guided Practice

Use 7 cubes. Snap off some.
Cross out. Write a subtraction sentence.

1. $7 - 2 = 5$

2. ___ − ___ = ___

3. ___ − ___ = ___

4. ___ − ___ = ___

5. ___ − ___ = ___

Explain Your Thinking What are all the ways to subtract from 7?

Independent Practice

Write each difference.
Use cubes if you want.

1. 7 − 3 = __4__

2. 5 − 3 = ___   3. 7 − 5 = ___   4. 7 − 0 = ___

5. 6 − 4 = ___   6. 7 − 4 = ___   7. 5 − 5 = ___

8. 7 − 6 = ___   9. 6 − 0 = ___   10. 7 − 7 = ___

11. 7 − 1 = ___   12. 6 − 5 = ___   13. 7 − 2 = ___

Problem Solving • Reasoning

Algebra Readiness • Number Sentences

Write each subtraction sentence.

14. Pat had 6 🍌 .
    He ate 2.
    How many 🍌 were left?

    ___ − ___ = ___

Draw or write to explain.

15. Rosa has 7 🍓 .
    She gives 5 to Pat.
    How many 🍓 does
    she have now?

    ___ − ___ = ___

Draw or write to explain.

At Home Show your child 7 objects. Take away some objects.
Ask your child to write a subtraction sentence.

Name _____

Subtract From 8 or Less

Standards
NS **2.5**, AF **1.3**
MR **1.2**

Learn About It

You can find ways to subtract from 8.

Use 8 cubes. Snap off one.

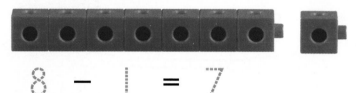

$$\underline{} - \underline{} = \underline{}$$

8 – 1 = 7

subtraction sentence

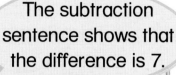

The subtraction sentence shows that the difference is 7.

Guided Practice

Use 8 cubes. Snap off some.
Cross out. Write a subtraction sentence.

1.    8 – 2 = 6

2. _____   ___ – ___ = ___

3.    ___ – ___ = ___

4. _____   ___ – ___ = ___

5. _____   ___ – ___ = ___

Explain Your Thinking What are all the ways to subtract from 8? How do you know?

Independent Practice

Write each difference.

Color the rabbit that can climb to 8.

7 − 0 = 7

7 − 1 = ___

7 − 2 = ___

7 − 3 = ___

7 − 4 = ___

7 − 5 = ___

7 − 6 = ___

7 − 7 = ___

8 − 0 = ___

8 − 1 = ___

8 − 2 = ___

8 − 3 = ___

8 − 4 = ___

8 − 5 = ___

8 − 6 = ___

8 − 7 = ___

8 − 8 = ___

At Home Give your child 8 objects. Take away 2 or 3. Ask him or her to write a subtraction sentence to describe what you did.

LESSON 9 Subtract in Vertical Form

Learn About It

You can write the same subtraction
fact in two ways.

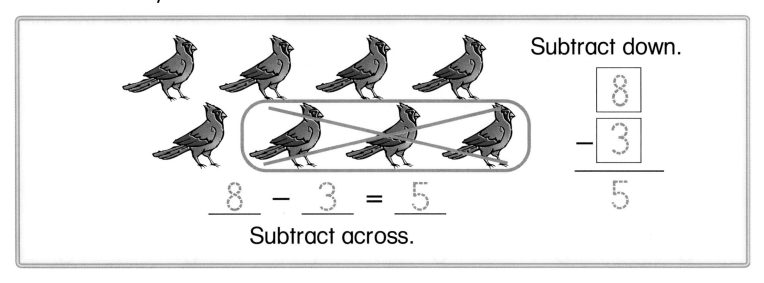

Subtract down.

$$\begin{array}{r} 8 \\ - 3 \\ \hline 5 \end{array}$$

8 – 3 = 5

Subtract across.

Guided Practice

Write each subtraction fact in two ways.

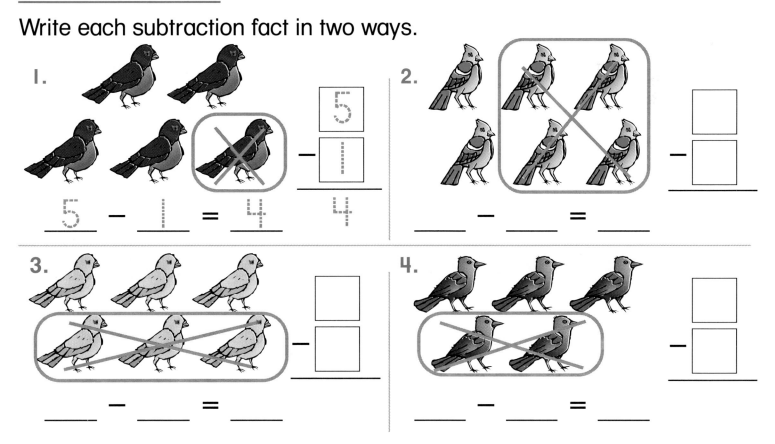

1.

5 – 1 = 4

$$\begin{array}{r} 5 \\ - 1 \\ \hline 4 \end{array}$$

2.

___ – ___ = ___

$$\begin{array}{r} \\ - \\ \hline \end{array}$$

3.

___ – ___ = ___

$$\begin{array}{r} \\ - \\ \hline \end{array}$$

4.

___ – ___ = ___

$$\begin{array}{r} \\ - \\ \hline \end{array}$$

Explain Your Thinking Whether you subtract across
or you subtract down, the difference is the same. Why?

Guided Practice

Solve.

1 There are 8 horses in the barn. 2 horses leave. How many horses are still in the barn?

> **Think:** How many horses are in the barn?

Draw or write to explain.

_6_ horses

---

2 5 cows are eating grass. 3 more join them. How many cows are eating now?

> **Think:** Do I add or subtract?

_____ cows

---

3 There are 7 pigs in the pen. 3 of them leave. How many pigs are still in the pen?

> **Think:** How many pigs are in the pen?

_____ pigs

---

4 2 chicks are eating grain. 4 more start to eat. How many chicks are eating now?

> **Think:** Do I add or subtract?

_____ chicks

At Home Tell addition or subtraction stories about your child's toys. Have your child tell whether to add or subtract and then solve.

Choose a Strategy

Solve.

1 There are 5 cows.
3 cows join them.
How many cows are
there now?

Draw or write to explain.

_____ cows

cow

2 7 donkeys are outside.
4 of them go into the barn.
How many donkeys are
still outside?

_____ donkeys

donkey

3 8 goats are eating.
5 of them leave. How many
goats are still eating?

_____ goats

goat

4 The farm has one rooster.
The farmer brings 5 more
roosters. How many roosters
are on the farm now?

_____ roosters

rooster

Name _____

Mixed Practice

Watch the signs. Add or subtract.

1. $5 - 1 = $ ___

2. $4 - 0 = $ ___

3. $6 - 3 = $ ___

4. $6 + 1 = $ ___

5. $5 + 3 = $ ___

6. $4 + 0 = $ ___

7. $\begin{array}{r} 5 \\ -3 \\ \hline \end{array}$

8. $\begin{array}{r} 6 \\ -1 \\ \hline \end{array}$

9. $\begin{array}{r} 8 \\ -2 \\ \hline \end{array}$

10. $\begin{array}{r} 6 \\ -2 \\ \hline \end{array}$

11. $\begin{array}{r} 4 \\ -3 \\ \hline \end{array}$

12. $\begin{array}{r} 7 \\ -4 \\ \hline \end{array}$

13. $\begin{array}{r} 2 \\ +3 \\ \hline \end{array}$

14. $\begin{array}{r} 2 \\ +0 \\ \hline \end{array}$

15. $\begin{array}{r} 4 \\ +1 \\ \hline \end{array}$

16. $\begin{array}{r} 1 \\ +1 \\ \hline \end{array}$

17. $\begin{array}{r} 3 \\ +5 \\ \hline \end{array}$

18. $\begin{array}{r} 4 \\ +3 \\ \hline \end{array}$

19. $\begin{array}{r} 8 \\ -6 \\ \hline \end{array}$

20. $\begin{array}{r} 7 \\ -3 \\ \hline \end{array}$

21. $\begin{array}{r} 6 \\ -6 \\ \hline \end{array}$

22. $\begin{array}{r} 7 \\ +1 \\ \hline \end{array}$

23. $\begin{array}{r} 5 \\ +0 \\ \hline \end{array}$

24. $\begin{array}{r} 5 \\ +2 \\ \hline \end{array}$

 Brain Teaser What's My Number?

Each shape stands for a number. Under each shape, write a number that it could stand for.

⬜   △   ⚫

___   ___   ___

 **Safe Site**

Internet Brain Teasers
Visit **www.eduplace.com/kids/mhm**
for more *Brain Teasers*.

Name_____

Check Your Understanding of Lessons 7–10

Write each difference.

1. $7 - 2 = $ _____   2. $6 - 4 = $ _____   3. $7 - 0 = $ _____

4. $7 - 1 = $ _____   5. $8 - 4 = $ _____   6. $7 - 6 = $ _____

7. $8 - 1 = $ _____   8. $8 - 6 = $ _____   9. $5 - 2 = $ _____

10. $8 - 3 = $ _____   11. $5 - 4 = $ _____   12. $8 - 2 = $ _____

13. $\begin{array}{r} 8 \\ -0 \\ \hline \end{array}$ 14. $\begin{array}{r} 7 \\ -4 \\ \hline \end{array}$ 15. $\begin{array}{r} 8 \\ -7 \\ \hline \end{array}$ 16. $\begin{array}{r} 7 \\ -3 \\ \hline \end{array}$ 17. $\begin{array}{r} 6 \\ -6 \\ \hline \end{array}$ 18. $\begin{array}{r} 8 \\ -5 \\ \hline \end{array}$

19. $\begin{array}{r} 7 \\ -7 \\ \hline \end{array}$ 20. $\begin{array}{r} 6 \\ -2 \\ \hline \end{array}$ 21. $\begin{array}{r} 5 \\ -0 \\ \hline \end{array}$ 22. $\begin{array}{r} 8 \\ -8 \\ \hline \end{array}$ 23. $\begin{array}{r} 7 \\ -5 \\ \hline \end{array}$ 24. $\begin{array}{r} 4 \\ -4 \\ \hline \end{array}$

Solve.

25. There were 7 rabbits. 5 hopped away. How many rabbits were left?

_____ rabbits

Draw or write to explain.

Name _____

Test Prep • Cumulative Review

Maintaining the Standards

Fill in the ○ for the correct answer.

1 Subtract. $7 - 5 = $ ■

2	3	4	5
○	○	○	○

2 José has 5 red apples and 2 green apples. How many apples does he have in all?

8	7	3	2
○	○	○	○

3 Add. $3 + 5 = $ ■

2	6	7	8
○	○	○	○

4 Subtract. $8 - 4 = $ ■

3	4	5	6
○	○	○	○

5 Subtract. $5 - 0 = $ ■

0	4	5	6
○	○	○	○

6 8 cats sat on a bed. 6 ran away. How many cats were left?

○ $7 - 5 = 2$

○ $8 - 6 = 2$

○ $8 + 0 = 8$

○ $8 - 2 = 6$

7 There were 5 birds. 3 flew away.

$$5 - 3 = 2$$

Explain why this number sentence shows how many birds were left.

_____

_____

_____

Safe Site

Internet Test Prep
Visit **www.eduplace.com/kids/mhm**
for more *Test Prep Practice*.

Name _____

Chapter Review

Use the words in the box.
Write the correct word on each line.

$$6 \; - \; 2 \; = \; 4$$

↑   ↑

1. _____   2. _____

3. Write a **subtraction sentence**.

____ ◯ ____ = ____

4. Circle the correct word.

You _____ to find how many are left.

add

subtract

Cross out to subtract.
Write how many are left.

5.

$$6 - 2 = \underline{\;\;\;}$$

6.

$$7 - 3 = \underline{\;\;\;}$$

Write each subtraction sentence.

7.

____ − ____ = ____

8.

____ − ____ = ____

Write each difference.

9. $3 - 0 = \underline{\;\;\;}$ 10. $6 - 6 = \underline{\;\;\;}$ 11. $8 - 5 = \underline{\;\;\;}$

Write each subtraction fact.

1. 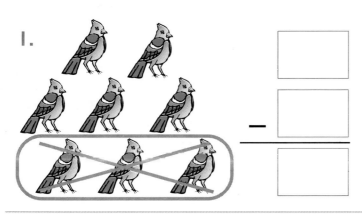 ☐ − ☐ ☐

2. 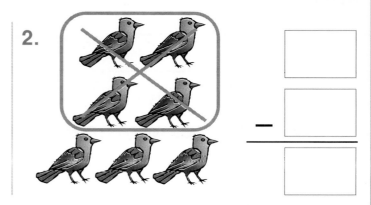 ☐ − ☐ ☐

Solve.

3. $7 - 7 = $ ___

4. $6 - 5 = $ ___

5. $8 - 2 = $ ___

6. $5 - 4 = $ ___

7. $2 - 0 = $ ___

8. $7 - 3 = $ ___

9. $\begin{array}{r} 8 \\ -6 \\ \hline \end{array}$

10. $\begin{array}{r} 6 \\ -0 \\ \hline \end{array}$

11. $\begin{array}{r} 4 \\ -3 \\ \hline \end{array}$

12. $\begin{array}{r} 7 \\ -5 \\ \hline \end{array}$

13. $\begin{array}{r} 8 \\ -3 \\ \hline \end{array}$

14. $\begin{array}{r} 6 \\ -1 \\ \hline \end{array}$

Solve.

15. Emma has 8 apples. She gives 5 to Van. How many apples does Emma have left?

Draw or write to explain.

____ apples left

16. Yoshi ate 4 berries. Toni ate 3 berries. How many berries in all did they eat?

Draw or write to explain.

____ berries in all

Name _____

Chapter Test

Cross out to subtract.
Write how many are left.

1.

   $6 - 1 =$ ___

2.

   $7 - 2 =$ ___

Write each subtraction sentence.

3.

   ___ $-$ ___ $=$ ___

4.

   ___ $-$ ___ $=$ ___

5.

   ___ $-$ ___ $=$ ___

6.

   ___ $-$ ___ $=$ ___

Write each difference.

7. $8 - 2 =$ ___   8. $3 - 2 =$ ___   9. $6 - 0 =$ ___

10. $3 - 3 =$ ___   11. $6 - 2 =$ ___   12. $5 - 4 =$ ___

13. $7 - 3 =$ ___   14. $8 - 5 =$ ___   15. $4 - 2 =$ ___

16. $\begin{array}{r} 4 \\ -4 \\ \hline \end{array}$ 17. $\begin{array}{r} 7 \\ -4 \\ \hline \end{array}$ 18. $\begin{array}{r} 2 \\ -1 \\ \hline \end{array}$ 19. $\begin{array}{r} 6 \\ -6 \\ \hline \end{array}$ 20. $\begin{array}{r} 8 \\ -6 \\ \hline \end{array}$ 21. $\begin{array}{r} 7 \\ -2 \\ \hline \end{array}$

Write each subtraction fact.

22.

$\boxed{} - \boxed{}$
$\overline{\boxed{}}$

23.

$\boxed{} - \boxed{}$
$\overline{\boxed{}}$

24. Jeff has 7 bananas.
He gives 6 to Berta.
How many bananas does
Jeff have left?

_____ banana left

Draw or write to explain.

25. Two rabbits were in the garden.
Six more rabbits joined them.
How many rabbits in all were in
the garden?

_____ rabbits in all

Draw or write to explain.

Write About It

Think of a subtraction story.
Draw a picture to show it.
Write the subtraction sentence.

_____ − _____ = _____

Draw or write to explain.

Explain why your story shows subtraction.

_____

_____

Name_____

It Makes a Difference!

What You Need

Spinner 1

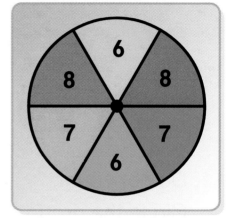

How to Play

❶ Take turns spinning both spinners.

❷ Write the numbers in the chart below. Find the difference.

❸ Take that many cubes.

❹ The first player with 16 cubes wins.

Spinner 2

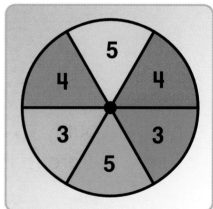

Spinner 1		Spinner 2		Difference
	−		=	
	−		=	
	−		=	
	−		=	
	−		=	

Enrichment

Estimate How Many

1. Do not count.

Circle the group that has more.

2. Do not count.

Circle the group that has more left.

3. Do not count.

Circle the group that has more than 5 left.

4. Do not count.

Circle the group that has less than 5 left.

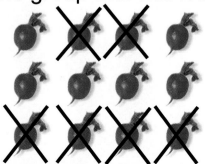 

CHAPTER 3

Addition and Subtraction Facts to 10

Accessing Prior Knowledge

This story will help you review
- Counting
- Addition and subtraction concepts

Bug Fun!

A Read-Aloud Story

written by Sarah Curran
illustrated by Kathy Couri

A Math Storybook for

_____

It is night, there is no sun.
The time has come to have some fun.
I'll get the others as I fly.
How many bugs do you spy?

_____ bugs

3 little ants soon strike out.

The others give a great big shout.

Now 4 ants wait to hit the ball.

How many ants are there in all?

3 + 4 = _____ ants

One little spider sings a song.
2 more spiders play along.
They'll sing and play their songs tonight.
How many spiders in the bright moonlight?

I + 2 = _____ spiders

8 little ladybugs like to chat,
Telling stories about this and that.
Then 5 little ladybugs fly away.
How many ladybugs are left to play?

8 − 5 = _____ ladybugs

All the grasshoppers take a dip.
They are careful not to slip.
Then 2 grasshoppers hop away.
How many grasshoppers stay to play?

6 − 2 = _____ grasshoppers

Oh, now look at the great big sun.
This is the end of our night of fun.
7 fireflies look around.
5 fly off without a sound.
How many fireflies are on the ground?

7 – 5 = _____ fireflies

Family Letter

addend Each of the numbers added in an addition problem.

sum The answer to an addition problem.

difference The answer to a subtraction problem.

fact family Related addition and subtraction facts.

Dear Family,

During the next few weeks, our math class will be learning addition and subtraction facts with sums and differences through 10.

You can expect to see work that provides practice with addition and subtraction facts.

As we learn about related facts and fact families, you may wish to use the following sample as a guide.

Related Facts

$8 + 1 = 9$ $9 - 1 = 8$

Fact Family

$$\begin{array}{r} 7 \\ + 3 \\ \hline 1\ 0 \end{array} \qquad \begin{array}{r} 3 \\ + 7 \\ \hline 1\ 0 \end{array} \qquad \begin{array}{r} 1\ 0 \\ - 3 \\ \hline 7 \end{array} \qquad \begin{array}{r} 1\ 0 \\ - 7 \\ \hline 3 \end{array}$$

Knowing addition facts can help children learn the related subtraction facts.

Sincerely,

Your child's teacher

LESSON 4 Use Doubles to Add

Learn About It

Two **addends** that are the same
make a double fact.

New Vocabulary
addend

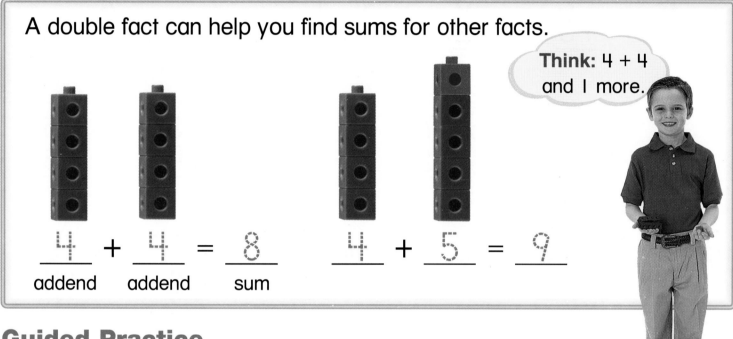

A double fact can help you find sums for other facts.

Think: 4 + 4
and 1 more.

$\underline{4} + \underline{4} = \underline{8}$
addend   addend   sum

$\underline{4} + \underline{5} = \underline{9}$

Guided Practice

Write the addition sentences.

1.

$\underline{3} + \underline{3} = \underline{6}$
double fact

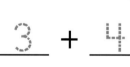

$\underline{3} + \underline{4} = \underline{7}$
double plus one

2.

_____ + _____ = _____
double fact

_____ + _____ = _____
double plus one

Explain Your Thinking How does knowing 4 + 4 = 8
help you find 5 + 4?

Independent Practice

Use a double fact to help you.

Write each sum.

1. $3 + 3 = \underline{6}$ $3 + 4 = \underline{7}$ $4 + 3 = \underline{7}$

2. $4 + 4 = \underline{}$ $4 + 5 = \underline{}$ $5 + 4 = \underline{}$

3.
$\begin{array}{r} 2 \\ +2 \\ \hline \end{array}$
$\begin{array}{r} 2 \\ +3 \\ \hline \end{array}$
$\begin{array}{r} 3 \\ +2 \\ \hline \end{array}$

4.
$\begin{array}{r} 1 \\ +1 \\ \hline \end{array}$
$\begin{array}{r} 1 \\ +2 \\ \hline \end{array}$
$\begin{array}{r} 2 \\ +1 \\ \hline \end{array}$

5.
$\begin{array}{r} 4 \\ +5 \\ \hline \end{array}$

6.
$\begin{array}{r} 5 \\ +2 \\ \hline \end{array}$

7.
$\begin{array}{r} 6 \\ +2 \\ \hline \end{array}$

8.
$\begin{array}{r} 3 \\ +6 \\ \hline \end{array}$

9.
$\begin{array}{r} 3 \\ +4 \\ \hline \end{array}$

10.
$\begin{array}{r} 5 \\ +5 \\ \hline \end{array}$

11.
$\begin{array}{r} 0 \\ +8 \\ \hline \end{array}$

12.
$\begin{array}{r} 3 \\ +7 \\ \hline \end{array}$

13.
$\begin{array}{r} 5 \\ +3 \\ \hline \end{array}$

14.
$\begin{array}{r} 2 \\ +4 \\ \hline \end{array}$

15.
$\begin{array}{r} 7 \\ +2 \\ \hline \end{array}$

16.
$\begin{array}{r} 5 \\ +4 \\ \hline \end{array}$

17.
$\begin{array}{r} 1 \\ +5 \\ \hline \end{array}$

18.
$\begin{array}{r} 2 \\ +8 \\ \hline \end{array}$

19.
$\begin{array}{r} 2 \\ +6 \\ \hline \end{array}$

20.
$\begin{array}{r} 9 \\ +0 \\ \hline \end{array}$

21.
$\begin{array}{r} 1 \\ +7 \\ \hline \end{array}$

22.
$\begin{array}{r} 4 \\ +3 \\ \hline \end{array}$

Problem Solving • Reasoning

Algebra Readiness · Missing Addends

Choose a number to make each double fact.

2	3
4	5

23.
$\begin{array}{r} 4 \\ + \square \\ \hline 8 \end{array}$

24.
$\begin{array}{r} \square \\ + 3 \\ \hline 6 \end{array}$

25.
$\begin{array}{r} \square \\ + 5 \\ \hline 10 \end{array}$

26.
$\begin{array}{r} 1 \\ + 1 \\ \hline \square \end{array}$

At Home Have your child add 4 to any number less than 6.

Standards
NS **2.1**, MR **1.2**

LESSON 5 Draw a Picture to Add

Review
Vocabulary
sum

Learn About It

You can draw a picture to help you find a **sum**.

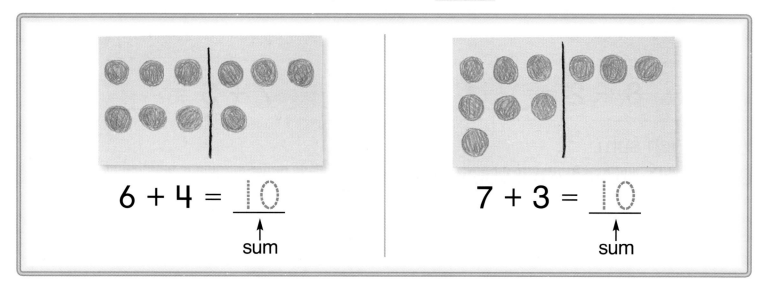

$6 + 4 = \underline{10}$
↑
sum

$7 + 3 = \underline{10}$
↑
sum

Guided Practice

Draw a picture for each addition sentence.
Write each sum.

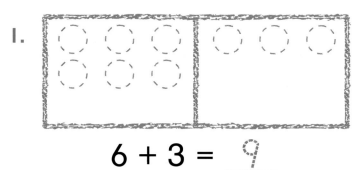

1. $6 + 3 = \underline{9}$

2. $9 + 0 = \underline{}$

3. $5 + 3 = \underline{}$

4. $5 + 4 = \underline{}$

Explain Your Thinking Why could you use
the same picture for $8 + 2$ and $2 + 8$?

Independent Practice

Draw a picture for each addition sentence.

Write each sum.

1.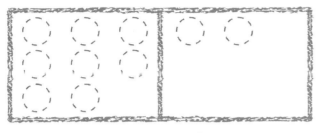

$8 + 2 = \underline{10}$

2.

$7 + 3 = \underline{}$

Write each sum.

Draw a picture to help if you want.

3. $\begin{array}{r} 4 \\ +6 \\ \hline \end{array}$ 4. $\begin{array}{r} 10 \\ +\ 0 \\ \hline \end{array}$ 5. $\begin{array}{r} 1 \\ +6 \\ \hline \end{array}$ 6. $\begin{array}{r} 2 \\ +8 \\ \hline \end{array}$ 7. $\begin{array}{r} 5 \\ +4 \\ \hline \end{array}$ 8. $\begin{array}{r} 3 \\ +6 \\ \hline \end{array}$

9. $\begin{array}{r} 3 \\ +5 \\ \hline \end{array}$ 10. $\begin{array}{r} 3 \\ +7 \\ \hline \end{array}$ 11. $\begin{array}{r} 4 \\ +5 \\ \hline \end{array}$ 12. $\begin{array}{r} 2 \\ +7 \\ \hline \end{array}$ 13. $\begin{array}{r} 6 \\ +4 \\ \hline \end{array}$ 14. $\begin{array}{r} 0 \\ +5 \\ \hline \end{array}$

15. $\begin{array}{r} 1 \\ +4 \\ \hline \end{array}$ 16. $\begin{array}{r} 2 \\ +6 \\ \hline \end{array}$ 17. $\begin{array}{r} 4 \\ +2 \\ \hline \end{array}$ 18. $\begin{array}{r} 7 \\ +0 \\ \hline \end{array}$ 19. $\begin{array}{r} 1 \\ +3 \\ \hline \end{array}$ 20. $\begin{array}{r} 0 \\ +8 \\ \hline \end{array}$

Problem Solving • Reasoning

Using Vocabulary

Answer each question.

21. The **addends** are ____ and ____ .

22. The **greater** addend is ____ .

23. The **sum** is ____ .

$8 + 2 = 10$

At Home Have your child draw a picture to solve $4 + 6$.

LESSON 6 Different Ways to Add

Learn About It

There are different ways you can find a sum.

Count on.

$$\begin{array}{r} 9 \\ +\ 1 \\ \hline 1\,0 \end{array}$$

9

Use a double fact.

$$\begin{array}{r} 4 \\ +5 \\ \hline 9 \end{array} \qquad \begin{array}{r} 5 \\ +4 \\ \hline 9 \end{array}$$

Think: 4 + 4 and 1 more.

Use counters.

$$\begin{array}{r} 3 \\ +6 \\ \hline 9 \end{array}$$

Draw a picture.

$$\begin{array}{r} 6 \\ +\ 4 \\ \hline 1\,0 \end{array}$$

Guided Practice

Choose a way to add.
Write each sum.

1. $\begin{array}{r} 4 \\ +5 \\ \hline 9 \end{array}$ **Think:** 4 + 4 and one more.

2. $\begin{array}{r} 6 \\ +4 \\ \hline \end{array}$

3. $\begin{array}{r} 3 \\ +4 \\ \hline \end{array}$

4. $\begin{array}{r} 4 \\ +6 \\ \hline \end{array}$

5. $\begin{array}{r} 1 \\ +8 \\ \hline \end{array}$

6. $\begin{array}{r} 5 \\ +5 \\ \hline \end{array}$

7. $\begin{array}{r} 4 \\ +2 \\ \hline \end{array}$

8. $\begin{array}{r} 7 \\ +3 \\ \hline \end{array}$

9. $\begin{array}{r} 0 \\ +6 \\ \hline \end{array}$

10. $\begin{array}{r} 1 \\ +2 \\ \hline \end{array}$

11. $\begin{array}{r} 6 \\ +3 \\ \hline \end{array}$

Explain Your Thinking For Exercise 11, which way did you choose to add? Why?

Independent Practice

Choose a way to add.
Write each sum.

1. 9
+1
10

2. 5
+3

3. 6
+0
___

4. 2
+5

5. 4
+5

6. 3
+3

7. 6
+4

8. 0
+9

9. 8
+2

10. 5
+5

11. 2
+4

12. 0
+10

13. 2
+6

14. 4
+6

15. 2
+2

16. 5 + 4 = ___

17. 2 + 8 = ___

18. 4 + 6 = ___

19. ___ = 6 + 4

20. ___ = 5 + 1

21. ___ = 1 + 1

Problem Solving • Reasoning

Logical Thinking

Use the clues to find each butterfly.
Write the correct letter under each butterfly.

Butterfly A has ╲╱ .

Butterfly B has ▨ .

Butterfly C has ∘∘ .

Butterfly D has ∴ .

____ ____ ____ ____

108 one hundred eight

At Home Ask your child to solve 6 + 3 and explain how he or she found the sum.

Quick ✓ Check

Check Your Understanding of Lessons 1–6

Count on to add.

1. $5 + 2 =$ ___

   $2 + 5 =$ ___

2. $6 + 1 =$ ___

   $1 + 6 =$ ___

3. $7 + 3 =$ ___

   $3 + 7 =$ ___

4. $9 + 1 =$ ___

   $1 + 9 =$ ___

5. $6 + 0 =$ ___

   $0 + 6 =$ ___

6. $8 + 2 =$ ___

   $2 + 8 =$ ___

Write each sum.

7. $\begin{array}{r} 2 \\ +2 \\ \hline \end{array}$ $\begin{array}{r} 2 \\ +3 \\ \hline \end{array}$

8. $\begin{array}{r} 4 \\ +4 \\ \hline \end{array}$ $\begin{array}{r} 4 \\ +5 \\ \hline \end{array}$

9. $\begin{array}{r} 3 \\ +3 \\ \hline \end{array}$ $\begin{array}{r} 3 \\ +4 \\ \hline \end{array}$

10. $\begin{array}{r} 5 \\ +5 \\ \hline \end{array}$

11. $\begin{array}{r} 6 \\ +0 \\ \hline \end{array}$

12. $\begin{array}{r} 7 \\ +2 \\ \hline \end{array}$

13. $\begin{array}{r} 1 \\ +8 \\ \hline \end{array}$

14. $\begin{array}{r} 6 \\ +4 \\ \hline \end{array}$

15. $\begin{array}{r} 1 \\ +7 \\ \hline \end{array}$

16. $\begin{array}{r} 0 \\ +9 \\ \hline \end{array}$

17. $\begin{array}{r} 3 \\ +6 \\ \hline \end{array}$

18. $\begin{array}{r} 2 \\ +6 \\ \hline \end{array}$

19. $\begin{array}{r} 6 \\ +3 \\ \hline \end{array}$

Test Prep • Cumulative Review

Maintaining the Standards

Fill in the ○ for the correct answer.

1 Add.

$$6$$
$$+4$$

7	8	9	10
○	○	○	○

2 Subtract.

$$8$$
$$-1$$

7	8	9	10
○	○	○	○

3 How many in all?

20	15	10	9
○	○	○	○

4 Which number is nine?

6	7	8	9
○	○	○	○

5 Which number sentence matches the problem?

Dale had 8 eggs. He broke 4 of them. How many does he have left?

○ $2 + 8 = 10$

○ $8 - 4 = 4$

○ $8 - 8 = 0$

○ $4 + 4 = 8$

6 Donna has 4 pink rings. She has the same number of purple rings.

Explain how you can find how many rings she has in all.

_____

_____

_____

Safe Site

Internet Test Prep
Visit **www.eduplace.com/kids/mhm**
for more *Test Prep Practice.*

LESSON 7 Count Back to Subtract

Learn About It

Counting back can help you subtract.

Start with 9. Count back 1.

9

$\underline{8}$

$9 - 1 = \underline{8}$

Start with 9. Count back 2.

9

$\underline{8}$, $\underline{7}$

$9 - 2 = \underline{7}$

Guided Practice

Count back to subtract.

1.

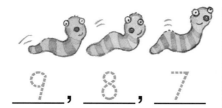

10

$\underline{9}$, $\underline{8}$, $\underline{7}$

$10 - 3 = \underline{7}$

2.

10

____ , ____

$10 - 2 = $ ___

3.

10

____

$10 - 1 = $ ___

4.

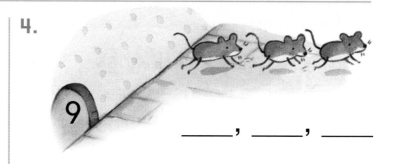

9

____ , ____ , ____

$9 - 3 = $ ___

Explain Your Thinking Why do you count back 2 to find $8 - 2$?

Independent Practice

Count back to subtract.

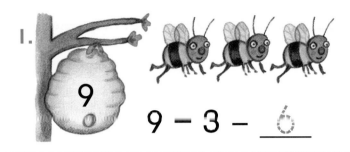

1. 9

   $9 - 3 - \underline{6}$

2. 10

   $10 \quad 2 = \underline{}$

3. $10 - 3 = \underline{}$ 4. $8 - 2 = \underline{}$ 5. $10 - 1 = \underline{}$

6. $7 - 2 = \underline{}$ 7. $9 - 1 = \underline{}$ 8. $2 - 2 = \underline{}$

9. $\begin{array}{r} 6 \\ -3 \\ \hline \end{array}$ 10. $\begin{array}{r} 10 \\ -1 \\ \hline \end{array}$ 11. $\begin{array}{r} 7 \\ -1 \\ \hline \end{array}$ 12. $\begin{array}{r} 6 \\ -2 \\ \hline \end{array}$ 13. $\begin{array}{r} 5 \\ -1 \\ \hline \end{array}$ 14. $\begin{array}{r} 7 \\ -2 \\ \hline \end{array}$

15. $\begin{array}{r} 9 \\ -3 \\ \hline \end{array}$ 16. $\begin{array}{r} 10 \\ -2 \\ \hline \end{array}$ 17. $\begin{array}{r} 8 \\ -3 \\ \hline \end{array}$ 18. $\begin{array}{r} 9 \\ -2 \\ \hline \end{array}$ 19. $\begin{array}{r} 8 \\ -2 \\ \hline \end{array}$ 20. $\begin{array}{r} 7 \\ -3 \\ \hline \end{array}$

21. $\begin{array}{r} 9 \\ -1 \\ \hline \end{array}$ 22. $\begin{array}{r} 10 \\ -3 \\ \hline \end{array}$ 23. $\begin{array}{r} 4 \\ -3 \\ \hline \end{array}$ 24. $\begin{array}{r} 8 \\ -1 \\ \hline \end{array}$ 25. $\begin{array}{r} 5 \\ -2 \\ \hline \end{array}$ 26. $\begin{array}{r} 6 \\ -1 \\ \hline \end{array}$

Problem Solving • Reasoning

27. A ladybug has 4 wings. Two are not used for flying. How many wings are used for flying?

    _____ wings

    Draw or write to explain.

At Home Pick a number from 3–10. Ask your child to start with that number and count back 3. Repeat with a different number.

LESSON 8 — Use a Number Line to Subtract

Learn About It

You can subtract by using a number line to count back.

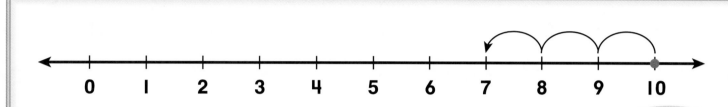

$$10 - 3 = \underline{7}$$

Start at 10.
Count back 3.
Say 9, 8, 7.

Guided Practice

Use the number line to count back.
Write each difference.

1. $9 - 3 = \underline{6}$
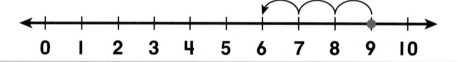

2. $10 - 1 = \underline{}$
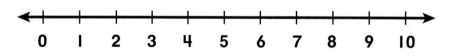

3. $10 - 2 = \underline{}$
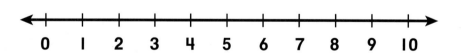

4. $9 - 2 = \underline{}$
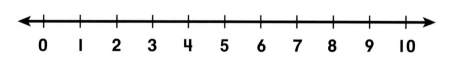

5. $8 - 3 = \underline{}$
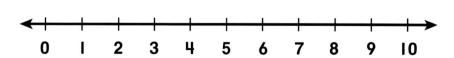

Explain Your Thinking How does knowing
$10 - 2$ help you know $10 - 8$?

Independent Practice

Use the number line.
Count back to find each difference.
Color to see what is hiding.

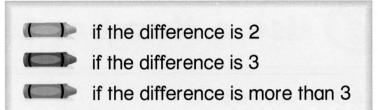

- if the difference is 2
- if the difference is 3
- if the difference is more than 3

0 1 2 3 4 5 6 7 8 9 10

10
− 2

9
− 3

7
− 1

9
− 2

4
− 2

6
− 1

3
− 1

6
− 3

4
− 1

5
− 3

10
− 3

7
− 2

5
− 2

8
− 1

7
− 3

6
− 2

10
− 1

8
− 2

9
− 1

8
− 3

At Home Ask your child to subtract 1, 2, and 3 from 10.

LESSON 9

Draw a Picture to Subtract

Learn About It

You can draw a picture to help you find a difference.

Cross out to show subtracting.

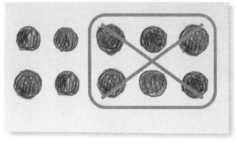

$10 - 6 = \underline{4}$

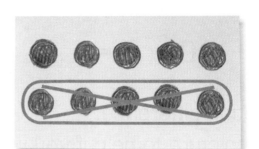

$10 - 5 = \underline{5}$

Guided Practice

Draw a picture for each subtracton sentence.

Cross out. Write each difference.

1.

$9 - 6 = \underline{3}$

2.

$8 - 5 = \underline{}$

3.

$10 - 9 = \underline{}$

4.

$10 - 4 = \underline{}$

Explain Your Thinking How could you use subtraction to solve $5 + \square = 10$?

Independent Practice

Draw a picture for each subtraction sentence.
Cross out. Write each difference.

1.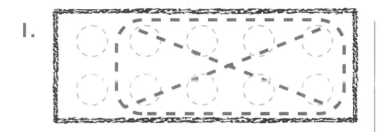

$$10 - 8 = \underline{2}$$

2.

$$9 - 5 = \underline{}$$

Write each difference.
Draw a picture to help if you want.

3. $\begin{array}{r} 6 \\ -0 \\ \hline \end{array}$
4. $\begin{array}{r} 5 \\ -3 \\ \hline \end{array}$
5. $\begin{array}{r} 8 \\ -8 \\ \hline \end{array}$
6. $\begin{array}{r} 8 \\ -6 \\ \hline \end{array}$
7. $\begin{array}{r} 9 \\ -6 \\ \hline \end{array}$
8. $\begin{array}{r} 10 \\ -\ 8 \\ \hline \end{array}$

9. $\begin{array}{r} 8 \\ -3 \\ \hline \end{array}$
10. $\begin{array}{r} 3 \\ -0 \\ \hline \end{array}$
11. $\begin{array}{r} 7 \\ -4 \\ \hline \end{array}$
12. $\begin{array}{r} 9 \\ -7 \\ \hline \end{array}$
13. $\begin{array}{r} 5 \\ -4 \\ \hline \end{array}$
14. $\begin{array}{r} 10 \\ -\ 9 \\ \hline \end{array}$

15. $\begin{array}{r} 9 \\ -9 \\ \hline \end{array}$
16. $\begin{array}{r} 6 \\ -4 \\ \hline \end{array}$
17. $\begin{array}{r} 8 \\ -5 \\ \hline \end{array}$
18. $\begin{array}{r} 9 \\ -8 \\ \hline \end{array}$
19. $\begin{array}{r} 7 \\ -5 \\ \hline \end{array}$
20. $\begin{array}{r} 10 \\ -\ 5 \\ \hline \end{array}$

Problem Solving • Reasoning

21. Phil sees 10 bugs.
5 crawl away.
How many bugs are left?

_____ bugs

Draw or write to explain.

At Home Ask your child to draw a picture to solve 10 − 7.

LESSON 10 Subtract to Compare

Learn About It

You can subtract to compare numbers.

Subtract to find how many more.

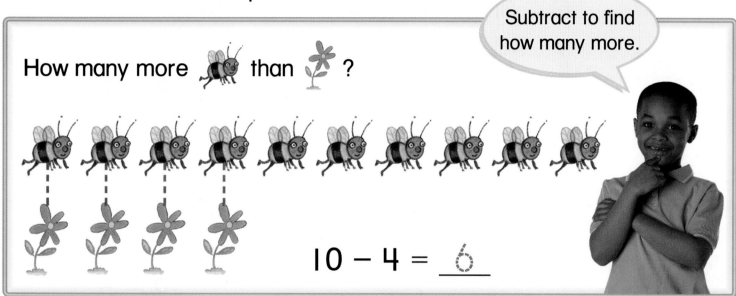

How many more 🐝 than 🌱 ?

$10 - 4 = \underline{6}$

Guided Practice

Match. Then subtract.

1. How many more 🐢 than 🐢 ?

$8 - 3 = \underline{5}$

2. How many more 🐞 than 🐞 ?

$9 - 4 = \underline{}$

Explain Your Thinking Can you add to compare numbers? Why or why not?

Independent Practice

Match. Then subtract.

1. How many more  than ?

$8 - 6 =$ _2_

2. How many more than ?

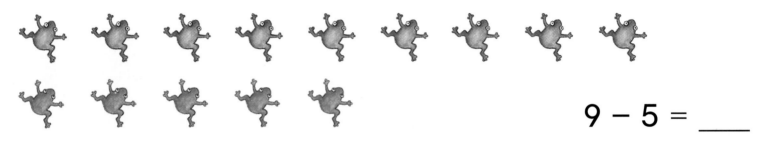

$9 - 5 =$ ___

3. How many more than ?

$10 - 4 =$ ___

Problem Solving • Reasoning

4. Robin saw 6 worms. Then she saw 4 more. How many worms did she see in all?

____ worms

Draw or write to explain.

At Home Ask your child to tell you how many more fingers than legs he or she has.

Name _____

LESSON 11

Problem Solving: Use Subtraction

Standards
NS **2.1, 2.5**
MR **1.0, 1.1**

Butterflies get food from flowers.
Crickets get food from plants.
You can see both in a garden.

You can compare to subtract.

9 crickets are by the plants.
There are 3 plants in the garden.
How many more crickets are
there than plants?

Think:
Find the numbers
in the story.
Subtract to compare.

☐ crickets

○ ☐ plants
_____
☐ more crickets

You can take away to subtract.

8 butterflies are on flowers.
6 butterflies fly away.
How many butterflies are left?

Think:
Find the numbers
in the story.
Subtract to find how
many are left.

☐ butterflies

○ ☐ fly away
_____
☐ are left

Guided Practice

Subtract.

1 There are 5 flowers. There is one bee. How many more flowers than bees are there?

Think: What do I need to find out?

___4___ more flowers

Draw or write to explain.

2 Cindy sees 4 grasshoppers. 2 hop under a bush. How many does she see now?

Think: What numbers do I use?

_____ grasshoppers

3 6 red ants crawl in line. 4 black ants crawl in line. How many more red ants than black ants are there?

Think: How can I find out how many more?

_____ more red ants

4 7 ladybugs are flying. 2 land on a leaf. How many ladybugs are still flying?

Think: What numbers do I subtract?

_____ ladybugs

At Home Give your child a subtraction story starting with a number under 9 and have him or her solve it.

120 one hundred twenty

Name_____

Choose a Strategy

Solve.

1 There are 4 caterpillars.
There are 2 leaves.
How many more caterpillars
are there than leaves?

_____ more caterpillars

Draw or write to explain.

caterpillar

2 Shelly saw 6 fireflies.
Then she saw 4 more.
How many did she
see in all.

_____ fireflies

firefly

3 8 beetles are looking for food.
3 beetles find food.
How many beetles are
still looking for food?

_____ beetles

beetle

4 There are 10 bumblebees.
6 of them fly away.
How many bumblebees
are there now?

_____ bumblebees

bumblebee

Test Prep • Cumulative Review

Maintaining the Standards

Fill in the ○ for the correct answer. NH means Not Here.

1 Which one shows the greatest amount?

○
○
○

○

2 Subtract.
$$\begin{array}{r} 6 \\ -5 \\ \hline \end{array}$$

1   2   3   NH
○   ○   ○   ○

3 Which fact has the same **sum** as $4 + 0 = 4$?

○ $4 + 4 = 8$

○ $4 - 4 = 0$

○ $0 + 4 = 4$

○ $8 - 4 = 4$

4 Frank had 7 stickers. He gave away 3 of them. How many does he have left?

6   5   4   3
○   ○   ○   ○

5 Which fact has the same **difference** as $10 - 3 = 7$?

○ $7 + 3 = 10$

○ $7 - 3 = 4$

○ $9 - 2 = 7$

○ $3 + 4 = 7$

6 **Explain** why $6 + 0$ and $0 + 6$ have the same sum.

_____

_____

Safe Site

Internet Test Prep
Visit **www.eduplace.com/kids/mhm**
for more *Test Prep Practice*.

LESSON 12

Algebra Readiness:
Relate Addition and Subtraction

Learn About It

Addition and subtraction facts that use
the same numbers are **related facts.**

New
Vocabulary
related fact

$\underline{6} + \underline{3} = \underline{9}$ $\underline{9} - \underline{3} = \underline{6}$

Guided Practice

Use Workmat 2 and cubes. Show the numbers.
Write the related facts.

Use two
different colors.

1. **8** and **1** $\underline{8} + \underline{1} = \underline{9}$ $\underline{9} - \underline{1} = \underline{8}$

2. **5** and **4**   ___ + ___ = ___   ___ − ___ = ___

3. **4** and **6**   ___ + ___ = ___   ___ − ___ = ___

4. **6** and **1**   ___ + ___ = ___   ___ − ___ = ___

5. **3** and **7**   ___ + ___ = ___   ___ − ___ = ___

Explain Your Thinking How are the number sentences
5 + 2 = 7 and 7 − 2 = 5 related?

Independent Practice

Add or subtract. Use cubes if you want.

1. $4 + 6 = \underline{10}$

   $10 - 6 = \underline{4}$

2. $3 + 5 = \underline{}$

   $8 - 5 = \underline{}$

3. $5 + 4 = \underline{}$

   $9 - 4 = \underline{}$

4. $2 + 7 = \underline{}$

   $9 - 7 = \underline{}$

5. $5 + 5 = \underline{}$

   $10 - 5 = \underline{}$

6. $\begin{array}{r} 2 \\ +8 \\ \hline \end{array}$ $\qquad$ $\begin{array}{r} 10 \\ -\ 8 \\ \hline \end{array}$

7. $\begin{array}{r} 4 \\ +3 \\ \hline \end{array}$ $\qquad$ $\begin{array}{r} 7 \\ -3 \\ \hline \end{array}$

8. $\begin{array}{r} 1 \\ +9 \\ \hline \end{array}$ $\qquad$ $\begin{array}{r} 10 \\ -\ 9 \\ \hline \end{array}$

9. $\begin{array}{r} 1 \\ +5 \\ \hline \end{array}$ $\qquad$ $\begin{array}{r} 6 \\ -5 \\ \hline \end{array}$

10. $\begin{array}{r} 5 \\ +2 \\ \hline \end{array}$ $\qquad$ $\begin{array}{r} 7 \\ -2 \\ \hline \end{array}$

11. $\begin{array}{r} 3 \\ +6 \\ \hline \end{array}$ $\qquad$ $\begin{array}{r} 9 \\ -6 \\ \hline \end{array}$

Problem Solving•Reasoning

Write each difference.
Circle the related addition fact.

12. $\begin{array}{r} 10 \\ -\ 4 \\ \hline \end{array}$

    $6 + 4 = 10$

    $5 + 4 = 9$

13. $\begin{array}{r} 9 \\ -5 \\ \hline \end{array}$

    $5 + 5 = 10$

    $4 + 5 = 9$

At Home Ask your child how the two number sentences in Exercise 11 are related.

Fact Families

LESSON **13**

Learn About It

New Vocabulary

fact family

A **fact family** is a set of related facts.

This fact family uses the numbers 9, 4, and 5.

Whole	
9	
Part	Part
4	5

9 is the whole.
4 and 5 are
the parts.

Workmat	
Whole	
Part	Part

$$\underline{4} + \underline{5} = \underline{9}$$

$$\underline{5} + \underline{4} = \underline{9}$$

Workmat	
Whole	
Part	Part

$$\underline{9} - \underline{5} = \underline{4}$$

$$\underline{9} - \underline{4} = \underline{5}$$

Guided Practice

Use Workmat 3 and cubes to show each fact.
Write each fact family.

1.

Whole	
10	
Part	Part
6	4

$$\underline{6} + \underline{4} = \underline{10}$$

$$\underline{} + \underline{} = \underline{}$$

$$\underline{10} - \underline{4} = \underline{6}$$

$$\underline{} - \underline{} = \underline{}$$

2.

Whole	
9	
Part	Part
6	3

$$\underline{} + \underline{} = \underline{}$$

$$\underline{} + \underline{} = \underline{}$$

$$\underline{} - \underline{} = \underline{}$$

$$\underline{} - \underline{} = \underline{}$$

Explain Your Thinking For a double fact like 4 + 4 = 8,
how many facts are in the fact family? Why?

Independent Practice

Use Workmat 3 and cubes to show each fact.
Write each fact family.

Think: Which numbers do I start with when I add?

1.

Whole	
10	
Part	Part
7	3

7 + 3 = 10   10 − 3 = 7

___ + ___ = ___   ___ − ___ = ___

2.

Whole	
8	
Part	Part
2	6

___ + ___ = ___   ___ − ___ = ___

___ + ___ = ___   ___ − ___ = ___

3.

Whole	
10	
Part	Part
2	8

___ + ___ = ___   ___ − ___ = ___

___ + ___ = ___   ___ − ___ = ___

4.

Whole	
9	
Part	Part
5	4

___ + ___ = ___   ___ − ___ = ___

___ + ___ = ___   ___ − ___ = ___

Problem Solving • Reasoning

Algebra Readiness · Missing Addends

Choose the number that
is the missing addend.

4   5   6   7

5. 10 = [ ] + 4   6. 10 = [ ] + 3   7. 9 = 5 + [ ]

At Home Ask your child to write a fact family for the numbers 4, 3, and 7.

Different Ways to Subtract

Learn About It

These are some ways you can find a difference.

Count back.
```
  7
- 2
-----
  5
```

Use counters.
```
  9
- 2
-----
  7
```

Draw a picture.
```
  8
- 6
-----
  2
```
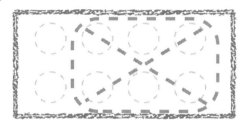

Use a related addition fact.
```
 10          5
- 5        + 5
-----      -----
  5         10
```

Guided Practice

Choose a way to subtract.
Write each difference.

1. 10   Think: 2. 10   3. 7   4. 6   5. 8
  - 3   Count back. - 6   - 6   - 3   - 0
  -----   ----- ----- ----- -----
     7

6. 7   7. 10   8. 8   9. 4   10. 5   11. 8
  - 7   - 4   - 7   - 3   - 5   - 4
  -----   -----   -----   -----   -----   -----

Explain Your Thinking For Exercise 11, which way
did you choose to subtract? Why?

Independent Practice

Choose a way to subtract.
Write each difference.

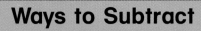

Ways to Subtract

Count back.
Use counters.
Draw a picture.
Use a related addition fact.

1. $7 - 0 = \underline{7}$

2. $3 - 2 = \underline{}$ 3. $6 - 5 = \underline{}$ 4. $8 - 6 = \underline{}$

5. $\begin{array}{r} 3 \\ -3 \\ \hline \end{array}$ 6. $\begin{array}{r} 5 \\ -0 \\ \hline \end{array}$ 7. $\begin{array}{r} 2 \\ -1 \\ \hline \end{array}$ 8. $\begin{array}{r} 8 \\ -5 \\ \hline \end{array}$ 9. $\begin{array}{r} 7 \\ -5 \\ \hline \end{array}$ 10. $\begin{array}{r} 6 \\ -6 \\ \hline \end{array}$

11. $\begin{array}{r} 9 \\ -7 \\ \hline \end{array}$ 12. $\begin{array}{r} 7 \\ -3 \\ \hline \end{array}$ 13. $\begin{array}{r} 9 \\ -0 \\ \hline \end{array}$ 14. $\begin{array}{r} 8 \\ -7 \\ \hline \end{array}$ 15. $\begin{array}{r} 10 \\ -10 \\ \hline \end{array}$ 16. $\begin{array}{r} 9 \\ -8 \\ \hline \end{array}$

17. $\begin{array}{r} 8 \\ -4 \\ \hline \end{array}$ 18. $\begin{array}{r} 8 \\ -0 \\ \hline \end{array}$ 19. $\begin{array}{r} 6 \\ -4 \\ \hline \end{array}$ 20. $\begin{array}{r} 1 \\ -0 \\ \hline \end{array}$ 21. $\begin{array}{r} 9 \\ -6 \\ \hline \end{array}$ 22. $\begin{array}{r} 7 \\ -4 \\ \hline \end{array}$

Problem Solving-Reasoning

Logical Thinking

Use the clues to find the number.

23. I am inside a shape.
    I am greater than 5.
    I am less than 9.
    I am not in the triangle.

    Which number am I? _____

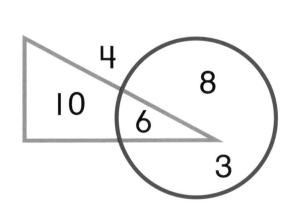

At Home Ask your child to solve $10 - 4$ and explain how he or she found the difference.

Name_____

LESSON 15 Problem Solving: Write a Number Sentence

Standards
NS **2.1**, AF **1.1**
MR **1.0**, **1.1**, **2.2**

You can write a number sentence to help you solve problems.

A fly has 2 wings.
A ladybug has 4 wings.
How many wings do they have in all?

Understand

What do you already know?

_____ wings on a fly

_____ wings on a ladybug

Plan

Circle how you would solve this problem.

add   subtract

Solve

Write a number sentence.

____ ◯ ____ = ____ wings in all

Look Back

Did you answer the question?

How do you know?

Guided Practice

Solve.

Write a number sentence.

Remember:
► Understand
► Plan
► Solve
► Look Back

Remember to use the 4 steps.

① One hornet has 4 wings.
One horse fly has 2 wings.
How many wings
do they have in all?

Draw or write to explain.

Think: Do I add or subtract?

$\underline{4} \; \oplus \; \underline{2} \; = \; \underline{6} \;$ wings

② A spider has 8 legs. An ant
has 6 legs. How many
more legs does a spider
have than an ant?

Think: How can I find out how many more?

____ ◯ ____ = ____ more legs

③ A walking stick has 6 legs.
It has 0 wings. How
many more legs than
wings does it have?

Think: How can I solve the problem?

____ ◯ ____ = ____ more legs

④ One butterfly has 4 wings.
One flea has no wings.
How many wings do
they have altogether?

Think: What do I need to find out?

____ ◯ ____ = ____

At Home Tell your child an insect has 6 legs. Ask him or her how
many more legs the insect has than he or she.

Name_____

Choose a Strategy

Solve.

1. A ladybug has 4 wings.
   How many wings do
   2 ladybugs have altogether?

   _____ wings

   Draw or write to explain.

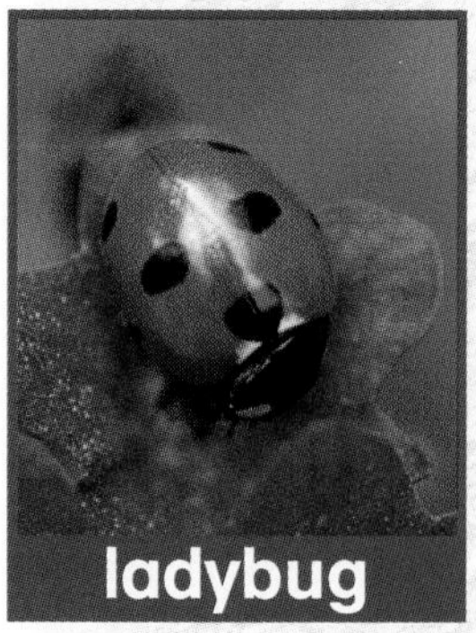

   ladybug

2. A moth has 6 legs.
   It has 4 wings.
   How many more legs does
   a moth have than wings?

   _____ more legs

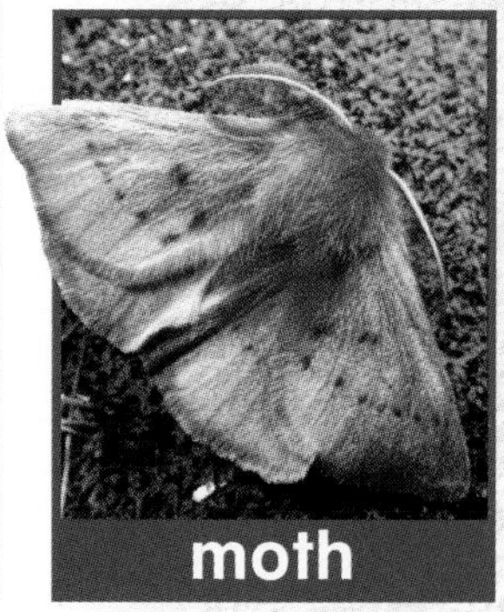

   moth

3. A dragonfly has 6 legs.
   How many legs do
   2 dragonflies have altogether?

   _____ legs

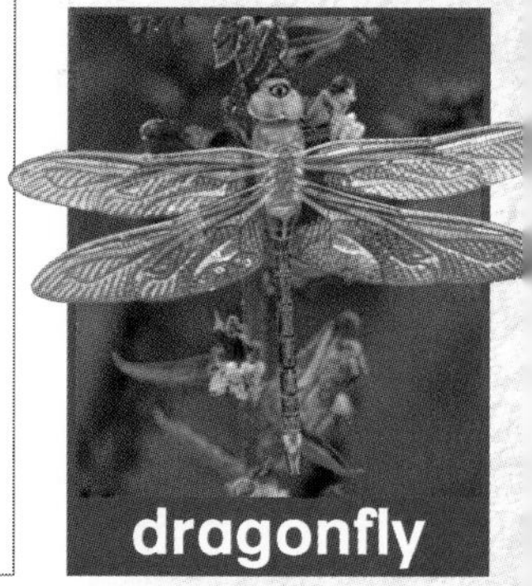

   dragonfly

4. A grasshopper has 4 short
   legs. It has 2 long legs.
   How many more short legs
   than long legs does it have?

   _____ more short legs

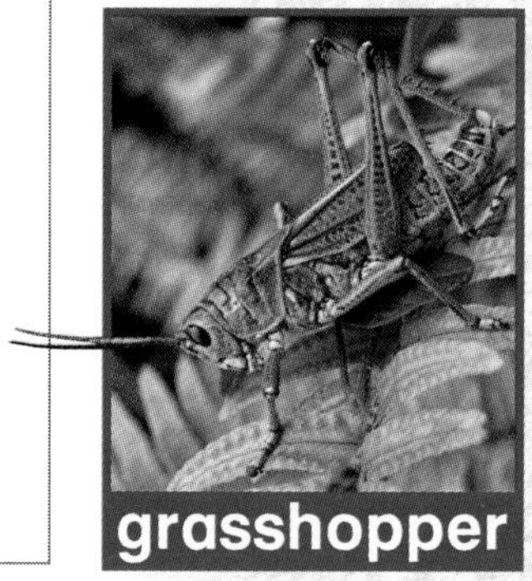

   grasshopper

Name _____

Mixed Practice

Memorize Your Facts

Watch the signs. Add or subtract.

1. 9 − 2 = ___   2. 6 + 3 = ___   3. 2 + 7 = ___

4. 3 − 1 = ___   5. 8 − 4 = ___   6. 4 + 5 = ___

7. 7   8. 8   9. 9   10. 6   11. 8   12. 1
   +3   − 1   − 4   +0   +2   − 1

13. 7   14. 9   15. 1   16. 9   17. 5   18. 1 0
    −5   +1   +6   −3   +5   − 6

19. 2   20. 9   21. 6   22. 5   23. 6   24. 1 0
    +3   −5   +2   +2   −4   − 4

 Brain Teaser The Rule

Look at the tables.
Write the rule for the
second table.

_____

Add the double			?
1	2	1	3
2	4	2	5
3	6	3	7
4	8	4	9

Safe Site

Internet Brain Teasers
Visit **www.eduplace.com/kids/mhm**
for more *Brain Teasers*.

Name _____

Check Your Understanding of Lessons 12–15

Add or subtract.

1. $7 + 3 =$ ___

   $10 - 3 =$ ___

2. $6 + 2 =$ ___

   $8 - 2 =$ ___

3. $5 + 5 =$ ___

   $10 - 5 =$ ___

Write each fact family.
Use cubes if you want.

4.
Whole	
10	
Part	Part
2	8

___ + ___ = ___   ___ − ___ = ___

___ + ___ = ___   ___ − ___ = ___

5.
Whole	
9	
Part	Part
5	4

___ + ___ = ___   ___ − ___ = ___

___ + ___ = ___   ___ − ___ = ___

Write a number sentence to solve each.

6. Nine ants march in a row. They carry 7 seeds. How many more ants are there than seeds?

   ___ ◯ ___ = ___

7. Angela put 3 flowers in one vase. She put 5 flowers in another vase. How many flowers are in both vases?

   ___ ◯ ___ = ___

Test Prep • Cumulative Review

Maintaining the Standards

Fill in the ○ for the correct answer. NH means Not Here.

1 Subtract.

$$9$$
$$-8$$

1	2	3	NH
○	○	○	○

2 Which is the same as 10 − 6?

0	4	6	8
○	○	○	○

3 Which number sentence is a related **addition** fact for 7 − 2 = 5?

○ 2 + 2 = 4

○ 5 + 5 = 10

○ 5 + 2 = 7

○ 7 − 5 = 2

4 Which number sentence is a related **subtraction** fact for 3 + 3 = 6?

○ 6 − 6 = 0

○ 3 − 3 = 0

○ 6 − 2 = 4

○ 6 − 3 = 3

5 Which is the same as 9 − 3?

9	5	3	NH
○	○	○	○

6 What number is 6 more than 2 + 2?
Explain how you found your answer.

_____

_____

_____

Safe Site

Internet Test Prep
Visit **www.eduplace.com/kids/mhm**
for more *Test Prep Practice*.

Chapter Review

1. Write a number sentence that has two **addends** that are the same. _____

2. The answer to an addition sentence is called the _____.

3. Write two **related facts**.

   _____   _____

4. Circle the number sentence that completes the fact family at the right.

   $9 - 9 = 0$ $9 - 7 = 2$

$7 + 2 = 9$
$2 + 7 = 9$
$9 - 2 = 7$

5. $\begin{array}{r} 8 \\ +1 \\ \hline \end{array}$
6. $\begin{array}{r} 4 \\ +3 \\ \hline \end{array}$
7. $\begin{array}{r} 5 \\ +2 \\ \hline \end{array}$
8. $\begin{array}{r} 9 \\ +1 \\ \hline \end{array}$
9. $\begin{array}{r} 7 \\ +0 \\ \hline \end{array}$
10. $\begin{array}{r} 5 \\ +3 \\ \hline \end{array}$

11. $\begin{array}{r} 3 \\ +3 \\ \hline \end{array}$ $\begin{array}{r} 4 \\ +3 \\ \hline \end{array}$
12. $\begin{array}{r} 2 \\ +2 \\ \hline \end{array}$ $\begin{array}{r} 3 \\ +2 \\ \hline \end{array}$
13. $\begin{array}{r} 4 \\ +4 \\ \hline \end{array}$ $\begin{array}{r} 5 \\ +4 \\ \hline \end{array}$

14. $6 + 1 =$ ___

    $1 + 6 =$ ___

15. $2 + 7 =$ ___

    $7 + 2 =$ ___

16. $6 + 3 =$ ___

    $3 + 6 =$ ___

1. 5
   +5

2. 4
   +0

3. 4
   +6

4. 5
   +3

5. 4
   +4

6. 2
   +7

7. 9
   −1

8. 8
   −3

9. 7
   −2

10. 10
    − 2

11. 9
    −3

12. 8
    −1

13. 8
    −6

14. 9
    −5

15. 10
    − 7

16. 7
    −5

17. 10
    − 9

18. 9
    −7

Write each fact family.

19.

Whole	
10	
Part	Part
6	4

___ + ___ = ___   ___ − ___ = ___

___ + ___ = ___   ___ − ___ = ___

20.

Whole	
9	
Part	Part
7	2

___ + ___ = ___   ___ − ___ = ___

___ + ___ = ___   ___ − ___ = ___

Write a number sentence to solve each.

21. Dino has 10 books and 5 bookmarks. How many more books than bookmarks does he have?

___ ◯ ___ = ___

22. Mattie has 2 stamps. She finds 8 more stamps. How many stamps does she have now?

___ ◯ ___ = ___

Chapter Test

Name_____

Add or subtract.

1. 1
   +8

2. 7
   +2

3. 9
   +1

4. 6
   +3

5. 8
   +2

6. 5
   +4

7. 3
   +7

8. 5
   +5

9. 4
   +6

10. 10
    − 1

11. 9
    −3

12. 8
    −2

13. 9
    −1

14. 10
    − 2

15. 9
    −6

16. 10
    − 8

17. 8
    −7

18. 9
    −5

19. 6 + 3 = _____

20. 1 + 7 = _____

21. 2 + 6 = _____

3 + 6 = _____

7 + 1 = _____

6 + 2 = _____

Write a number sentence to solve.

22. Marcus has 8 red model cars. He has 2 black model cars. How many cars does he have altogether?

23. There are 9 big bottles and 7 small bottles on the table. How many more big bottles are there?

____ ◯ ____ = ____

____ ◯ ____ = ____

Write the fact family.

24.

Whole	
9	
Part	**Part**
1	8

___ + ___ = ___ | ___ − ___ = ___

___ + ___ = ___ | ___ − ___ = ___

25.

Whole	
10	
Part	**Part**
7	3

___ + ___ = ___ | ___ − ___ = ___

___ + ___ = ___ | ___ − ___ = ___

 Write About It

1. Jean said that she could subtract a number from 10 and still have 10 left.

   Explain whether she is right or wrong. Tell how you know.

   _____

   _____

2. **Explain** how you know $5 + 3 - 3 - 5$?

   _____

   _____

Name _____

Spinning Solutions

What You Need

How to Play

1 Choose or .

2 Spin to get an answer.

3 Find a box below in which to write that answer. Lose a turn if you can't find a box.

4 The player who has the most boxes with answers wins.

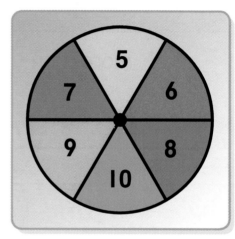

9 −0	4 +3	9 −4	4 +2	5 +3	1 0 − 0
9 −3	1 0 − 2	6 +4	9 −2	5 +4	3 +2

Standards
NS 3.0, 3.1

Enrichment

Estimate Sums and Differences

Circle the correct estimate.
Do not find the exact answer.
Tell how you found your answer.

1. $9 + 1$

more than 9

less than 9

2. $5 + 3$

more than 6

less than 6

3. $10 + 1$

more than 10

less than 10

4. $8 + 3$

more than 9

less than 9

5. $8 - 2$

more than 8

less than 8

6. $7 + 3$

more than 7

less than 7

7. $10 - 3$

more than 9

less than 9

8. $9 - 4$

more than 8

less than 8

From Here to There

A Read-Aloud Story

written by Yael Resnick
illustrated by Doris Barrette

Accessing Prior Knowledge

This story will
help you review
- Counting
- Comparing
  numbers

A Math Storybook for

_____

You can sit high up on a camel's hump
or hold onto your hat when your truck goes bump —

if you have to go across the hot, hot desert.

There are _____ camels and _____ trucks.

Are there more camels or trucks? _____

You can ride through the valley on a bike
or glide in a riverboat if you like —

if you want to see the countryside.

There are _____ bikes and _____ boats.

Are there fewer bikes or boats? _____

You can take a high-flying plane trip
or zoom through the stars in a rocket ship —

if you want to reach the sky!

There are ____ planes and ____ rocket ship.

Which will take you to the moon? _____

Family Letter

Vocabulary

tally mark A mark used to record a number.

picture graph A graph that uses pictures to show information.

bar graph A graph that uses bars to show information.

Dear Family,

During the next few weeks, our math class will be learning about data by using charts and graphs.

You can expect to see work that provides practice with charts and graphs. You may wish to use the following sample as a guide.

Tally Marks

1   2   5   10

Bar Graph

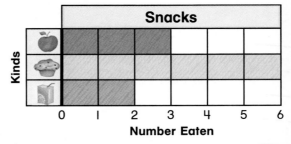

Snacks

Kinds

0   1   2   3   4   5   6

Number Eaten

Picture Graph

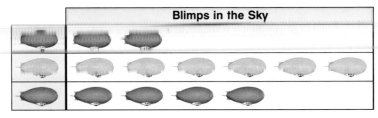

Blimps in the Sky

Knowing how to read and make charts and graphs can help children in their lives.

Sincerely,
Your child's teacher

150

Name_____

Standards
SDP **1.1, 1.2, 2.0, 2.1**
MG **2.0, 2.2,** MR **1.2**

Sorting Objects

Learn About It

Sort the shapes in different ways.
Then draw one of the ways.

Explain Your Thinking What other objects could you sort?
Explain how you could sort them.

Try It Out

Circle all the shapes that belong in each group.

1. Circles

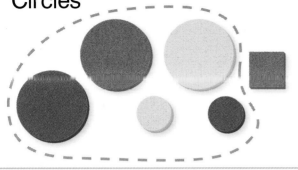

2. Large shapes

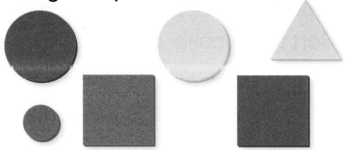

3. Red shapes

4. Squares

5. Small shapes

6. Blue shapes

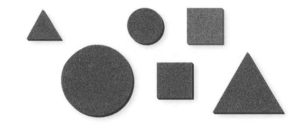

Problem Solving • Reasoning

Patterns

Draw and color what is likely to come next.

7.

_____

8.

_____

At Home Ask your child to sort some household items such as laundry, shoes, or cards.

152 one hundred fifty-two

Standards
NS **1.3**
SDP **1.0, 1.1, 1.2**

Hands-On Activity

LESSON 2

Make a Tally Chart

New Vocabulary
tally mark

Learn About It

You can make a tally chart to show how many.
Make one **tally mark** for each dot.

Draw a line across for the fifth one.

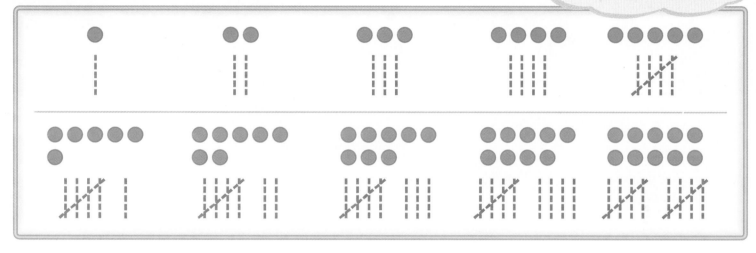

Ask 10 classmates which activity they like best.
Complete the tally chart.

Make a tally mark for each answer.

Activity	Tally	Total

Use the chart. Write how many.

1.  _____

2. _____

3. _____

Explain Your Thinking How can you show 14 by using tally marks?

Try It Out

Use the picture to complete the tally chart.

As you make a tally mark, cross off the picture.

Activity	Tally	Total
	⫶	

Use the chart.

1. How many are there?

   _____

2. How many are there?

   _____

3. Circle the activity that has the largest number.

4. Circle the activity that has the smallest number.

Name_____

LESSON 3 Read a Picture Graph

New
Vocabulary
picture graph

Learn About It

A **picture graph** uses pictures to show information.

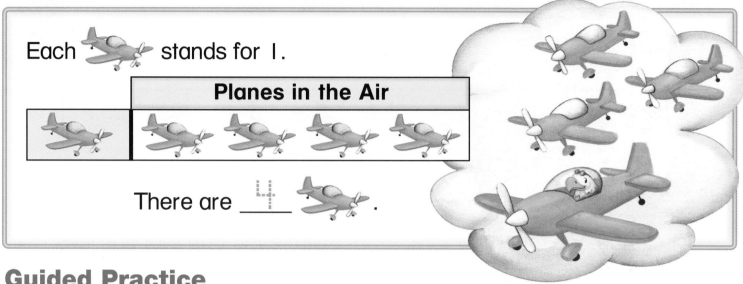

Each ✈ stands for 1.

Planes in the Air

There are ___4___ ✈.

Guided Practice

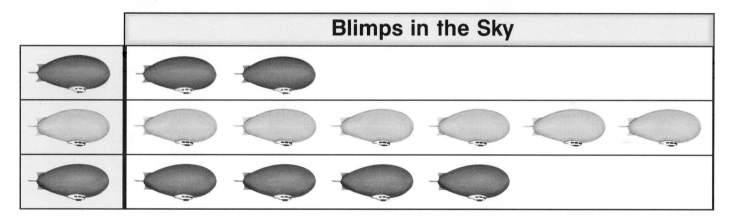

Blimps in the Sky

Use the picture graph.

1. The largest number is

2. The smallest number is

3. How many 🛩 and 🛩

are there? _____ in all

4. How many less 🛩 than

🛩 are there? _____ less

Explain Your Thinking How many more would you need in order to have the same number as 🛩 ?

Independent Practice

Each picture stands for 1 trip into space.

Trips Into Space

Use the graph.

1. Circle the one that has more.

 ()

2. Circle the one that has less.

3. How many less than are there?

_____ less

4. How many and are there?

_____ in all

5. How many more than are there? _____ more

Problem Solving • Reasoning

Algebra Readiness · Number Sentences

Write the number sentence.

6. There are 10 .
4 fly away.
How many  are left?

_____ ◯ _____ = _____

At Home Ask your child to use the Trips Into Space graph to tell you how many trips were taken in all.

LESSON 4 **Make a Picture Graph**

Learn About It

You can show information by
using a picture graph.

I cross off one
ticket as I color
each picture.

Color one picture on the graph
for each ticket shown.

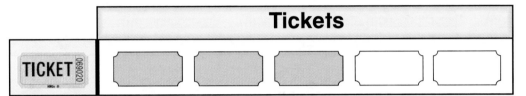

	Tickets				
TICKET 069020					

Guided Practice

Use the picture to make a graph.
Color to show how many of each.

	Toys				
train					
fire truck					
helicopter					

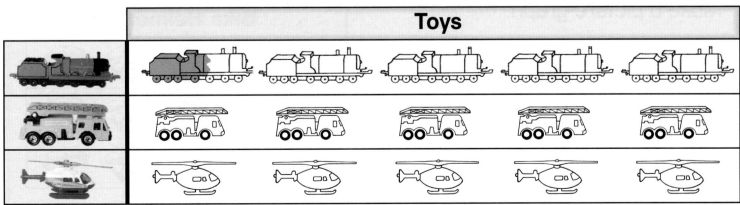

Explain Your Thinking How can you tell which toy there is the most of?

Independent Practice

Use the picture to make a graph.
Color to show how many.

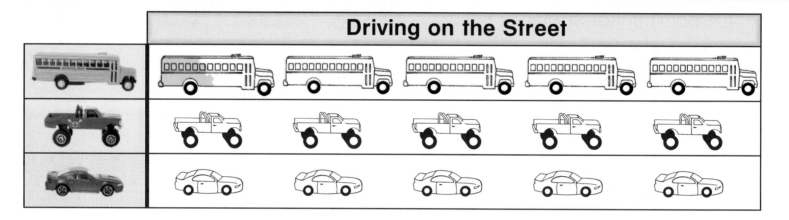

Driving on the Street

Use the picture graph.

1. How many more than are there? _____ more

2. How many and are there? _____ in all

Problem Solving•Reasoning

Logical Thinking

Make a picture graph.

3. There are 3 🪖 .
   There are 2 less 🪖 than 🪖 .
   There is 1 more 🪖 than 🪖 .

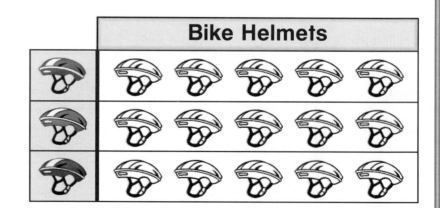

Bike Helmets

At Home Ask your child to use the Bike Helmets graph to tell you which color helmet is the greatest in number.

Name _____

Problem Solving: Use Logical Thinking

LESSON 5

Standards
MR **1.0, 1.1, 2.2**

You can use clues to help you solve problems.

Shannon has a favorite balloon. It has red and has only 2 colors. Which is her favorite balloon?

Understand

Circle what you need to find out.

Which is her favorite?

How many there are.

Plan

Circle how you would solve this problem.

Use clues.

Add.

Solve

Follow the clues.
Cross out what does not match.
Circle Shannon's favorite balloon.

has red   only 2 colors

Look Back

Does your answer match the clues?
Explain why.

Guided Practice

Solve. Circle the one
that matches the clues.

Remember
to use the
4 steps.

1 It has 4 wheels.
Children pull it to play.

Think:
Which ones have
4 wheels?

---

2 It has a driver.
More than 10 people can
ride in it at the same time.

Think:
Which ones have
a driver?

---

3 It has more than 2 wheels.
It carries cars, not people.

Think:
Which ones have
more than 2 wheels?

---

4 It has more than 2 wheels.
It rides on a track.

Think:
Which one matches
the clues?

---

160 one hundred sixty

At Home Help your child make up clues to describe his or her
favorite way to travel on land.

Name_____

Choose a Strategy

Use the clues to solve.

1 It goes very fast.
It travels into space.
What is it?

_____

Draw or write to explain.

helicopter

2 It flies in the air.
It is made of cloth.
What is it?

_____

space
shuttle

3 10 people got on the jet.
2 more people sat on the right
side than the left. How many
people are on each side?

_____ right   _____ left

hang glider

4 The helicopter made 9 trips.
5 trips were to the city.
How many trips were not
to the city?

_____ trips

jet

Name _____

Mixed Practice

Watch the signs. Find each sum or difference.

1. 0 + 3 = ___

2. 8 − 4 = ___

3. 5 + 4 = ___

4. 10 − 2 = ___

5. 8 + 0 = ___

6. 4 + 6 = ___

7. 9 − 1 = ___

8. 8 − 7 = ___

9. 2 + 5 = ___

10. 3
    +3
    ___

11. 5
    −5
    ___

12. 9
    −6
    ___

13. 9
    −0
    ___

14. 1
    +8
    ___

15. 6
    −5
    ___

16. 9
    −5
    ___

17. 1
    +9
    ___

18. 4
    +4
    ___

19. 9
    −7
    ___

20. 10
    − 3
    ___

21. 2
    +8
    ___

 Brain Teaser Favorite Color

Write the colors in the chart.
Use these clues.

- Blue had the most votes.
- More children voted for red than green.

Favorite Colors	
Color	**Tally**
_____	||
_____	ⅢⅠ
_____	Ⅲ

 Safe Site

Internet Brain Teasers
Visit www.eduplace.com/kids/mhm
for more *Brain Teasers.*

Name_____

Check Your Understanding of Lessons 1–5

1. Circle all the blue shapes.

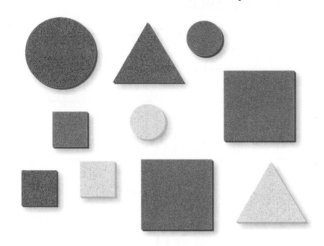

2. Make a tally chart to show the shapes from Exercise 1.

Shape	Tally	Total
◯		_____
△		_____
☐		_____

3. Use the tally chart to make a picture graph.

Shapes					
◯	◯	◯	◯	◯	◯
△	△	△	△	△	△
☐	☐	☐	☐	☐	☐

Use the picture graph for Exercises 4 and 5.

4. How many more ☐ than △?

_____ more

5. How many ◯ and ☐ are there in all?

_____ in all

Circle the one that matches the clues.

6. I am not red.
   I can fly in the air.

Test Prep • Cumulative Review

Maintaining the Standards

Fill in the ○ for the correct answer. NH means Not Here.

1 Subtract.

$$8 - 5 = \blacksquare$$

5	4	3	NH
○	○	○	○

2 There are 9 birds.
Four fly away.
How many are left?

6	5	4	3
○	○	○	○

3 Add.
$$\begin{array}{r} 4 \\ +5 \\ \hline \end{array}$$

9	8	7	6
○	○	○	○

4 Which number will make this a double fact?

$$4 + \blacksquare = 8$$

1	2	3	4
○	○	○	○

Use the chart for Exercises 5–7.

Bug	Number
bee	||||
ladybug	|||| ||
ant	|||

5 How many less bee than ladybug are there?

1	2	3	5
○	○	○	○

6 How many more ladybug than ant are there?

4	3	2	1
○	○	○	○

7 Which bug has the most tally marks?
Explain how you know.

_____

_____

Safe Site

Internet Test Prep
Visit **www.eduplace.com/kids/mhm**
for more *Test Prep Practice.*

Standards
NS **1.1, 1.3**
SDP **1.0, 1.2**

LESSON 6 Read a Bar Graph

New
Vocabulary
bar graph

Learn About it

A **bar graph** can help you compare numbers.

The longest bar shows which snack was chosen the most.

This graph shows the snack each child chose.

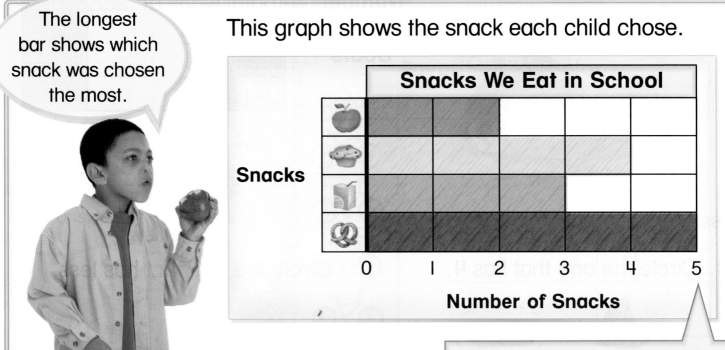

Look at the number where the shading ends to know how many.

Guided Practice

Use the bar graph.

1. How many kinds of snacks are there?

   __4__ kinds

2. How many more than are eaten?

   _____ more

3. Circle the snack that is eaten most often.

4. Circle the snack that is eaten least often.

Explain Your Thinking How would the graph change if someone switched from to ?

Try It Out

Use the picture to make a bar graph.

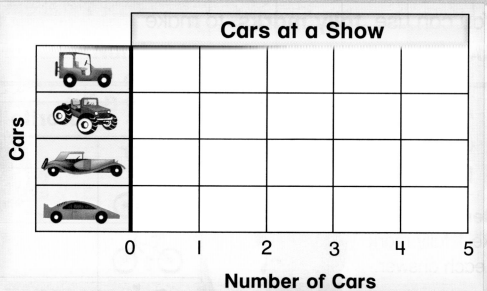

Remember: Color 1 box for each car.

Cars at a Show

Cars

0   1   2   3   4   5

Number of Cars

Use the bar graph.

1. How many are there?

   _____

2. How many 🚗 and 🚙 are there? _____ in all

3. Circle the one that has less.

4. Circle the one that has 2 more than 🚗.

Problem Solving · Reasoning

Logical Thinking

5. Make a bar graph to show that ⚪ has the greatest, ⚫ has the least, and ⚫ has more than ⚫.

Favorite Colors

Colors

0   1   2   3   4   5

Number of Children

6. **Write About It** Will everyone's graph look the same? Explain.

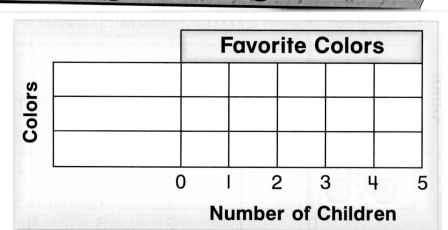

At Home Ask your child to make a bar graph that shows how many chairs are in 3 rooms in your home.

LESSON 8 # Different Ways to Show Data

Learn About It

You can show data on a tally chart or on a bar graph.

Count the
tally marks.

Color 1 box on the bar graph for each tally mark.

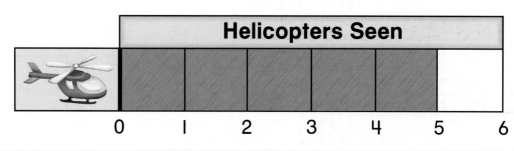

Guided Practice

Use the tally chart.
Complete the bar graph.

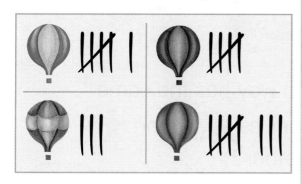

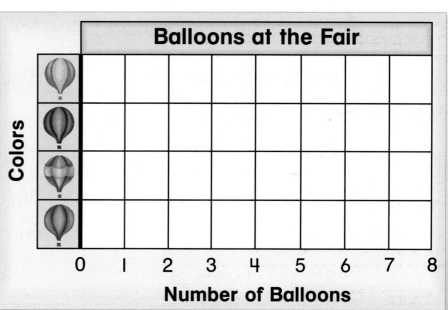

Use the graph.

1. How many are there?

____

2. How many and

are there? ____ in all

3. Circle the one that has 2 more
than .

4. Circle the one that has 3 less
than .

Explain Your Thinking How many balloons in all are at the fair?

Independent Practice

Use the tally chart.
Make a bar graph.

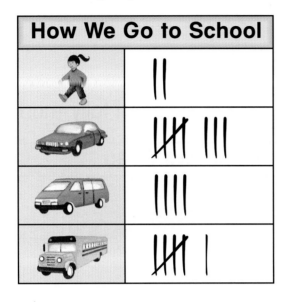

How We Go to School	
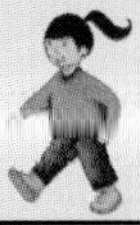	II
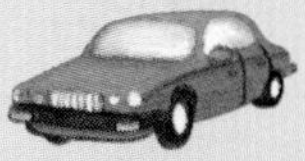	卌 III
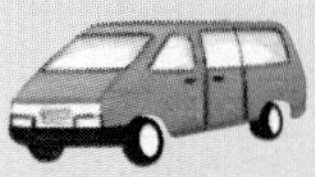	IIII
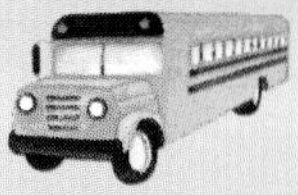	卌 I

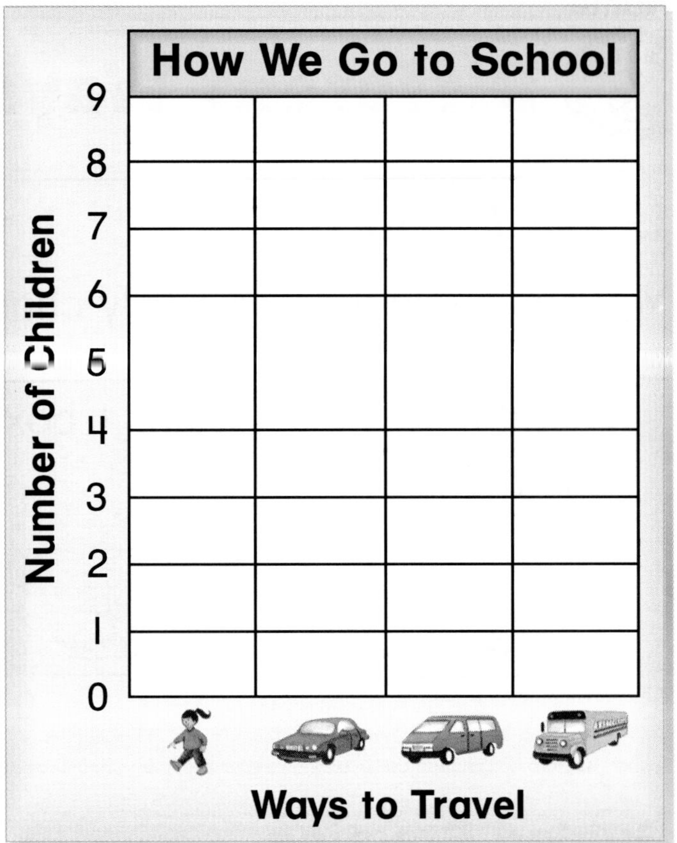
How We Go to School
Number of Children
0
1
2
3
4
5
6
7
8
9
Ways to Travel

Use the graph. Circle each answer.

1. Which way has fewer?

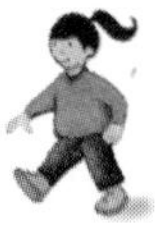 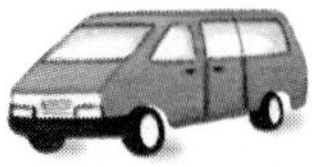

2. Which way has 4 more than 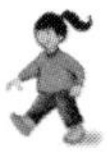 ?

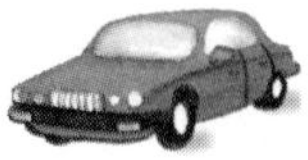 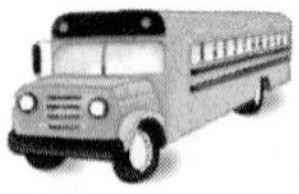

3. Which way has 2 fewer than 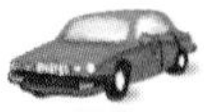 ?

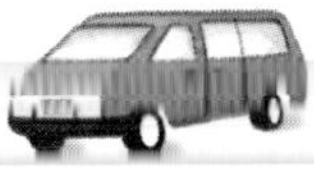 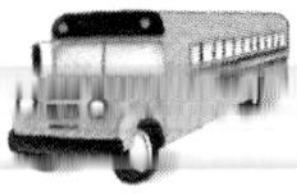

4. Which way has the same number as 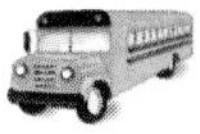 and 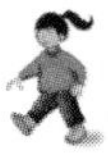 altogether?

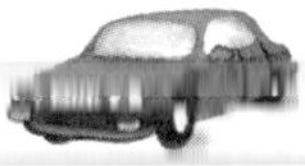 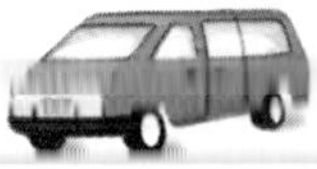

Problem Solving • Reasoning

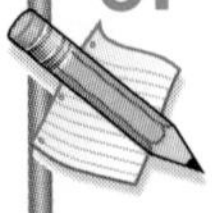

5. **Write Your Own** Write a question about this graph.

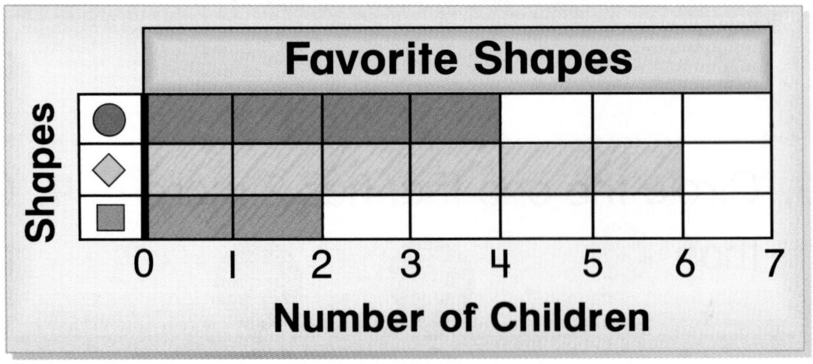
Favorite Shapes
Shapes
0
1
2
3
4
5
6
7
Number of Children

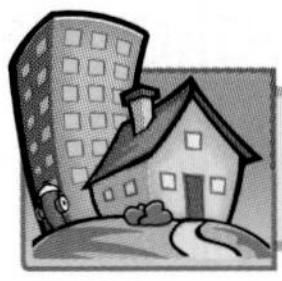

At Home Have your child explain how he or she found the answer for Exercise 4.

Name_____

Problem Solving:
Use a Bar Graph

Standards
NS 2.0, SDP 1.0, 1.2
MR 1.0, 1.1, 3.0

You can travel on water in different kinds of boats. This graph shows how many boats are at one dock.

Boats at the Dock

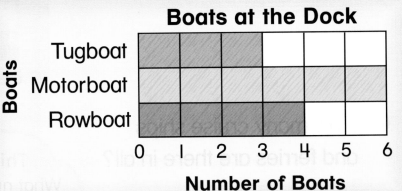

Boats — Tugboat, Motorboat, Rowboat

0 1 2 3 4 5 6
Number of Boats

You can use a graph and add to solve a problem.

How many tugboats and motorboats are there in all?

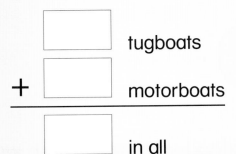

[ ] tugboats
+ [ ] motorboats
_____
[ ] in all

Think: Find the numbers on the graph. Add to find how many in all.

You can use a graph and subtract to solve a problem.

How many more motorboats are there than rowboats?

[ ] motorboats
− [ ] rowboats
_____
[ ] more motorboats

Think: Find the numbers on the graph. Subtract to find the difference.

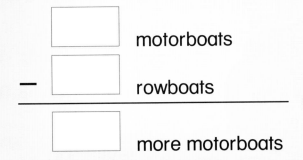

Name _____

Mixed Practice

Memorize
Your Facts

Watch the signs. Find each sum or difference.

1. $10 - 4 = $ ___

2. $8 - 5 = $ ___

3. $3 + 2 = $ ___

4. $0 + 9 = $ ___

5. $7 - 6 = $ ___

6. $6 + 2 = $ ___

7.
$$\begin{array}{r} 6 \\ -6 \\ \hline \end{array}$$

8.
$$\begin{array}{r} 10 \\ -\ 1 \\ \hline \end{array}$$

9.
$$\begin{array}{r} 8 \\ -6 \\ \hline \end{array}$$

10.
$$\begin{array}{r} 1 \\ +1 \\ \hline \end{array}$$

11.
$$\begin{array}{r} 7 \\ +2 \\ \hline \end{array}$$

12.
$$\begin{array}{r} 5 \\ +3 \\ \hline \end{array}$$

13.
$$\begin{array}{r} 3 \\ +7 \\ \hline \end{array}$$

14.
$$\begin{array}{r} 1 \\ +9 \\ \hline \end{array}$$

15.
$$\begin{array}{r} 5 \\ +4 \\ \hline \end{array}$$

16.
$$\begin{array}{r} 10 \\ -\ 7 \\ \hline \end{array}$$

17.
$$\begin{array}{r} 6 \\ -0 \\ \hline \end{array}$$

18.
$$\begin{array}{r} 10 \\ -\ 5 \\ \hline \end{array}$$

 Brain Teaser

Label the graph.
There are 2 more
red than yellow.
There is 1 less
blue than green.

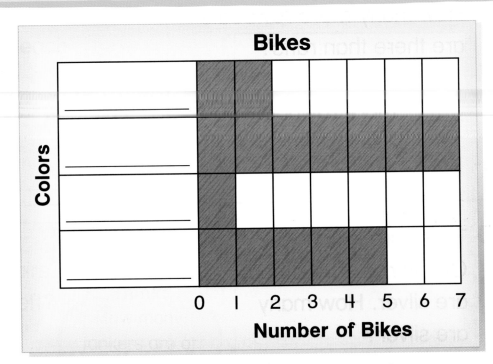

Safe Site
Internet Brain Teasers
Visit **www.eduplace.com/kids/mhm**
for more *Brain Teasers*.

Quick ✓ Check

Check Your Understanding of Lessons 6–9

Use the picture to make a bar graph. Then solve.

1.

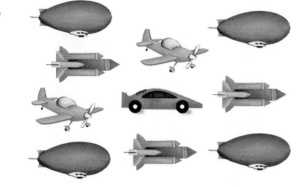

Ways to Travel

Ways				

0   1   2   3   4

Number

2. How many more 🎈 than ✈️ ?

_____ more

3. How many 🚀 and 🚗 in all?

_____ in all

Use the tally chart to make the bar graph. Then solve.

Ways to the Park	
🚶	IIII I
🚐	II
🚗	IIII II

Ways to the Park

Ways						
🚶						
🚐						
🚗						

0   1   2   3   4   5   6

Number

4. How many less 🚐 than 🚗 ?

_____ less

5. How many and in all?

_____ in all

Name_____

Test Prep • Cumulative Review

Maintaining the Standards

Fill in the ○ for the correct answer.

Use the graph for Exercises 1–3.

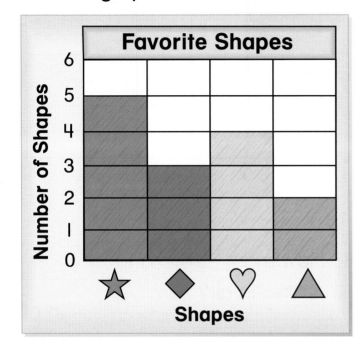

Favorite Shapes

Number of Shapes

6
5
4
3
2
1
0

Shapes

1 Which has the most?

○   ○   ○   ○

2 How many more than ▲ are there?

1   2   3   4

○   ○   ○   ○

3 How many ◆ and ♡ are there in all?

9   7   6   5

○   ○   ○   ○

4 Subtract.

$$10 - 6 = \blacksquare$$

6   5   4   3

○   ○   ○   ○

5 Add.
$$\begin{array}{r} 7 \\ +2 \\ \hline \end{array}$$

9   8   7   6

○   ○   ○   ○

6 Which number matches these tally marks?

‖‖‖ ‖‖‖

three   five   seven   eight

○   ○   ○   ○

7 Write a related **subtraction** fact for $5 + 3 = 8$. **Explain.**

_____

_____

176 one hundred seventy-six

Safe Site

Internet Test Prep
Visit **www.eduplace.com/kids/mhm**
for more *Test Prep Practice.*

Chapter Review

Circle the correct word.

1. A **picture graph** uses _____ to show information.

   pictures   bars

2. A **bar graph** uses _____ to show information.

   pictures   bars

Write the **tally marks** for each number.

3. four _____   4. ten _____   5. seven _____

6. Circle all the red shapes.

Shape	Tally	Total
◯		_____
△		_____
▢		_____

7. Use the shapes from Exercise 6 to make a tally chart.

8. Use the tally chart to make a picture graph.

Shapes

◯	◯ ◯ ◯ ◯ ◯
△	△ △ △ △ △
▢	▢ ▢ ▢ ▢ ▢

Use the picture graph for Exercise 9.

9. How many less ◯ than △ are there?   _____ less ◯

1. Use the pictures to make a bar graph. Then solve.

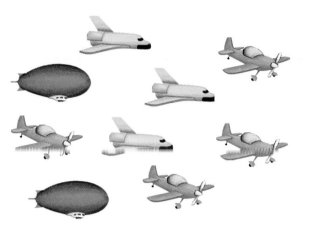

In the Air				
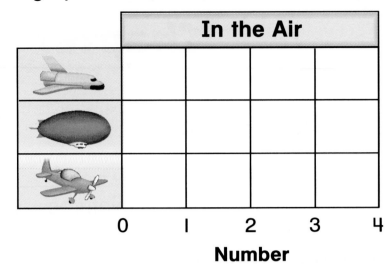				

Kinds

0   1   2   3   4

Number

2. How many more than are there?

_____ more

3. How many and are there in all?

_____ in all

4. Use the tally chart to complete the bar graph. Then solve.

Activity	Tally
	|||||
	|||

Favorite Activities						
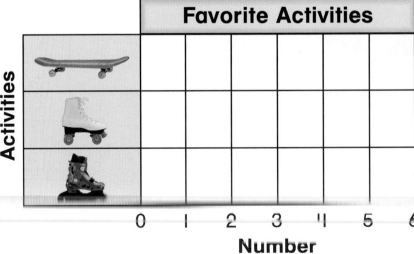						

Activities

0   1   2   3   4   5   6

Number

5. Which was chosen least often?

6. Which was chosen most often?

7. Circle the one that matches the clues.

It does not ride on tracks.
It only has 2 wheels.

Name _____

Chapter Test

1. Circle all the yellow shapes.

2. Make a tally chart to show the shapes from Exercise 1.

Shape	Tally	Total
⬤		
△		
☐		

3. Use the tally chart to make a graph. Then solve.

Shapes					
⬤	○	○	○	○	○
△	△	△	△	△	△
☐	☐	☐	☐	☐	☐

4. How many more ◯ than ☐ are there?

____ more

5. How many △ and ◯ are there in all?

____ in all

6. Circle the one that has 4 more than ☐.

△ ◯

7. Circle the one that has the smallest number.

△ ☐

8. Use the tally chart to make the bar graph.

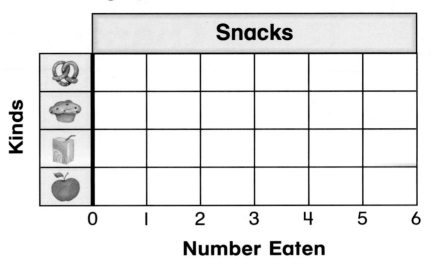

Snacks	
🥨	IIII I
🧁	III
🧃	IIII
🍎	IIII

Snacks

Kinds

Number Eaten
0 1 2 3 4 5 6

Use the bar graph for Exercises 9 and 10.

9. Circle the snack with the largest number.

10. Circle the snack with 2 less than .

✏️ **Write About It**

1. Use the pictures to make a graph.

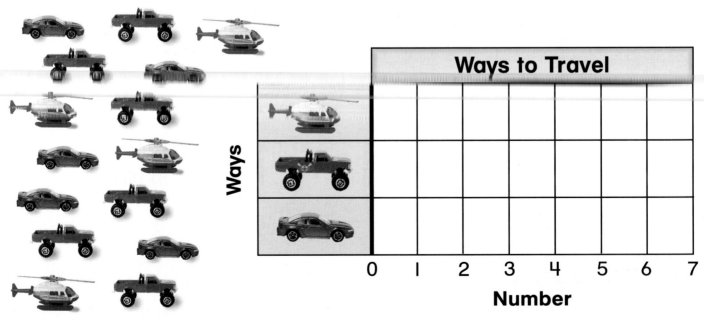

Ways to Travel

Ways

Number
0 1 2 3 4 5 6 7

2. Write a question about the graph.

_____

Name_____

Numbers Are Great!

Players
2

What You Need

number cards 1–20

How to Play

❶ Cards are placed facedown in a pile.

❷ Each player turns over the top card.

❸ The player with the greater number colors 1 box on the graph below.

❹ Players continue until all the cards are turned over. The player with the most colored boxes wins.

	The Greater Number									
_____ Name										
_____ Name										
	0	1	2	3	4	5	6	7	8	9	10

Standards
SDP **1.0, 1.1, 1.2**

Enrichment

Logical Thinking

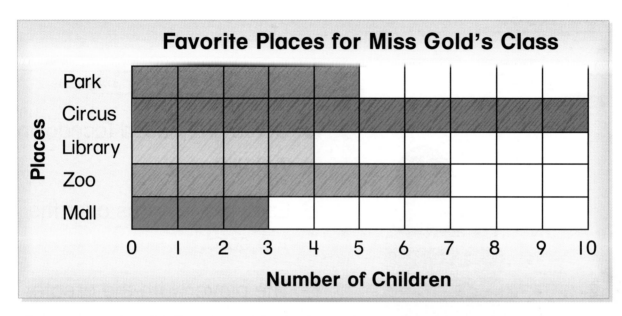

Favorite Places for Miss Gold's Class

Places: Park, Circus, Library, Zoo, Mall

Number of Children (0 to 10)

Mr. Suntag asked his class their favorite sports.
Fill in the graph below.
Use the clues and the graph above.

1. T-ball has 4 less votes than the circus.

2. Soccer has 3 more votes than the zoo.

3. Hockey has double the amount of votes that the library has.

4. Swimming has more votes than the mall and less than the park.

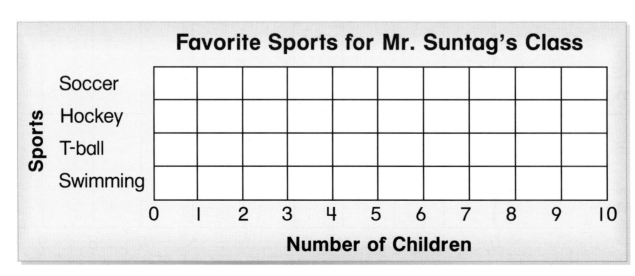

Favorite Sports for Mr. Suntag's Class

Sports: Soccer, Hockey, T-ball, Swimming

Number of Children (0 to 10)

Numbers and Patterns to 100

Accessing Prior Knowledge

This story will help you review
- Counting
- Ordering numbers

Party Under the Sea

A Read-Aloud Story

written by Laura Black
illustrated by Janet Skiles

A Math Storybook for

_____

The fish are having a party.
They're inviting us to come.
Why don't we join them
For some counting fun?

Finish counting the fish: 1, 2, _____, _____.

First a game of soccer.
The octopus can't be beat!
I wonder if it's because
She has so many feet!

Finish counting the octopus feet: 5, 6, _____, _____.

The catfish and dogfish are dancing.
I've never seen this before!
How many dancers do you see
Out on the big dance floor?

Finish counting the dancers: 9, 10, _____, _____.

Some seals all got together
And started a big sack race.
Be careful when you count them
So you don't lose your place!

Finish counting the seals: 13, 14, _____, _____.

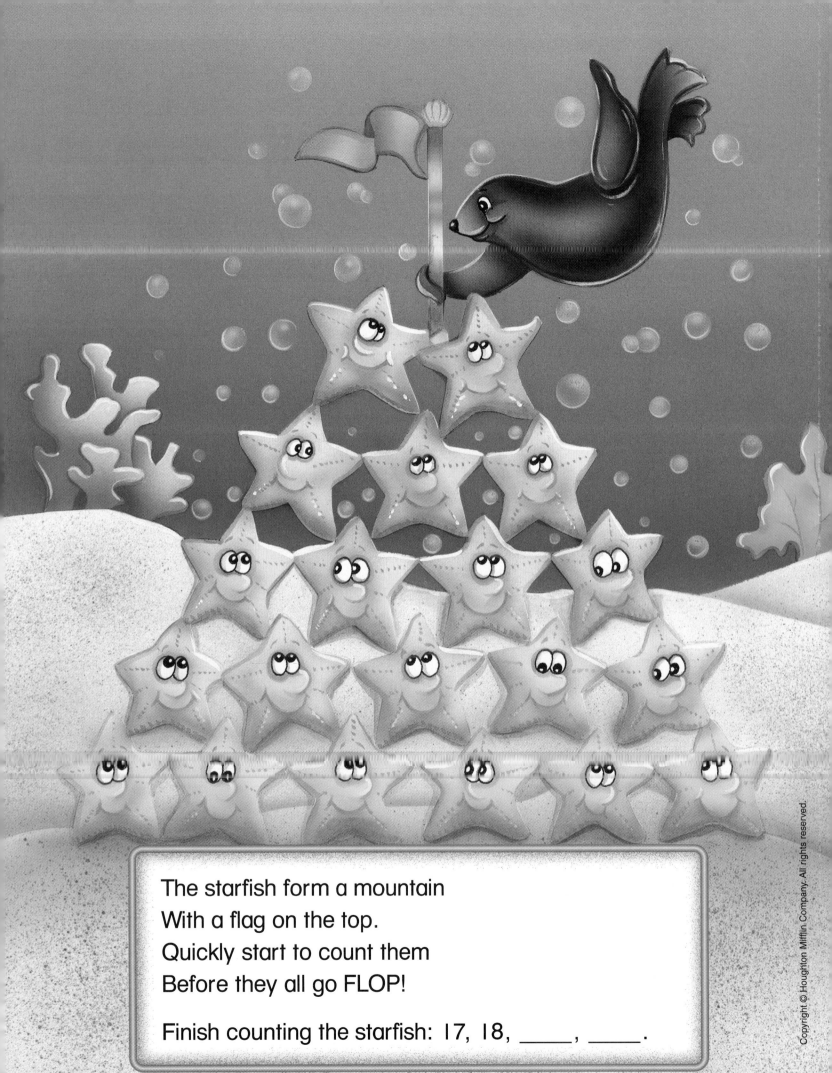

The starfish form a mountain
With a flag on the top.
Quickly start to count them
Before they all go FLOP!

Finish counting the starfish: 17, 18, _____, _____.

Now the day is over.

We're all so glad we came.

We hope that you had fun

Playing the counting game.

Finish counting the sea friends: 22, 23, _____, _____.

Family Letter

Dear Family,

During the next few weeks, our math class will be learning and practicing place value through 100.

You can expect to see work that provides practice with writing and counting numbers from 1 through 100.

As we learn about place value, you may wish to use the following sample as a guide.

Different Ways to Show a Number

Tens	Ones

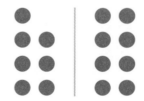

Fifteen
1 ten 5 ones
15

Comparing Numbers

7 is less than 8.
7 < 8
You can also say 8 is greater than 7.
8 > 7

Knowing place value can help children read, write, count, and compare greater numbers and quantities.

Sincerely,

Your child's teacher

Hands-On Activity

LESSON 1

Teen Numbers

Learn About It

You can show teen numbers by using **tens** and **ones**.

New Vocabulary
ones
tens

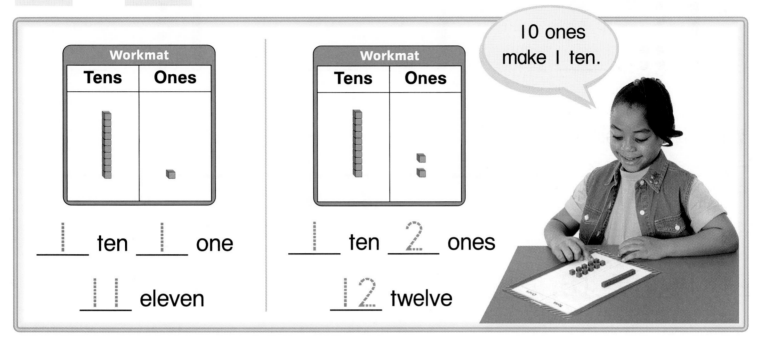

10 ones make 1 ten.

Workmat	
Tens	**Ones**

___1___ ten ___1___ one

___11___ eleven

Workmat	
Tens	**Ones**

___1___ ten ___2___ ones

___12___ twelve

Guided Practice

Use Workmat 4 with ▭▭▭▭ and ▪.
Show and write each number.

1. 13 thirteen ___1___ ten ___3___ ones = ___13___

2. 14 fourteen _____ ten _____ ones = _____

3. 15 fifteen _____ ten _____ ones = _____

4. 16 sixteen _____ ten _____ ones = _____

5. 17 seventeen _____ ten _____ ones = _____

Explain Your Thinking What teen numbers come after 17?

Independent Practice

Write each number.

1.  _18_

2.  ____

3.  ____

4. ____

5. ____

6. ____

Write the missing numbers.

7.
10   11   12   ____   ____   15   16   ____   ____   19   20

8. 16, 17, 18, ____, ____

9. 12, 13, 14, ____, ____

10. 15, 14, 13, ____, ____

11. 20, 19, 18, ____, ____

Problem Solving•Reasoning

Write About It

12. Write each teen number in order.
    Explain why this is a pattern for teen numbers.

    10 and 3 = _13_,   10 and 4 = ____,   10 and 5 = ____,

    10 and 6 = ____,   ____ and ____ = ____,

    ____ and ____ = ____,   ____ and 9 = ____

At Home Count aloud with your child from 1 to 20 and from 20 back to 1.

LESSON 2 Count by Tens

Learn About It

You can count groups of 10.

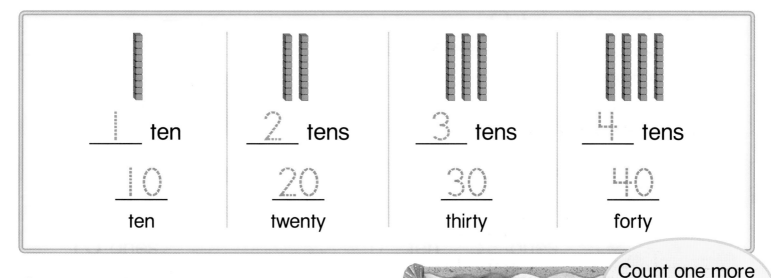

__1__ ten	__2__ tens	__3__ tens	__4__ tens
__10__	__20__	__30__	__40__
ten	twenty	thirty	forty

Guided Practice

Write each number.

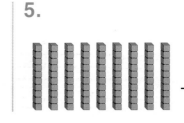

Count one more 10 each time: 10, 20, 30, 40.

1. __5__ tens = __50__
   fifty

2. 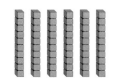 ____ tens = ____
   sixty

3. 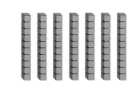 ____ tens = ____
   seventy

4. 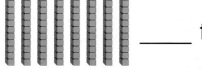 ____ tens = ____
   eighty

5. ____ tens = ____
   ninety

Explain Your Thinking Why would you want to count by tens instead of counting by ones?

Independent Practice

Write each number.

Use ▱▱▱▱▱▱ and ▪ if you want.

1.
Tens	Ones
3	8

_38_
thirty-eight

2.
Tens	Ones
4	5

____
forty-five

3.
Tens	Ones
3	2

____
thirty-two

4.
Tens	Ones
3	1

____
thirty-one

5.
Tens	Ones
3	3

____
thirty-three

6.
Tens	Ones
4	6

____
forty-six

7.
Tens	Ones
3	7

____
thirty-seven

8.
Tens	Ones
4	1

____
forty-one

9.
Tens	Ones
3	4

____
thirty-four

10.
Tens	Ones
4	3

____
forty-three

11.
Tens	Ones
3	6

____
thirty-six

12.
Tens	Ones
4	4

____
forty-four

Problem Solving•Reasoning

Patterns

Write the missing numbers.

13. 15 = _10_ and _5_

25 = _20_ and ____

35 = _30_ and ____

45 = ____ and ____

14. 37 = _30_ and _7_

38 = ____ and ____

39 = ____ and ____

40 = ____ and ____

At Home Say some numbers between 20 and 50.
Ask your child how many tens and ones are in each number.

Check Your Understanding of Lessons 1–4

Write the number for each word name.

1. eleven _____   2. twelve _____   3. thirteen _____

4. eighteen _____   5. nineteen _____   6. twenty _____

Write each number.

7.

_____ tens _____ ones

8.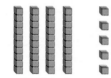

_____ tens _____ ones

9.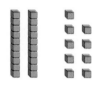

_____ tens _____ ones

10.

_____ tens _____ ones

11. Count by tens. Write the numbers.

_10_, _____, _____, _____, _____, _____, _____, _____, _____

Regroup. Write the tens and ones. Then write the number.

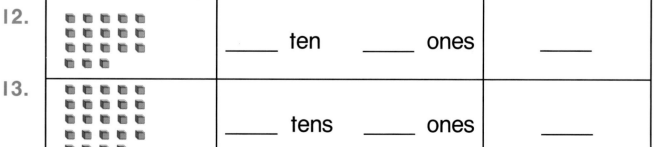

12.		_____ ten _____ ones	_____
13.		_____ tens _____ ones	_____

Name _____

Test Prep • Cumulative Review

Maintaining the Standards

Fill in the ○ for the correct answer. NH means Not Here.

Use the table for Exercises 1–3.

Tony's Hats	
Blue	6
Black	9
Red	4
Green	4

1 How many more black hats are there than red hats?

2 ○   4 ○   5 ○   6 ○

2 How many blue and red hats are there altogether?

11 ○   10 ○   9 ○   NH ○

3 How many hats are green?

4 ○   6 ○   9 ○   10 ○

4 Which number is thirty-five?

25 ○   30 ○   35 ○   53 ○

5 Count by tens. Which number comes next?

10	20	30	40	

40 ○   50 ○   60 ○   70 ○

6 Which number is 1 ten 6 ones?

6 ○   7 ○   16 ○   61 ○

7 Use these digits to make the largest number possible.

3	6

Explain how you know you are right.

_____

_____

_____

Safe Site

Internet Test Prep
Visit **www.eduplace.com/kids/mhm**
for more Test Prep Practice.

Numbers to 99

Learn About It

You can show a number as tens and ones.

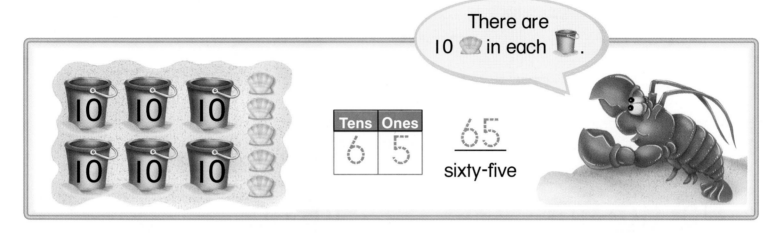

There are 10 🐚 in each 🪣.

Tens	Ones
6	5

65

sixty-five

Guided Practice

Write how many.

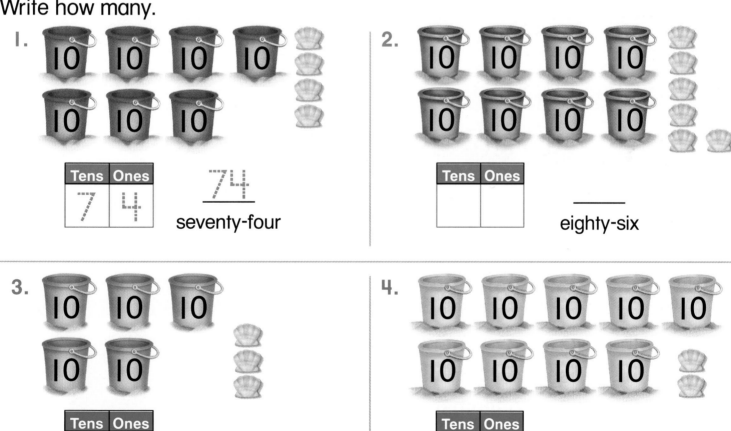

1.

Tens	Ones
7	4

74

seventy-four

2.

Tens	Ones

_____

eighty-six

3.

Tens	Ones

_____

fifty-three

4.

Tens	Ones

_____

ninety-two

Explain Your Thinking How would you show
the number 75 with tens and ones blocks?

Independent Practice

Write how many.

1.

Tens	Ones
7	1

71

seventy-one

2.

Tens	Ones

_____

ninety-two

3.

Tens	Ones

_____

sixty-eight

4.

Tens	Ones

_____

fifty-six

5.

Tens	Ones

_____

eighty-three

6.

Tens	Ones

_____

seventy-nine

Problem Solving•Reasoning

7. Feather starfish live in the ocean. Each starfish has 10 arms. How many arms will 6 feather starfish have?

_____ arms

At Home Ask your child how many tens and ones there are in 54, 79, 86, and 98.

LESSON 6 — One Hundred

Learn About It

New Vocabulary
one hundred

The number after 99 is **one hundred**.

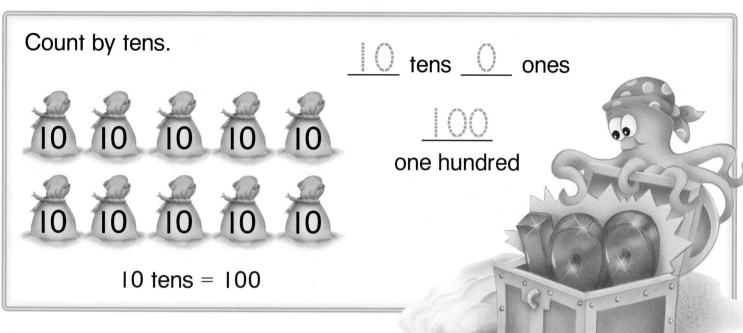

Count by tens.

___10___ tens ___0___ ones

___100___
one hundred

10 10 10 10 10
10 10 10 10 10

10 tens = 100

Guided Practice

Write how many.

1.   10 10 10 10

10 10 10 10 10 10

___10___ tens ____ ones

___100___
one hundred

2. 10 10 10 10 10 10 10

10 10 10

____ tens ____ ones

_____
one hundred

Explain Your Thinking How is 100 different
from numbers like 80 and 90?

Independent Practice

Connect the dots from 60 to 100.
Start at 60. Finish at 100.

At Home Have your child count by tens to 100.

	Standards
	NS 1.0, 1.3, 1.4

LESSON 7 Different Ways to Show Numbers

Learn About It

You can write a number in different ways.

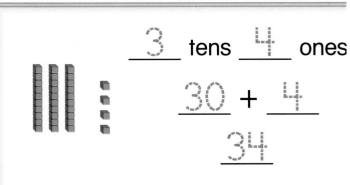

___3___ tens ___4___ ones

__30__ + __4__

__34__

3 tens is the same as 30.

So 30 + 4 = 34.

30 + 4 = 34

Guided Practice

Write each number.

1.

___7___ tens ___5___ ones

__70__ + __5__ = __75__

2.

____ tens ____ ones

___ + ___ = ___

3.

____ tens ____ ones

___ + ___ = ___

4.

____ tens ____ ones

___ + ___ = ___

Explain Your Thinking In the number 45, does the number 4 mean 40 or 4? How do you know?

Independent Practice

Write each number.

1.  __2__ tens __6__ ones   __20__ + __6__ = __26__

2. 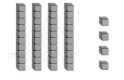 ____ tens ____ ones   ___ + ___ = ___

3.  ____ tens ____ ones   ___ + ___ = ___

4.  ____ tens ____ ones   ___ + ___ = ___

5.   ____ tens ____ ones   ___ + ___ = ___

Problem Solving • Reasoning

Number Sense

6. Circle the sign that matches the snail's number.

52

5 + 2   50 + 2   50 + 20

 **At Home** Look for two-digit numbers in magazines and newspapers. Ask your child to tell how many tens and ones are in each number.

Name _____

Check Your Understanding of Lessons 5–7

Write how many.

1.

Tens	Ones

_____ fifty-four

2.

Tens	Ones

_____ seventy-seven

Write each number.

3.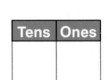

_____ tens _____ ones

_____ + _____ = _____

4.

_____ tens _____ ones

_____ + _____ = _____

5.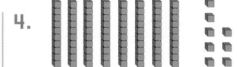

_____ tens _____ ones

_____ + _____ = _____

6.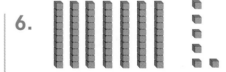

_____ tens _____ ones

_____ + _____ = _____

Test Prep • Cumulative Review

Maintaining the Standards

Fill in the ○ for the correct answer.

1 What number is one hundred?

0   l   10   100

○   ○   ○   ○

Use the graph to answer
Exercises 2 and 3.

In the Sea			

2 How many are **not** ?

3   6   8   ll

○   ○   ○   ○

3 How many more 🐚 than
🦀 are there?

l   2   3   4

○   ○   ○   ○

4 What number is 70 + 5?

705   75   57   12

○   ○   ○   ○

5 Subtract.

$$\begin{array}{r} 9 \\ -7 \\ \hline \end{array}$$

2   3   4   5

○   ○   ○   ○

6 Three dogs are brown. Six
dogs are white. How many
dogs are there altogether?

Explain why this problem is
about addition.

_____

_____

_____

_____

Count by Twos

Learn About It

To skip count by twos, count two at a time.

> Count by twos to count the shoes.

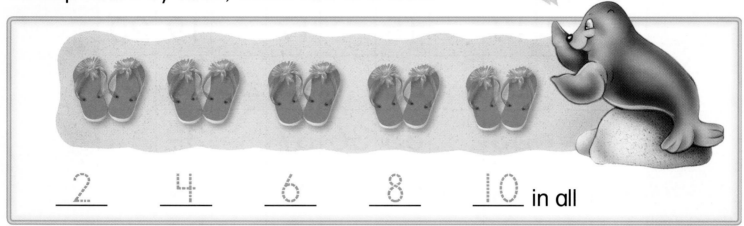

2 ___ 4 ___ 6 ___ 8 ___ 10 in all

Guided Practice

Skip count by twos.

1.

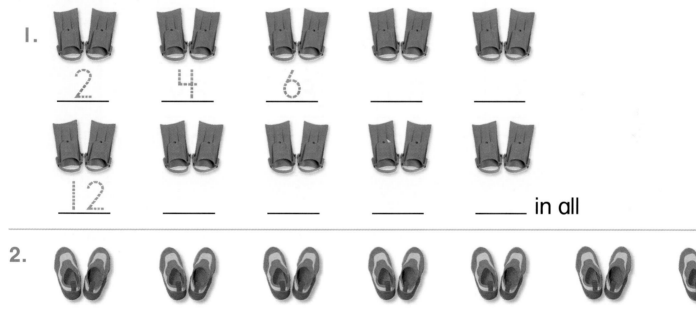

2 ___ 4 ___ 6 ___ ___ ___

12 ___ ___ ___ ___ ___ in all

2.

___ ___ ___ ___ ___ ___ ___

___ ___ ___ ___ ___ ___ in all

Explain Your Thinking What pattern do you see when
you skip count by twos?

Independent Practice

1. Write the missing numbers.
2. Count by twos. Color the numbers you counted [ ].

1	2	3	4	5		7	8	9	
11	12	13		15		17		19	20
21		23		25		27	28	29	
31		33		35	36	37		39	
41		43	44	45		47		49	50
51	52	53		55	56	57		59	
61		63	64	65		67	68	69	
71		73		75	76	77		79	
81	82	83		85		87		89	90
91		93	94	95		97		99	100

Problem Solving·Reasoning

Write About It

3. Some sea gulls are standing on the beach. There are 14 legs. How many sea gulls are there?

   _____ sea gulls

4. Explain how you found your answer.

Draw or write to explain.

At Home Ask your child to skip count by twos aloud. Help him or her count to 50 or higher.

Standards
NS 1.1, 1.2, 2.4
SDP 2.1

LESSON 9 Count by Fives

Learn About It

To skip count by fives, count five at a time.

> Count by fives to count the arms on starfish.

__5__ __10__ __15__ __20__ __25__ arms in all

Guided Practice

Skip count by fives.

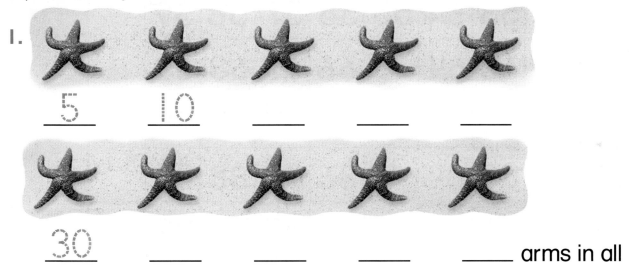

1. __5__ __10__ ____ ____ ____

__30__ ____ ____ ____ ____ arms in all

2. ____ ____ ____ ____ ____ ____ ____

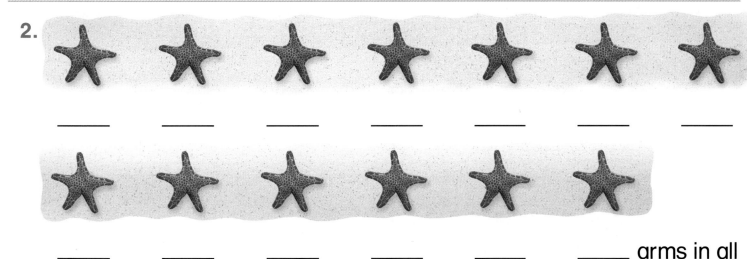

____ ____ ____ ____ ____ arms in all

Explain Your Thinking When could you use skip counting?

Independent Practice

1. Write the missing numbers.
2. Count by fives. Color the numbers you counted .
3. Count by tens. Circle the tens.

1	2	3	4	5	6	7	8	9	10
11	12	13	14		16	17	18	19	
21	22	23	24		26	27	28	29	
31	32	33	34		36	37	38	39	
41	42	43	44		46	47	48	49	
51	52	53	54	55	56	57	58	59	
61	62	63	64		66	67	68	69	
71	72	73	74		76	77	78	79	80
81	82	83	84		86	87	88	89	
91	92	93	94		96	97	98	99	100

Problem Solving•Reasoning

Logical Thinking

Draw or write to explain.

Write the mystery number.

4. It is greater than 80.

   It is less than 90.

   You say it when counting by fives.

   What number is it? _____

At Home Ask your child to count by fives to 100.

LESSON 10 Number Patterns

New
Vocabulary
more than
less than

Learn About It

You can use the words **more than** and **less than** to compare numbers.

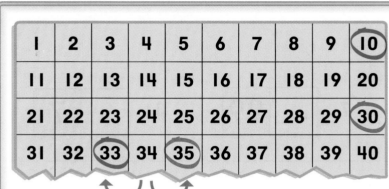

1	2	3	4	5	6	7	8	9	⑩
11	12	13	14	15	16	17	18	19	20
21	22	23	24	25	26	27	28	29	㉚
31	32	㉝	34	㉟	36	37	38	39	40

10 less than 20

10 more than 20

1 less than 34   1 more than 34

There are 10 numbers in each row.

Guided Practice

Use the number chart above.
Write the number that is 1 more.

1. | 13 | 14 |
2. | 8 | |
3. | 21 | |
4. | 35 | |

Write the number that is 1 less.

5. | 4 | 5 |
6. | | 22 |
7. | | 20 |
8. | | 38 |

Write the number that is 10 more.

9. | 5 |
   | 15 |
10. | 10 |
    | |
11. | 21 |
    | |
12. | 28 |
    | |
13. | 16 |
    | |

Explain Your Thinking How can you find the number that is 10 less than 26?

two hundred thirteen **213**

Independent Practice

Write the number that is 1 more.

1	2	3	4	5	6	7	8	9	10
11	12	13	14	15	16	17	18	19	20
21	22	23	24	25	26	27	28	29	30
31	32	33	34	35	36	37	38	39	40
41	42	43	44	45	46	47	48	49	50
51	52	53	54	55	56	57	58	59	60

1. 25 | 26
2. 19 | ☐

3. 48 | ☐
4. 36 | ☐

Write the number that is 1 less.

5. ☐ | 40
6. ☐ | 32
7. ☐ | 29
8. ☐ | 7

Write the number that is 10 more.

9. 6
10. 22
11. 18
12. 20
13. 35

Write the number that is 10 less.

14. 45
15. 16
16. 23
17. 12
18. 50

Problem Solving • Reasoning

Number Sense

19. Follow the pattern on a hundred chart. Write the missing numbers.

44	45		
		56	57
64	65		

Ordinal Numbers

LESSON 11

Learn About It

Some words help you know the position
of something or someone.

first   second   third   fourth   fifth   sixth   seventh   eighth   ninth   tenth

Guided Practice

Color.

1.

first   ▭   fifth   ▭   eighth   ▭

third   ▭   seventh   ▭   ninth   ▭

2.

second   ▭   sixth   ▭   ninth   ▭

fourth   ▭   seventh   ▭   tenth   ▭

Explain Your Thinking If you were fifth in line,
how many people would be in front of you?

Independent Practice

Color.

1.

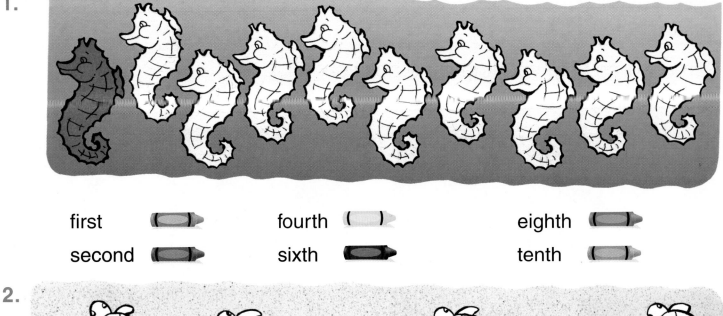

| first |  | fourth | | eighth | |
| second | | sixth | | tenth | |

2.

first		tenth		sixth	
eighth		second		ninth	
fifth		seventh			

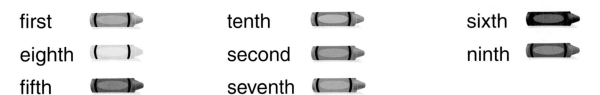

Problem Solving · Reasoning

3. Find the third 🦭. Count 2 more. Color it ✏.

4. Find the ninth 🦭. Count back 6. Color it ✏.

At Home Line up 8 to 10 objects. Ask your child to tell you the position of each object.

Name_____

LESSON 12

Problem Solving: Find a Pattern

Standards
NS **2.4**, SDP **2.1**
MR **1.0**, **1.1**, **2.2**

Finding a pattern can help you solve problems.

One lobster has 2 claws.
Two lobsters have 4 claws.
Three lobsters have 6 claws.
How many claws do 4 lobsters have?

Understand

What do you already know?

1 lobster has _____ claws.
2 lobsters have _____ claws.
3 lobsters have _____ claws.

Plan

Look for a pattern.
The pattern is to add _____ claws for each lobster.

Solve

Continue the pattern.

1 lobster	2 lobsters	3 lobsters	4 lobsters
2	4	6	

Look Back

Does your answer continue the pattern? Explain why.

Name _____

Test Prep • Cumulative Review

Maintaining the Standards

Fill in the ○ for the correct answer. NH means Not Here.

1 Mom gave Claire 3 pennies. Dad gave Claire 6 pennies. How many pennies does Claire have now?

7	8	9	NH
○	○	○	○

2 What number is likely to come next in this pattern?

6, 8, 10, 12, ___

11	12	13	14
○	○	○	○

3 What number is missing?

50, ___ 70, 80, 90

40	50	60	70
○	○	○	○

4 Subtract. 9 − 4 = ___

6	5	4	3
○	○	○	○

5 Choose a sign to make the sentence true.

8 ○ 2 = 10

+	−	=	¢
○	○	○	○

6 What number is likely to come next in this pattern?

15, 20, 25, ___

30	35	40	45
○	○	○	○

7 Regroup 10 ones as 1 ten. Write the number. **Explain** your thinking.

_____

_____

_____

Safe Site

Internet Test Prep
Visit **www.eduplace.com/kids/mhm**
for more *Test Prep Practice.*

LESSON 13 Use Ten to Estimate

Learn About It

When you need to find about how many,
you can **estimate**.

New
Vocabulary
estimate

About how many fish are there?

Circle 10.
Then estimate.

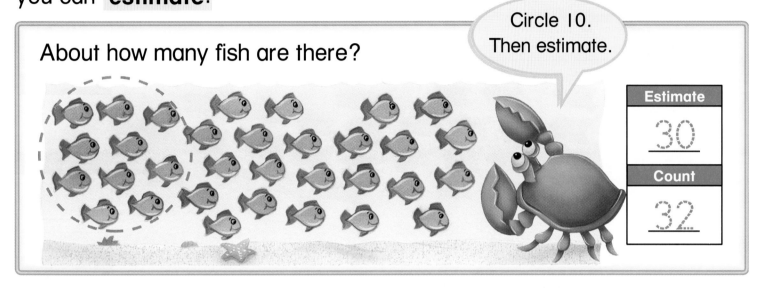

Estimate
30

Count
32

Guided Practice

Circle one group of ten.
Estimate how many in all. Then count.

1.

Estimate
40

Count
42

2.

Estimate
____

Count
____

Explain Your Thinking Why does it help to look
for groups of ten when you estimate?

Independent Practice

Circle one group of ten. Estimate. Then count.

1.

Estimate
20
Count
19

2.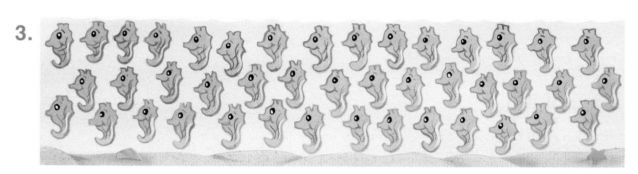

Estimate
_____
Count
_____

3.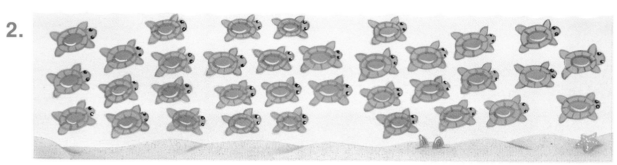

Estimate
_____
Count
_____

Problem Solving • Reasoning

Using Data

Use the graph.

Write how many of each.

Shells Found

4. _____

5.  _____

6. _____

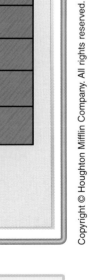

At Home Ask your child to estimate the number of items in a jar.

LESSON 14 Compare Numbers

Learn About It

You can use the words **is greater than** and **is less than** to compare numbers.

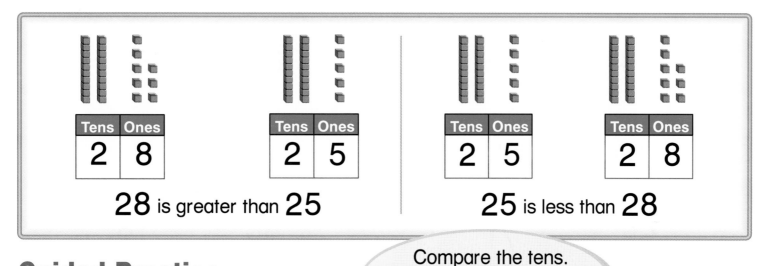

Tens	Ones
2	8

Tens	Ones
2	5

28 is greater than 25

Tens	Ones
2	5

Tens	Ones
2	8

25 is less than 28

Guided Practice

Compare the numbers.
Circle **is greater than** or **is less than**.

Compare the tens.
If the tens are the same,
compare the ones.

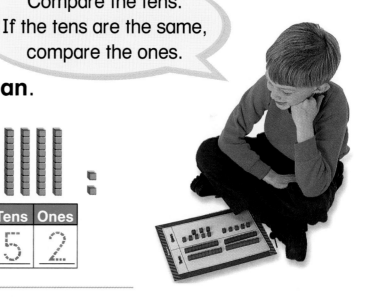

1.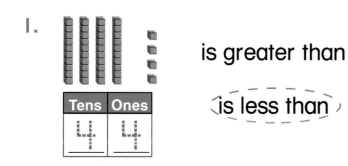

is greater than

is less than

Tens	Ones
4	4

Tens	Ones
5	2

2.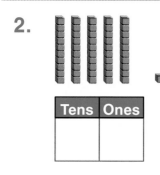

is greater than

is less than

Tens	Ones

Tens	Ones

Explain Your Thinking Why is 56 greater than 46?

Independent Practice

Circle the number that is greater.

1.
   27   39

2.
   31   19

3.
   64   46

4.
   83   87

Circle the number that is less.

5.
   54   71

6.
   29   19

7.
   62   66

8.
   94   49

Problem Solving · Reasoning

Visual Thinking

9. Write each number.
   Circle the number that is less.

_____   _____

At Home Write pairs of numbers such as 45, 51 and 28, 22.
Ask your child which number in each pair is greater and how he or she knows.

Standards
NS 1.1, 1.2, 1.3, 1.4

LESSON 15 Use Symbols to Compare Numbers

Learn About It

You can compare numbers using **is greater than**, **is less than**, and **is equal to**.

25	19

25 is greater than 19

25 > 19

19   25

19 is less than 25

19 < 25

19   19

19 equals 19

19 = 19

Guided Practice

Write and compare.
Circle >, <, or =.

> is greater than

< is less than

= is equal to

1.

$>$
$=$
$<$

Tens	Ones
4	2

Tens	Ones
3	7

2.

$>$
$=$
$<$

Tens	Ones

Tens	Ones

3.

$>$
$=$
$<$

Tens	Ones

Tens	Ones

4.

$>$
$=$
$<$

Tens	Ones

Tens	Ones

Explain Your Thinking How can you use > to compare 15 and 18?

Independent Practice

Compare. Circle >, <, or =.

1.  33   > (<) =    36

2. 72   > < =    65

3.  49   > < =    49

4.  94   > < =    96

5.  54   > < =    45

6.  55   > < =    55

7.  27   > < =    72

8. 33   > < =    13

9. 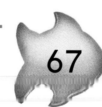 67   > < =    76

Problem Solving • Reasoning

Number Sense

10. Circle the ways that show 35. Explain how you know.

 :   3 tens 5 ones    10 10   30 + 5

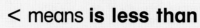

At Home Ask your child to compare 46 and 48. Ask him or her to explain which is greater.

Name _____

LESSON 16 Order Numbers

New
Vocabulary
before
after
between

Learn About It

A number line can help you write numbers in order.

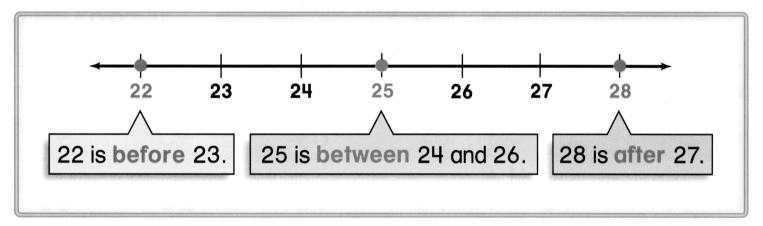

22 is **before** 23.   25 is **between** 24 and 26.   28 is **after** 27.

Guided Practice

Use the number line.

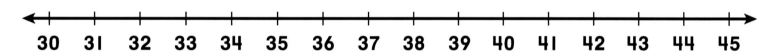

30 31 32 33 34 35 36 37 38 39 40 41 42 43 44 45

Write the number that comes **before**.

1. _36_, 37   2. ___, 43   3. ___, 35   4. ___, 32

Write the number that comes **after**.

5. 44, _45_   6. 37, ___   7. 41, ___   8. 30, ___

Write the number that comes **between**.

9. 39, _40_, 41   10. 38, ___, 40   11. 33, ___, 35

Explain Your Thinking Use **before, after,** and **between** to tell about 34, 37, and 40.

Guided Practice

Cross out the information
you do not need. Solve.

① Two cod swim in the ocean. ~~One cod~~
~~has 2 fins.~~ Two more cod join them.
How many cod are there now?

__4__ cod

> **Think:**
> What do I need
> to find out?

Draw or write to explain.

---

② 8 trout are near the shore. There are
10 different kinds of fish in the lake.
One trout swims away. How many
trout are near the shore?

_____ trout

> **Think:**
> What information do I need
> to solve the problem?

---

③ There are 9 crabs on the beach.
Crabs have 10 legs. 6 crabs crawl
into the water. How many crabs are
left on the beach?

_____ crabs

> **Think:**
> What information do I need
> to solve the problem?

At Home Create a story problem. Include facts that are not needed. Ask your
child to identify the unnecessary information and then solve the problem.

Name_____

Choose a Strategy

Solve.

① 7 goldfish swim in the stream. A goldfish has 4 fins. 3 more goldfish join them. How many goldfish are swimming?

_____ goldfish

Draw or write to explain.

goldfish

Draw a Picture
Write a Number Sentence
Use Models to Act It Out

② Nine angelfish swim in 2 different groups. There are 3 more fish in one group than the other. How many fish are in each group?

Group 1 _____ Group 2 _____

angelfish

③ There are 5 blue tangs. 2 more join them. One is 10 years old. How many blue tangs are there in all?

_____ blue tangs

blue tang

④ 10 eels are in the ocean. 4 eels are black. 8 clown fish are in the ocean. How many more eels are there than clown fish?

_____ more eels

clown fish

Name _____

Mixed Practice

Memorize Your Facts

Watch the signs. Find each sum or difference.

1. $8 - 3 =$ _____
2. $9 - 0 =$ _____
3. $2 + 3 =$ _____

4. $3 + 5 =$ _____
5. $9 - 3 =$ _____
6. $6 + 1 =$ _____

7. $6 + 2 =$ _____
8. $5 + 5 =$ _____
9. $8 - 0 =$ _____

10.
$$\begin{array}{r} 9 \\ -6 \\ \hline \end{array}$$

11.
$$\begin{array}{r} 7 \\ -3 \\ \hline \end{array}$$

12.
$$\begin{array}{r} 6 \\ -4 \\ \hline \end{array}$$

13.
$$\begin{array}{r} 0 \\ +5 \\ \hline \end{array}$$

14.
$$\begin{array}{r} 2 \\ +6 \\ \hline \end{array}$$

15.
$$\begin{array}{r} 4 \\ +5 \\ \hline \end{array}$$

16.
$$\begin{array}{r} 8 \\ -8 \\ \hline \end{array}$$

17.
$$\begin{array}{r} 8 \\ +1 \\ \hline \end{array}$$

18.
$$\begin{array}{r} 7 \\ +3 \\ \hline \end{array}$$

19.
$$\begin{array}{r} 6 \\ -0 \\ \hline \end{array}$$

20.
$$\begin{array}{r} 3 \\ +6 \\ \hline \end{array}$$

21.
$$\begin{array}{r} 10 \\ -\ 5 \\ \hline \end{array}$$

22.
$$\begin{array}{r} 5 \\ -0 \\ \hline \end{array}$$

23.
$$\begin{array}{r} 10 \\ -\ 3 \\ \hline \end{array}$$

24.
$$\begin{array}{r} 8 \\ -5 \\ \hline \end{array}$$

25.
$$\begin{array}{r} 0 \\ +4 \\ \hline \end{array}$$

26.
$$\begin{array}{r} 1 \\ +8 \\ \hline \end{array}$$

27.
$$\begin{array}{r} 4 \\ +6 \\ \hline \end{array}$$

 Brain Teaser Guess the Number

I am between 30 and 40. You can say my name when you count by fives.

What number am I? _____

I am between 70 and 80. I have 2 more tens than ones. What number am I? _____

Safe Site

Internet Brain Teasers
Visit **www.eduplace.com/kids/mhm**
for more *Brain Teasers*.

Name_____

Make It Big and Win!

What You Need

number cube with 5, 7, 8, 9, 10, 20

▭▭▭▭▭ and ▫

How to Play

1. Toss the cube and take that many ▭▭▭▭▭ and ▫.

2. Take turns until each player tosses the cube 5 times.

3. Regroup ones as tens.

4. The player with the greatest number wins.

Enrichment

Standards
NS **1.1**

Even and Odd Numbers

Here are 10 counters.

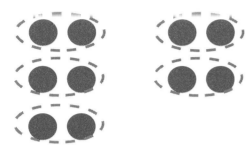

If you can circle groups of two with none left over, the number is **even**.

Here are 11 counters.

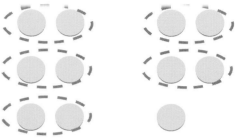

If you can circle groups of two and one is left over, the number is **odd**.

Circle groups of two. Write **E** for **even** or **O** for **odd**.

1. 15 ____

2. 18 ____

3. 12 ____

4. 11 ____

5. 9 ____

6. 6 ____

CHAPTER 6

Addition and Subtraction Facts to 12

Accessing Prior Knowledge

This story will help you review
- Addition facts
- Subtraction facts

A Walk Around the Farm

A Read-Aloud Story

written by Margaret Lena
illustrated by C.D. Hullinger

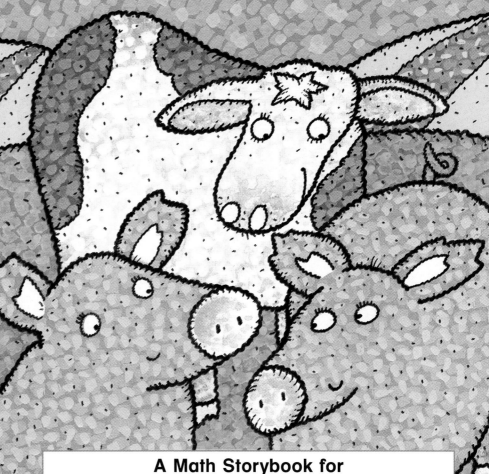

A Math Storybook for

_____

We stroll with Grandpa arm in arm,
To take a walk around the farm.
In the pigsty, 4 piglets squeal,
While 3 others wait for their meal.

How many piglets are there in all?

4 piglets + 3 piglets = _____ piglets

Mother sheep watch and guard
Their little lambs in the yard.
3 little lambs are fast asleep,
While 5 woolly lambs play and leap.

How many lambs are in the yard?

3 lambs + 5 lambs = _____ lambs

We stop to look and say, "Hi"
To 7 calves as we walk by.
2 calves turn and run away.
The other calves stay to play.

How many calves stay to play?

7 calves − 2 calves = _____ calves

Across the field and beyond,
6 downy ducklings swim on a pond.
3 more decide to leave the nest.
They wish to swim with all the rest.

How many ducklings are there in all?

6 ducklings + 3 ducklings = _____ ducklings

In the barn and behind the plow,
We hear the sound of a cat's meow.
We see 6 kittens near the door.
Then 4 go off to explore.

How many kittens stay in the barn?

6 kittens − 4 kittens = _____ kittens

Now our morning walk is done.
Seeing the animals was lots of fun!
Thank you, Grandpa, thanks a bunch.
Now we're hungry for some lunch!

How many children are ready for lunch?

1 child + 1 child = _____ children

Family Letter

Dear Family,

During the next few weeks, our math class will be learning and practicing addition and subtraction facts to 12.

You can expect to see work that provides practice with addition and subtraction facts.

As we learn about related facts and fact families, you may wish to use the following sample as a guide.

Related Facts
7 + 3 = 10   10 − 3 = 7

Fact Family
4 + 5 = 9   9 − 5 = 4
5 + 4 = 9   9 − 4 = 5

Knowing addition facts can help children learn the related subtraction facts.

Sincerely,

Your child's teacher

Vocabulary

addend Each of the numbers added in an addition problem.

related facts Addition and subtraction facts that use the same numbers.

fact family Related addition and subtraction facts that use the same numbers.

Count On to Add

Review
Vocabulary
number line

Learn About It

A **number line** can help you count on to add.

Here are three new facts.

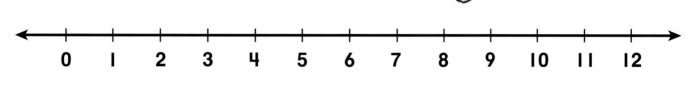

$$\begin{array}{r} 8 \\ + \ 3 \\ \hline 11 \end{array}$$
Start at 8.
Count on 3.

$$\begin{array}{r} 9 \\ + \ 2 \\ \hline 11 \end{array}$$
Start at 9.
Count on 2.

$$\begin{array}{r} 9 \\ + \ 3 \\ \hline 12 \end{array}$$
Start at 9.
Count on 3.

Guided Practice

Start with the greater number.
Write each sum.

1. $\begin{array}{r} 3 \\ + \ 9 \\ \hline 12 \end{array}$ **Think:** 10, 11, 12

2. $\begin{array}{r} 1 \\ +8 \\ \hline \end{array}$

3. $\begin{array}{r} 9 \\ +2 \\ \hline \end{array}$

4. $\begin{array}{r} 7 \\ +3 \\ \hline \end{array}$

5. $\begin{array}{r} 2 \\ +8 \\ \hline \end{array}$

6. $\begin{array}{r} 6 \\ +3 \\ \hline \end{array}$

7. $\begin{array}{r} 9 \\ +1 \\ \hline \end{array}$

8. $\begin{array}{r} 2 \\ +6 \\ \hline \end{array}$

9. $\begin{array}{r} 3 \\ +8 \\ \hline \end{array}$

10. $\begin{array}{r} 4 \\ +3 \\ \hline \end{array}$

11. $\begin{array}{r} 9 \\ +3 \\ \hline \end{array}$

12. $7 + 2 =$ _____

13. $2 + 9 =$ _____

14. $5 + 3 =$ _____

15. $3 + 7 =$ _____

16. $8 + 2 =$ _____

17. $1 + 9 =$ _____

Explain Your Thinking When you find the answer to 9 + 2, will the sum be greater than 9? Why or why not?

Independent Practice

Write each sum.

Use the number line if you want.

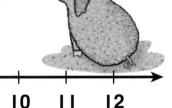

```
←|——|——|——|——|——|——|——|——|——|——|——|——|→
  0   1   2   3   4   5   6   7   8   9   10  11  12
```

1. 6 + 3 = _9_   2. 4 + 6 = ___   3. 2 + 9 = ___

4. 1 + 8 = ___   5. 8 + 3 = ___   6. 3 + 9 = ___

7. 3 + 7 = ___   8. 9 + 2 = ___   9. 5 + 1 = ___

10. 9 + 3 = ___   11. 1 + 9 = ___   12. 3 + 8 = ___

13. 8 + 2 = ___   14. 8 + 1 = ___   15. 7 + 3 = ___

16. 4 + 2 = ___   17. 5 + 3 = ___   18. 9 + 1 = ___

19. 2 + 7 = ___   20. 2 + 8 - ___   21. 10 + 2 = ___

Problem Solving • Reasoning

22. Sam and Amy saw 8 mother cows. They also saw 3 baby cows. How many cows did they see in all?

_____ cows

 At Home Ask your child to add 1, 2, or 3 to any number less than 10.

LESSON 2 Sums to 11

Here are two new facts with sums of 11.

Learn About It

Knowing one addition fact can help you find another fact.

$4 + 7 = \underline{11}$

$7 + 4 = \underline{11}$

$6 + 5 = \underline{11}$

$5 + 6 = \underline{11}$

Guided Practice

Write each sum.

1. $9 + 2 = \underline{11}$

   $2 + 9 = \underline{11}$

2. $3 + 8 = \underline{}$

   $8 + 3 = \underline{}$

3. $10 + 1 = \underline{}$

   $1 + 10 = \underline{}$

4. $7 + 4 = \underline{}$

   $4 + 7 = \underline{}$

5.
$$\begin{array}{r} 5 \\ +6 \\ \hline \end{array} \qquad \begin{array}{r} 6 \\ +5 \\ \hline \end{array}$$

6.
$$\begin{array}{r} 11 \\ +\ 0 \\ \hline \end{array} \qquad \begin{array}{r} 0 \\ +11 \\ \hline \end{array}$$

7.
$$\begin{array}{r} 2 \\ +9 \\ \hline \end{array} \qquad \begin{array}{r} 9 \\ +2 \\ \hline \end{array}$$

Explain Your Thinking If you know that $7 + 4 = 11$, what other addition fact do you know?

Independent Practice

Write each sum.

1.
$$4 + 7 = 11$$
$$7 + 4 = 11$$

2.
$$6 + 3$$
$$3 + 6$$

3.
$$2 + 8$$
$$8 + 2$$

4.
$$8 + 3$$
$$3 + 8$$

5.
$$7 + 2$$
$$2 + 7$$

6.
$$6 + 4$$
$$4 + 6$$

7.
$$7 + 3$$
$$3 + 7$$

8.
$$6 + 5$$
$$5 + 6$$

9.
$$5 + 4$$
$$4 + 5$$

10.
$$9 + 2$$
$$2 + 9$$

11.
$$5 + 3$$
$$3 + 5$$

12.
$$10 + 0$$
$$0 + 10$$

13. $10 + 1 = $ ___

$1 + 10 = $ ___

14. $0 + 9 = $ ___

$9 + 0 = $ ___

15. $11 + 0 = $ ___

$0 + 11 = $ ___

Problem Solving • Reasoning

Algebra Readiness • Number Sentences

Write each sum.

16. ___ $= 6 + 3$

17. ___ $= 6 + 5$

At Home Ask your child to name two numbers that have a sum of 11.

Sums to 12

Learn About It

Knowing one addition fact can help you find a related fact.

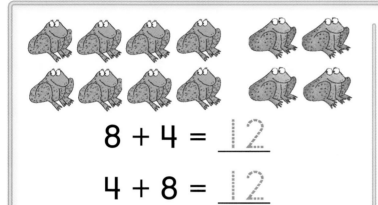

$8 + 4 = \underline{12}$

$4 + 8 = \underline{12}$

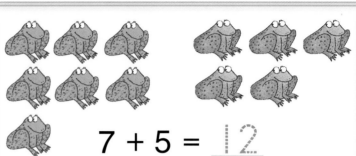

$7 + 5 = \underline{12}$

$5 + 7 = \underline{12}$

$6 + 6 = \underline{12}$

Here are three new facts with sums of 12.

Guided Practice

Write each sum.

1. $9 + 3 = \underline{12}$

   $3 + 9 = \underline{12}$

2. $12 + 0 = \underline{}$

   $0 + 12 = \underline{}$

3.
$$\begin{array}{r} 5 \\ +7 \\ \hline \end{array} \qquad \begin{array}{r} 7 \\ +5 \\ \hline \end{array}$$

4.
$$\begin{array}{r} 4 \\ +8 \\ \hline \end{array} \qquad \begin{array}{r} 8 \\ +4 \\ \hline \end{array}$$

5.
$$\begin{array}{r} 6 \\ +6 \\ \hline \end{array}$$

Explain Your Thinking If you know $7 + 5 = 12$, what other addition fact do you know?

Independent Practice

Write each sum.

1. $\begin{array}{r} 5 \\ + \ 7 \\ \hline 12 \end{array}$ $\begin{array}{r} 7 \\ + \ 5 \\ \hline 12 \end{array}$

2. $\begin{array}{r} 8 \\ +3 \\ \hline \end{array}$ $\begin{array}{r} 3 \\ +8 \\ \hline \end{array}$

3. $\begin{array}{r} 5 \\ +4 \\ \hline \end{array}$ $\begin{array}{r} 4 \\ +5 \\ \hline \end{array}$

4. $\begin{array}{r} 4 \\ +6 \\ \hline \end{array}$ $\begin{array}{r} 6 \\ +4 \\ \hline \end{array}$

5. $\begin{array}{r} 3 \\ +9 \\ \hline \end{array}$ $\begin{array}{r} 9 \\ +3 \\ \hline \end{array}$

6. $\begin{array}{r} 4 \\ +7 \\ \hline \end{array}$ $\begin{array}{r} 7 \\ +4 \\ \hline \end{array}$

7. $\begin{array}{r} 4 \\ +8 \\ \hline \end{array}$ $\begin{array}{r} 8 \\ +4 \\ \hline \end{array}$

8. $\begin{array}{r} 7 \\ +3 \\ \hline \end{array}$ $\begin{array}{r} 3 \\ +7 \\ \hline \end{array}$

9. $\begin{array}{r} 6 \\ +2 \\ \hline \end{array}$ $\begin{array}{r} 2 \\ +6 \\ \hline \end{array}$

10. $\begin{array}{r} 2 \\ +8 \\ \hline \end{array}$ $\begin{array}{r} 8 \\ +2 \\ \hline \end{array}$

11. $\begin{array}{r} 2 \\ +7 \\ \hline \end{array}$ $\begin{array}{r} 7 \\ +2 \\ \hline \end{array}$

12. $\begin{array}{r} 5 \\ +6 \\ \hline \end{array}$ $\begin{array}{r} 6 \\ +5 \\ \hline \end{array}$

13. $9 + 1 = $ ___

    $1 + 9 = $ ___

14. $12 + 0 = $ ___

    $0 + 12 = $ ___

15. $2 + 9 = $ ___

    $9 + 2 = $ ___

Problem Solving·Reasoning

16. **Write Your Own** Write a story about the pictures. Then write a number sentence.

    ___ ◯ ___ = ___

At Home Ask your child to solve 8 + 4 and 4 + 8 and tell how he or she found each sum.

LESSON 4 Add Three Numbers

Learn About It

You can add three numbers in any order.

Look for facts you know.

⑥
②
+4   →   8   + 4
           12

Think: 8 + 4

6
②
+④   →   6   + 6
           12

Think: 6 + 6

⑥
2
+④   →   10   + 2
           12

Think: 10 + 2

The sum is the same each way.

Guided Practice

Write each sum.

1. ⑥
   ①   →   7
  +2   + 2
          9

2. 4
  ③   →   4
  +③   + ☐

3. ②
  ③   →   ☐
  +4   + 4

4. 2
  3
 +5

5. 5
  5
 +2

6. 1
  8
 +2

7. 6
  2
 +3

8. 2
  2
 +4

9. 1
  9
 +0

10. $5 + 3 + 3 =$ ___

11. $6 + 4 + 1 =$ ___

Explain Your Thinking Which numbers would you add first to find the sum of $6 + 3 + 4$?

Independent Practice

Write each sum.

1. 2
    3
   +3

    8

2. 7
    3
   +1
   ----

3. 3
    4
   +2
   ----

4. 2
    4
   +6
   ----

5. 2
    2
   +3
   ----

6. 2
    8
   +1
   ----

7. 1
    9
   +2
   ----

8. 5
    3
   +2
   ----

9. 1
    1
   +7
   ----

10. 5
    4
   +2
   ----

11. 2
    7
   +1
   ----

12. 4
    4
   +3
   ----

13. 4
    1
   +6
   ----

14. 2
    3
   +7
   ----

15. 5
    2
   +1
   ----

16. 8
    2
   +2
   ----

17. 3
    3
   +6
   ----

18. 2
    1
   +1
   ----

19. $4 + 2 + 3 =$ _____

20. $6 + 1 + 5 =$ _____

21. $4 + 4 + 2 =$

22. $1 + 5 + 5 =$ _____

Problem Solving•Reasoning

Number Sense

23. Fill in each ◯ with the number 2, 5, or 7. The sum of each side should equal 12.

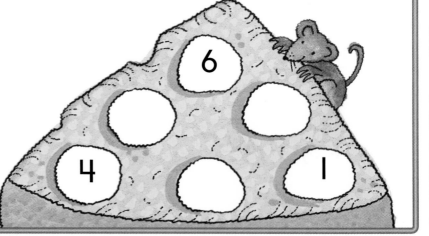

At Home Give your child three numbers such as 2, 4, and 5. Ask him or her to find the sum.

Standards
NS **2.1**, AF **1.1**
MR **1.1, 1.2**

Hands-On Activity
LESSON 5
Algebra Readiness: Missing Addends

Review Vocabulary
addend
sum

Learn About It

Sometimes you know one **addend** and the **sum**.

How many cubes do you add to get 8 in all?

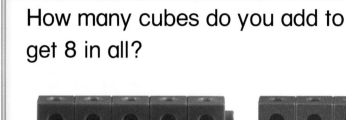

$$5 + \boxed{3} = 8$$

addend   addend   sum

I added 3 more cubes.

Guided Practice

Add cubes to find each missing addend.

1.

   $$6 + \boxed{2} = 8$$

2.

   $$\boxed{} + 7 = 12$$

3.

   $$6 + \boxed{} = 12$$

4.

   $$\boxed{} + 3 = 10$$

Explain Your Thinking How could you use subtraction to find the missing addend for $4 + \boxed{} = 10$?

Independent Practice

Find each missing addend.
Use cubes if you want.

1.  $\boxed{4} + 5 = 9$

2.  $6 + \boxed{} = 10$

3. $2 + \boxed{} = 8$

4. $5 + \boxed{} = 11$

5. $\boxed{} + 4 = 9$

6.
$$\begin{array}{r} 5 \\ + \boxed{} \\ \hline 7 \end{array}$$

7.
$$\begin{array}{r} \boxed{} \\ + \ 2 \\ \hline 10 \end{array}$$

8.
$$\begin{array}{r} 7 \\ + \boxed{} \\ \hline 12 \end{array}$$

9.
$$\begin{array}{r} 4 \\ + \boxed{} \\ \hline 7 \end{array}$$

10.
$$\begin{array}{r} \boxed{} \\ + \ 8 \\ \hline 11 \end{array}$$

11.
$$\begin{array}{r} \boxed{} \\ + \ 9 \\ \hline 11 \end{array}$$

12.
$$\begin{array}{r} 5 \\ + \boxed{} \\ \hline 10 \end{array}$$

13.
$$\begin{array}{r} 3 \\ + \boxed{} \\ \hline 12 \end{array}$$

14.
$$\begin{array}{r} \boxed{} \\ + \ 6 \\ \hline 11 \end{array}$$

15.
$$\begin{array}{r} 4 \\ + \boxed{} \\ \hline 11 \end{array}$$

Problem Solving • Reasoning

Algebra Readiness • Missing Addends

16. Mia has 6 people in her family.
The table is set for 10 people.
How many guests are coming
to dinner?

_____ guests

Draw or write to explain.

At Home Ask your child questions such as, "What number plus six equals twelve?"

Name_____

LESSON 6

Problem Solving:
Make a Table

Standards
AF 1.1, SDP 1.0, 1.2
MR 1.0, 1.1, 2.2

You can make a table to help you solve problems.

Many animals are born on a farm. Count the animals. Write the numbers in the table. How many more pigs are there than mules?

Understand

Circle the animals that the question asks about.

Pigs   Sheep   Mules

Kind of Animal	Number of Babies
Pigs	
Sheep	
Mules	

Plan

Circle how would you solve this problem.   add   subtract

Solve

Use the table.

_____ ◯ _____ = _____ more pigs

Look Back

Use the picture above to check your answer.

Guided Practice

Solve. Complete the table.

Animals	Number
Chickens	7
Ducks	
Turkeys	

① There are 3 fewer ducks than chickens. How many ducks are there?

Think: How many chickens are there?

Draw or write to explain.

___4___ ducks

② There are 4 more turkeys than chickens. How many turkeys are there?

Think: Do I add or subtract?

_____ turkeys

③ How many chickens and ducks are there in all?

Think: How many ducks are there?

_____ chickens and ducks

④ How many more turkeys are there than ducks?

Think: What numbers do I use?

_____ turkeys

At Home Have your child make a table showing the number of three kinds of clothing items he or she has. For example, show shoes, shirts, and pajamas.

Name_____

Baby Animals

Animals	Number
Kittens	6
Colts	3
Lambs	

Choose a Strategy

Solve. Complete the table.

① There are three lambs.
Then six more lambs
are born. How many lambs
are there?

_____ lambs

Draw or write to explain.

lamb

② How many lambs and colts
are there altogether?

_____ lambs and colts

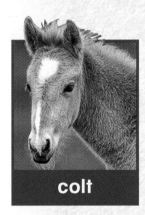

colt

③ How many more lambs
are there than kittens?

_____ lambs

kitten

two hundred sixty-three **263**

Mixed Practice

Find each sum or difference.

1. 8 – 2 = ___
2. 9 + 2 = ___
3. 5 + 6 = ___

4. 4 + 5 = ___
5. 8 – 3 = ___
6. 6 + 3 = ___

7. 6 – 3 = ___
8. 10 – 7 = ___
9. 5 + 3 = ___

10. 2
+4

11. 5
–0

12. 10
– 4

13. 0
+6

14. 4
+6

15. 7
–4

16. 5
–2

17. 6
+6

18. 7
+4

19. 8
–5

20. 9
+3

21. 10
– 3

 Brain Teaser The Elevator Story

Some people get in the elevator on the first floor. The elevator goes up. 4 people get on. 2 people get off. Now there are 9 people. How many people got in the elevator on the first floor?

_____ people

Safe Site

Internet Brain Teasers
Visit www.eduplace.com/kids/mhm
for more *Brain Teasers*.

Quick ✓ Check

Check Your Understanding of Lessons 1–6

Write each sum.

1. $7 + 3 =$ ____   2. $8 + 2 =$ ____   3. $5 + 3 =$ ____

4. $8 + 3 =$ ____   5. $6 + 5 =$ ____   6. $7 + 4 =$ ____

7. $\begin{array}{r} 9 \\ +3 \\ \hline \end{array}$ 8. $\begin{array}{r} 7 \\ +5 \\ \hline \end{array}$ 9. $\begin{array}{r} 8 \\ +4 \\ \hline \end{array}$ 10. $\begin{array}{r} 5 \\ +6 \\ \hline \end{array}$ 11. $\begin{array}{r} 6 \\ +6 \\ \hline \end{array}$

12. $\begin{array}{r} 4 \\ 3 \\ +4 \\ \hline \end{array}$ 13. $\begin{array}{r} 7 \\ 1 \\ +3 \\ \hline \end{array}$ 14. $\begin{array}{r} 8 \\ 2 \\ +2 \\ \hline \end{array}$ 15. $\begin{array}{r} 2 \\ 4 \\ +4 \\ \hline \end{array}$ 16. $\begin{array}{r} 5 \\ 2 \\ +3 \\ \hline \end{array}$

Find each missing addend. Use cubes if you want.

17. ☐ $+ 4 = 11$ 18. $8 +$ ☐ $= 12$

Solve. Use the answers to complete the table.

19. The number of blue hats is 2 less than the number of red hats. How many blue hats are there?

____ blue hats

20. There are 4 more green hats than blue hats. How many green hats are there?

____ green hats

Hats	
Color	**Number**
Red	5
Blue	
Green	

Test Prep • Cumulative Review

Maintaining the Standards

Fill in the ○ for the correct answer. NH means Not Here.

1 Which is the sum? $\begin{array}{r} 7 \\ +2 \\ \hline \end{array}$

9	8	7	5
○	○	○	○

2 Walt drew 3 pictures today and 0 pictures yesterday. How many pictures did Walt draw in all?

0	1	2	3
○	○	○	○

3 Leanne had 11 carrots. She ate 5 of them. How many carrots did she have left?

5	6	7	8
○	○	○	○

4 Which is the sum?

$$5 + 4 + 2 = \blacksquare$$

12	11	10	NH
○	○	○	○

5 Look at the tally chart.

Animals	Tally
Cows	卌 ||||
Pigs	|||
Horses	卌 ||

How many more cows than horses are there?

4	3	2	1
○	○	○	○

6 **Explain** how you can use subtraction to find the missing addend in $5 + \blacksquare = 8$?

_____

_____

_____

_____

Safe Site

Internet Test Prep
Visit **www.eduplace.com/kids/mhm**
for more *Test Prep Practice.*

Standards
NS **2.1**, **2.6** AF **1.3**
SDP **1.2**, MR **1.0**

LESSON 7 Count Back to Subtract

Learn About It

A number line can help you count back to **subtract**.

Here are three new facts.

Review
Vocabulary
subtract

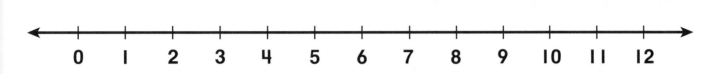

0 1 2 3 4 5 6 7 8 9 10 11 12

$$\begin{array}{r} 11 \\ -\ 3 \\ \hline 8 \end{array}$$

Start at 11.
Count back 3.

$$\begin{array}{r} 11 \\ -\ 2 \\ \hline 9 \end{array}$$

Start at 11.
Count back 2.

$$\begin{array}{r} 12 \\ -\ 3 \\ \hline 9 \end{array}$$

Start at 12.
Count back 3.

Guided Practice

Subtract.

1.
$$\begin{array}{r} 10 \\ -\ 3 \\ \hline 7 \end{array}$$
Think:
9, 8, 7

2.
$$\begin{array}{r} 7 \\ -1 \\ \hline \end{array}$$

3.
$$\begin{array}{r} 9 \\ -1 \\ \hline \end{array}$$

4.
$$\begin{array}{r} 8 \\ -3 \\ \hline \end{array}$$

5.
$$\begin{array}{r} 10 \\ -\ 2 \\ \hline \end{array}$$

6.
$$\begin{array}{r} 11 \\ -\ 2 \\ \hline \end{array}$$

7.
$$\begin{array}{r} 9 \\ -3 \\ \hline \end{array}$$

8.
$$\begin{array}{r} 7 \\ -3 \\ \hline \end{array}$$

9.
$$\begin{array}{r} 5 \\ -3 \\ \hline \end{array}$$

10.
$$\begin{array}{r} 8 \\ -2 \\ \hline \end{array}$$

11.
$$\begin{array}{r} 11 \\ -\ 3 \\ \hline \end{array}$$

12. $6 - 2 =$ _____

13. $8 - 1 =$ _____

14. $10 - 1 =$ _____

15. $9 - 2 =$ _____

16. $7 - 2 =$ _____

17. $12 - 3 =$ _____

Explain Your Thinking When you find $11 - 3$, will the answer be greater than 11? Why or why not?

Independent Practice

Subtract.

Use the number line if you want.

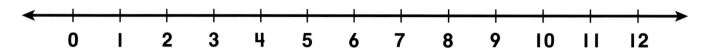

1. 8 − 1 = _7_

2. 12 − 3 = ___

3. 11 − 3 = ___

4. 11 − 2 = ___

5. 9 − 3 = ___

6. 10 − 2 = ___

7. 7 − 1 = ___

8. 5 − 2 = ___

9. 10 − 3 = ___

10. 8 − 3 = ___

11. 10 − 1 = ___

12. 7 − 2 = ___

13. 7 − 3 = ___

14. 8 − 2 = ___

15. 9 − 2 = ___

Problem Solving • Reasoning

Write About It

16. Write a subtraction question that you can answer by using this graph.

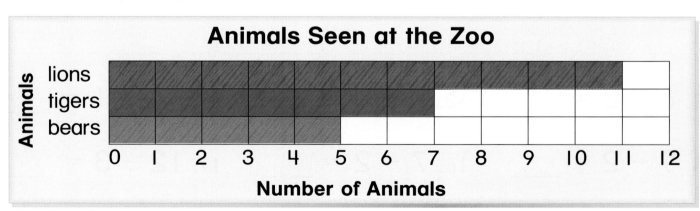

At Home Ask your child to subtract 1, 2, or 3 from 12 and then from 11.

Standards
NS **2.1, 2.2, 2.6**

LESSON 8 Subtract From 11 and Less

Learn About It

Knowing one subtraction fact can help you find another fact.

Here are four new facts.

$11 - 5 = \underline{6}$

$11 - 6 = \underline{5}$

$11 - 4 = \underline{7}$

$11 - 7 = \underline{4}$

Guided Practice

Write each difference.

1. $11 - 2 = \underline{9}$

   $11 - 9 = \underline{2}$

2. $11 - 3 = \underline{}$

   $11 - 8 = \underline{}$

3. $10 - 7 = \underline{}$

   $10 - 3 = \underline{}$

4. $10 - 6 = \underline{}$

   $10 - 4 = \underline{}$

5. $\begin{array}{r} 11 \\ -\ 7 \\ \hline \end{array}$ $\begin{array}{r} 11 \\ -\ 4 \\ \hline \end{array}$

6. $\begin{array}{r} 11 \\ -\ 6 \\ \hline \end{array}$ $\begin{array}{r} 11 \\ -\ 5 \\ \hline \end{array}$

7. $\begin{array}{r} 10 \\ -\ 8 \\ \hline \end{array}$ $\begin{array}{r} 10 \\ -\ 2 \\ \hline \end{array}$

Explain Your Thinking How does knowing $11 - 4 = 7$ help you find the answer to $11 - 7$?

Independent Practice

Write each difference.

1.   1 1   1 1
   – 3   – 8
      8   3

2.   1 0   1 0
   – 6   – 4

3.   1 1   1 1
   – 2   – 9

4.   1 1   1 1
   – 7   – 4

5.   9   9
   –6   –3

6.   1 0   1 0
   – 8   – 2

7.   1 0   1 0
   – 3   – 7

8.   1 1   1 1
   – 5   – 6

9.   9   9
   –5   –4

10. 8   8
   –5   –3

11. 9   9
   –1   –8

12. 1 0   1 0
   – 9   – 1

13. 1 1 – 8 = ____

11 – 3 = ____

14. 1 1 – 4 = ____

11 – 7 = ____

15. 1 0 – 4 = ____

10 – 6 =

Problem Solving • Reasoning

Using Vocabulary

16. What number would you subtract from eleven to get a difference of seven?

____

17. Write two addends that have a sum of eleven.

____ and ____

At Home Ask your child to tell you the difference in each of the following: 11 – 6, 11 – 5, 11 – 7, 11 – 4, 11 – 9, and 11 – 2.

LESSON 9 Subtract From 12 and Less

Learn About It

If you know one subtraction fact, it can help
you find another fact.

$$12 - 5 = \underline{7}$$

$$12 - 7 = \underline{5}$$

$$12 - 4 = \underline{8}$$

$$12 - 8 = \underline{4}$$

$$12 - 6 = \underline{6}$$

Here are five
new facts.

Guided Practice

Write each difference.

1. $12 - 3 = \underline{9}$

   $12 - 9 = \underline{3}$

2. $11 - 3 = \underline{}$

   $11 - 8 = \underline{}$

3. $\begin{array}{r} 12 \\ -\ 8 \\ \hline \end{array}$ $\begin{array}{r} 12 \\ -\ 4 \\ \hline \end{array}$

4. $\begin{array}{r} 12 \\ -\ 5 \\ \hline \end{array}$ $\begin{array}{r} 12 \\ -\ 7 \\ \hline \end{array}$

5. $\begin{array}{r} 11 \\ -\ 7 \\ \hline \end{array}$ $\begin{array}{r} 11 \\ -\ 4 \\ \hline \end{array}$

Explain Your Thinking How does knowing
$12 - 5 = 7$ help you find the answer to $12 - 7$?

Independent Practice

Write each difference.

1.
$$\begin{array}{r} 12 \\ -\ 7 \\ \hline 5 \end{array}$$
$$\begin{array}{r} 12 \\ -\ 5 \\ \hline 7 \end{array}$$

2.
$$\begin{array}{r} 10 \\ -\ 8 \\ \hline \end{array}$$
$$\begin{array}{r} 10 \\ -\ 2 \\ \hline \end{array}$$

3.
$$\begin{array}{r} 9 \\ -6 \\ \hline \end{array}$$
$$\begin{array}{r} 9 \\ -3 \\ \hline \end{array}$$

4.
$$\begin{array}{r} 12 \\ -\ 3 \\ \hline \end{array}$$
$$\begin{array}{r} 12 \\ -\ 9 \\ \hline \end{array}$$

5.
$$\begin{array}{r} 11 \\ -\ 7 \\ \hline \end{array}$$
$$\begin{array}{r} 11 \\ -\ 4 \\ \hline \end{array}$$

6.
$$\begin{array}{r} 10 \\ -\ 3 \\ \hline \end{array}$$
$$\begin{array}{r} 10 \\ -\ 7 \\ \hline \end{array}$$

7.
$$\begin{array}{r} 11 \\ -\ 8 \\ \hline \end{array}$$
$$\begin{array}{r} 11 \\ -\ 3 \\ \hline \end{array}$$

8.
$$\begin{array}{r} 12 \\ -\ 8 \\ \hline \end{array}$$
$$\begin{array}{r} 12 \\ -\ 4 \\ \hline \end{array}$$

9.
$$\begin{array}{r} 11 \\ -\ 5 \\ \hline \end{array}$$
$$\begin{array}{r} 11 \\ -\ 6 \\ \hline \end{array}$$

10. $9 - 5 =$ ___

$9 - 4 =$ ___

11. $10 - 4 =$ ___

$10 - 6 =$ ___

12. $9 - 7 =$ ___

$9 - 2 =$ ___

Problem Solving • Reasoning

Algebra Readiness · Functions

Follow the rule to find each difference.

13.

Subtract 3	
12	9
11	
10	
9	

14.

Subtract 2	
3	
4	
5	
6	

15.

Subtract 4	
12	
11	
10	
9	

At Home Ask your child to name a related subtraction fact for $12 - 8 = 4$.

Name _____

Check Your Understanding of Lessons 7–9

Write each difference.

1. $\begin{array}{r} 9 \\ -3 \\ \hline \end{array}$ 2. $\begin{array}{r} 9 \\ -2 \\ \hline \end{array}$ 3. $\begin{array}{r} 8 \\ -3 \\ \hline \end{array}$ 4. $\begin{array}{r} 10 \\ -3 \\ \hline \end{array}$ 5. $\begin{array}{r} 11 \\ -2 \\ \hline \end{array}$ 6. $\begin{array}{r} 10 \\ -2 \\ \hline \end{array}$

7. $\begin{array}{r} 12 \\ -7 \\ \hline \end{array}$ $\begin{array}{r} 12 \\ -5 \\ \hline \end{array}$ 8. $\begin{array}{r} 11 \\ -3 \\ \hline \end{array}$ $\begin{array}{r} 11 \\ -8 \\ \hline \end{array}$ 9. $\begin{array}{r} 11 \\ -5 \\ \hline \end{array}$ $\begin{array}{r} 11 \\ -6 \\ \hline \end{array}$

10. $\begin{array}{r} 11 \\ -2 \\ \hline \end{array}$ $\begin{array}{r} 11 \\ -9 \\ \hline \end{array}$ 11. $\begin{array}{r} 12 \\ -4 \\ \hline \end{array}$ $\begin{array}{r} 12 \\ -8 \\ \hline \end{array}$ 12. $\begin{array}{r} 11 \\ -7 \\ \hline \end{array}$ $\begin{array}{r} 11 \\ -4 \\ \hline \end{array}$

13. $\begin{array}{r} 12 \\ -3 \\ \hline \end{array}$ $\begin{array}{r} 12 \\ -9 \\ \hline \end{array}$ 14. $\begin{array}{r} 10 \\ -4 \\ \hline \end{array}$ $\begin{array}{r} 10 \\ -6 \\ \hline \end{array}$ 15. $\begin{array}{r} 9 \\ -7 \\ \hline \end{array}$ $\begin{array}{r} 9 \\ -2 \\ \hline \end{array}$

16. $12 - 8 =$ ___

17. $11 - 3 =$ ___

18. $10 - 5 =$ ___

19. $11 - 9 =$ ___

20. $11 - 4 =$ ___

21. $12 - 6 =$ ___

Test Prep • Cumulative Review

Maintaining the Standards

Fill in the ○ for the correct answer.

1 Add.

$$0 + 8$$

0	8	9	10
○	○	○	○

2 Subtract.

$$11 - 2$$

10	9	8	7
○	○	○	○

3 If $12 - 3 = 9$, what is $12 - 9$?

12	9	6	3
○	○	○	○

4 Which addend will make a double fact?

$$6 + \blacksquare = 12$$

12	8	6	2
○	○	○	○

5 Tomás is making a tally chart of home runs made by his team. The team made 5 home runs. Then they made 1 more. Which tally mark names the number of home runs?

II	IIII I	IIII I	IIII II
○	○	○	○

6 Kaya found 11 seashells. She gave some away. She has 6 seashells left.

Explain how you can find how many seashells Kaya gave away.

_____

_____

_____

_____

Safe Site

Internet Test Prep
Visit **www.eduplace.com/kids/mhm**
for more *Test Prep Practice.*

LESSON 10
Algebra Readiness:
Relate Addition and Subtraction

Learn About It

An addition fact and a subtraction fact that use the same numbers are **related facts**.

Review
Vocabulary
related facts

$$\begin{array}{r} 4 \\ +\ 6 \\ \hline 10 \end{array} \qquad \begin{array}{r} 10 \\ -\ 6 \\ \hline 4 \end{array}$$

I know 4 + 6 = 10.
I can use that fact
to find 10 − 6 = 4.

Guided Practice

Add. Then subtract.

1.
$$\begin{array}{r} 3 \\ 9 \\ \hline 12 \end{array} \qquad \begin{array}{r} 12 \\ -\ 9 \\ \hline 3 \end{array}$$

2.
$$\begin{array}{r} 7 \\ +3 \\ \hline \end{array} \qquad \begin{array}{r} 10 \\ -\ 3 \\ \hline \end{array}$$

3.
$$\begin{array}{r} 8 \\ +3 \\ \hline \end{array} \qquad \begin{array}{r} 11 \\ -\ 3 \\ \hline \end{array}$$

4.
$$\begin{array}{r} 5 \\ +6 \\ \hline \end{array} \qquad \begin{array}{r} 11 \\ -\ 6 \\ \hline \end{array}$$

5.
$$\begin{array}{r} 6 \\ +3 \\ \hline \end{array} \qquad \begin{array}{r} 9 \\ -3 \\ \hline \end{array}$$

6.
$$\begin{array}{r} 8 \\ +4 \\ \hline \end{array} \qquad \begin{array}{r} 12 \\ -\ 4 \\ \hline \end{array}$$

7.
$$\begin{array}{r} 6 \\ 6 \\ \hline \end{array} \qquad \begin{array}{r} 12 \\ -\ 6 \\ \hline \end{array}$$

8.
$$\begin{array}{r} 9 \\ +2 \\ \hline \end{array} \qquad \begin{array}{r} 11 \\ -\ 2 \\ \hline \end{array}$$

9.
$$\begin{array}{r} 5 \\ +7 \\ \hline \end{array} \qquad \begin{array}{r} 12 \\ -\ 7 \\ \hline \end{array}$$

Explain Your Thinking How does knowing
5 + 6 = 11 help you find the answer to 11 − 6?

Independent Practice

Solve. Then draw a path for the puppy to get to the bone.

3	11
+8	− 8
11	3

4	9
+5	−5

4	12
+8	− 8

8	10
+2	− 2

9	12
+3	− 3

2	8
+6	−6

7	12
+5	− 5

3	10
+7	− 7

4	11
+7	− 7

6	10
+4	− 4

6	11
+5	− 5

5	10
+5	− 5

At Home Tell your child an addition fact like 8 + 3 = 11. Then ask your child to name a related subtraction fact.

Standards
NS **1.3, 2.1, 2.2, 2.6**
MR **2.0**

Algebra Readiness:
Fact Families for 11

Learn About It

Review
Vocabulary

fact family

A **fact family** uses the same numbers.

This fact family uses the numbers 11, 4, and 7.

11 is the whole.
4 and 7 are the parts.

$4 + 7 = \underline{11}$ $11 - 4 = \underline{7}$

$7 + 4 = \underline{11}$ $11 - 7 = \underline{4}$

Guided Practice

Complete each fact family.

1.

$3 + 8 = \underline{11}$

$8 + 3 = \underline{11}$

$11 - 8 = \underline{3}$

$11 - 3 = \underline{8}$

2.

$6 + 5 = \underline{}$

$5 + 6 = \underline{}$

$11 - 6 = \underline{}$

$11 - 5 = \underline{}$

Explain Your Thinking Are $6 - 4$ and $6 + 4$ in the same fact family? Why or why not?

Independent Practice

Remember: A fact family uses the same numbers.

Complete each fact family.

1. 10

$6 + 4 =$ __10__

$4 + 6 =$ __10__

$10 - 6 =$ __4__

$10 - 4 =$ __6__

2. 9

$5 + 4 =$ ___

$4 + 5 =$ ___

$9 - 5 =$ ___

$9 - 4 =$ ___

3.

$9 + 2 =$ ___

$2 + 9 =$ ___

$11 - 9 =$ ___

$11 - 2 =$ ___

4.

$7 + 4 =$ ___

$4 + 7 =$ ___

$11 - 7 =$ ___

$11 - 4 =$ ___

Problem Solving·Reasoning

Write About It

5. Brad says he can make 2 groups of 6 pennies. Is he right? Explain.

At Home Ask your child to write a fact family using 8, 2, and 10.

Algebra Readiness: Fact Families for 12

Learn About It

The facts in a fact family are all related.

The numbers 12, 4, and 8 make a fact family.

Fact families always use the same numbers.

Whole	
12	
Part	**Part**
8	4

$8 + 4 = \underline{12}$ $12 - 8 = \underline{4}$

$4 + 8 = \underline{12}$ $12 - 4 = \underline{8}$

Guided Practice

Add or subtract. Write the missing fact.

1.

12	
5	7

   $5 + 7 = \underline{12}$ $12 - 5 = \underline{7}$

   $12 - 7 = \underline{5}$ $\underline{7} \oplus \underline{5} = \underline{12}$

2.
12	
9	3

   $9 + 3 = \underline{}$ $12 - 3 = \underline{}$

   $3 + 9 = \underline{}$ $\underline{} \bigcirc \underline{} = \underline{}$

3.
12	
6	6

   $6 + 6 = \underline{}$ $\underline{} \bigcirc \underline{} = \underline{}$

Explain Your Thinking Can a fact family use only 2 numbers? Give an example.

Independent Practice

Add or subtract.

Write the missing fact.

1.

12	
7	5

   7 + 5 = _12_   12 − 7 = ___

   12 − 5 = ___   ___ ◯ ___ = ___

2.

12	
4	8

   4 + 8 = ___   12 − 8 = ___

   8 + 4 = ___   ___ ◯ ___ = ___

3.

11	
7	4

   11 − 7 = ___   11 − 4 = ___

   7 + 4 = ___   ___ ◯ ___ = ___

Problem Solving•Reasoning

Complete each fact family.

4.   9 + 3 = ___

   ___ ◯ ___ = ___

   ___ ◯ ___ = ___

   ___ ◯ ___ = ___

5.   11 − 6 = ___

   ___ ◯ ___ = ___

   ___ ◯ ___ = ___

   ___ ◯ ___ = ___

6. **Write Your Own** Write another fact family using 3 different numbers.

At Home Ask your child to write the fact family that uses the numbers 5, 7, and 12. Repeat with other numbers.

Names for Numbers

Learn About It

You can get the same answer in different ways.

4 + 5 and 12 – 3 are facts.

Circle the names for 9.

| 9 | $\begin{array}{r} 4 \\ +5 \\ \hline 9 \end{array}$ | $\begin{array}{r} 7 \\ -2 \\ \hline 5 \end{array}$ | $\begin{array}{r} 5 \\ +6 \\ \hline 11 \end{array}$ | $\begin{array}{r} 12 \\ -\ 3 \\ \hline 9 \end{array}$ |

Guided Practice

Write each sum and difference.
Circle the names for each number on the left.

1.

| 10 | $\begin{array}{r} 9 \\ -1 \\ \hline 8 \end{array}$ | $\begin{array}{r} 3 \\ +\ 7 \\ \hline 10 \end{array}$ | $\begin{array}{r} 10 \\ -\ 0 \\ \hline 10 \end{array}$ | $\begin{array}{r} 12 \\ -\ 4 \\ \hline 8 \end{array}$ | $\begin{array}{r} 6 \\ +\ 4 \\ \hline 10 \end{array}$ |

2.

| 8 | $\begin{array}{r} 7 \\ +1 \\ \hline \end{array}$ | $\begin{array}{r} 8 \\ -2 \\ \hline \end{array}$ | $\begin{array}{r} 11 \\ -\ 3 \\ \hline \end{array}$ | $\begin{array}{r} 6 \\ +2 \\ \hline \end{array}$ | $\begin{array}{r} 10 \\ -\ 4 \\ \hline \end{array}$ |

Circle the names for the number on the left.

3.

| 7 | 5 + 3 | 12 – 5 | 4 + 1 + 2 |

Explain Your Thinking Tell as many different names for ten as you can.

Independent Practice

Circle the names for each number on the left.

1. 5

$(3 + 2)$ $5 + 2$ $(1 + 2 + 2)$

$(11 - 6)$ $(9 - 4)$ $4 + 0 + 3$

2. 10

$4 + 6$ $9 + 1$ $6 + 3 + 2$

$12 - 3$ $8 - 4$ $7 + 2 + 1$

3. 9

$6 + 3$ $12 - 3$ $5 + 3 + 2$

$11 - 2$ $9 - 1$ $7 + 1 + 1$

4. 8

$12 - 5$ $5 + 3$ $1 + 6 + 3$

$8 - 3$ $11 - 3$ $4 + 0 + 4$

5. 4

$11 - 7$ $3 + 1$ $2 + 2 + 4$

$9 - 5$ $2 + 5$ $6 + 2 + 0$

Problem Solving • Reasoning

Patterns

6. Write each sum. Look for a pattern.
   Write the facts likely to come next.

$$\begin{array}{cccccc}
0 & 1 & 2 & 3 & & \\
+7 & +6 & +5 & +4 & +\square & +\square \\
\hline
\end{array}$$

At Home Give your child 3 or 4 facts that have the same answers, such as 6 + 2, 10 − 2, 3 + 5. Ask what number the facts name.

Name

Problem Solving:
Choose the Operation

Standards
NS 2.1, 2.6
MR 1.0, 1.1, 3.0

Animals need food to grow. They
eat different kinds of foods.

**You can use addition to solve a
problem.**

One cub eats 3 bowls of food. Another
eats 4 bowls of food. How many bowls
of food do they eat in all?

☐ bowls

○ ☐ bowls
———
☐ bowls

Think:
Find the numbers
in the problem.
Add to find the total.

**You can use subtraction to
solve a problem.**

There are 12 seals. The zookeeper
feeds 9 seals. How many seals still
need to be fed?

☐ seals

○ ☐ seals
———
☐ seals

Think:
Find the numbers
in the problem.
Subtract to find the
difference.

Guided Practice

Add or subtract to solve.

1 One baby monkey has 8 bananas.
Another baby monkey takes 3 of them.
How many bananas are left?

_5_ bananas

Think: Do I add or subtract?

2 One baby camel eats 4 bags of hay.
Another eats 6 bags of hay.
How many bags of hay do the baby camels eat?

_____ bags of hay

Think: How can I solve the problem?

3 The baby buffalo ate 5 bags of grass on Monday and 6 bags on Tuesday. How many bags of grass did they eat on both days?

_____ bags of grass

Think: What do I need to find out?

At Home Create a story problem about a baby animal. Help your child write a number sentence, choose the operation, and solve the problem.

Name_____

Choose a Strategy

Solve.

1 There are 2 chicks under a tree. Soon 4 chicks join them. Then 3 more chicks come under the tree. How many chicks are under the tree?

Draw or write to explain.

_____ chicks

chick

2 The piglets ate 5 pails of grain. Then they ate 3 more pails of grain. How many pails of grain did they eat?

_____ pails of grain

piglet

3 There are 9 ducklings in the pond. 3 ducklings get out of the pond. Now how many ducklings are in the pond?

_____ ducklings

duckling

4 The puppies had 12 treats. They ate 9 of them. How many treats were not eaten?

_____ treats

puppy

Name_____

Mixed Practice

Find each sum or difference.

1. 11 − 2 = ___
2. 7 + 5 = ___
3. 5 + 5 − ___

4. 8 − 4 = ___
5. 6 − 2 = ___
6. 3 + 5 = ___

7. 6 + 0 = ___
8. 9 + 3 = ___
9. 11 − 3 = ___

10.   1
    +8
    ———

11.   4
    −2
    ———

12.   5
    −4
    ———

13.   4
    +0
    ———

14.   6
    +5
    ———

15.   8
    −5
    ———

16.   11
    − 8
    ———

17.   6
    +6
    ———

18.   7
    +4
    ———

19.   7
    −6
    ———

20.   12
    − 3
    ———

21.   8
    +3
    ———

22.   3
    +7
    ———

23.   4
    +6
    ———

24.   7
    −2
    ———

25.   12
    − 4
    ———

26.   4
    +4
    ———

27.   4
    +7
    ———

 Brain Teaser Less Than

Write as many numbers as you can
that make each sentence true.

7 + ▨ is less than 12.   5 + ▨ is less than 11.

_____   _____

Safe Site

Internet Test Prep
Visit **www.eduplace.com/kids/mhm**
for more *Brain Teasers*.

Quick ✓ Check

Check Your Understanding of Lessons 10–14

Add or subtract.

1. $\begin{array}{r} 3 \\ +9 \\ \hline \end{array}$ $\begin{array}{r} 12 \\ -\ 9 \\ \hline \end{array}$

2. $\begin{array}{r} 4 \\ +6 \\ \hline \end{array}$ $\begin{array}{r} 10 \\ -\ 6 \\ \hline \end{array}$

3. $\begin{array}{r} 9 \\ +2 \\ \hline \end{array}$ $\begin{array}{r} 11 \\ -\ 2 \\ \hline \end{array}$

Complete each fact family.

4. $11 - 6 =$ ___

    ___ $-$ ___ $=$ ___

    ___ $+$ ___ $=$ ___

    ___ $+$ ___ $=$ ___

5. $3 + 9 =$ ___

    ___ $+$ ___ $=$ ___

    ___ $-$ ___ $=$ ___

    ___ $-$ ___ $=$ ___

6. Circle the names for 8.

   $12 - 5$ $5 + 3$ $11 - 3$ $6 + 3$ $6 + 0 + 2$

Solve.

7. Three boys are playing tag. Four girls join them. Then two more girls join the game. How many children are playing tag?

   ____ children

8. Mona has 12 cards. She gives away 5 of them. How many does she have left?

   ____ cards

Name_____

Test Prep • Cumulative Review

Maintaining the Standards

Fill in the ○ for the correct answer. NH means Not Here.

1 What number comes after 42?

24   40   43   41
○   ○   ○   ○

2 Which is the sum?

$$4 + 6 + 2 = \blacksquare$$

8   10   11   NH
○   ○   ○   ○

3 Which number sentence is a related subtraction fact for 8 + 3 = 11?

○ 8 − 3 − 5

○ 11 − 8 = 3

○ 11 − 7 = 4

○ NH

4 Which number names 12 − 3?

7   8   9   10
○   ○   ○   ○

Use this graph for Exercises 5 and 6.

5 How many more ☾ does Lora have than ♥?

4   3   2   1
○   ○   ○   ○

6 **Explain** how you can find out how many stickers Lora has in all.

_____

_____

Internet Test Prep
Visit www.eduplace.com/kids/mhm
for more *Test Prep Practice.*

Chapter Review

1. Write a number sentence that has three **addends**.

   ___ ◯ ___ ◯ ___ = ___

2. Write three **related facts** for $8 + 4 = 12$.

   ___ ◯ ___ = ___   ___ ◯ ___ = ___

   ___ ◯ ___ = ___

3. Write a **fact family** using 3 different numbers.

   ___ ◯ ___ = ___   ___ ◯ ___ = ___

   ___ ◯ ___ = ___   ___ ◯ ___ = ___

Add.

4.
$$\begin{array}{r} 4 \\ +7 \\ \hline \end{array}$$

5.
$$\begin{array}{r} 5 \\ +6 \\ \hline \end{array}$$

6.
$$\begin{array}{r} 8 \\ +4 \\ \hline \end{array}$$

7.
$$\begin{array}{r} 3 \\ +9 \\ \hline \end{array}$$

8.
$$\begin{array}{r} 3 \\ +8 \\ \hline \end{array}$$

9.
$$\begin{array}{r} 7 \\ +5 \\ \hline \end{array}$$

10. $6 + 2 + 3 =$ ___

11. $4 + 3 + 3 =$ ___

Write the missing addend.

12. ☐ $+ 4 = 9$

13. $7 +$ ☐ $= 11$

Subtract.

14. $11 - 3 =$ ___

15. $12 - 7 =$ ___

16. $12 - 4 =$ ___

17. $11 - 5 =$ ___

Subtract.

1. $\begin{array}{r} 1\,2 \\ -\ \ 3 \\ \hline \end{array}$
2. $\begin{array}{r} 1\,1 \\ -\ \ 7 \\ \hline \end{array}$
3. $\begin{array}{r} 1\,2 \\ -\ \ 5 \\ \hline \end{array}$
4. $\begin{array}{r} 1\,2 \\ -\ \ 8 \\ \hline \end{array}$
5. $\begin{array}{r} 1\,1 \\ -\ \ 6 \\ \hline \end{array}$

6. Circle the related fact for $11 - 3 = 8$.

$8 + 3 = 11$ $11 - 2 = 9$

7. Write a fact family using the numbers 12, 9, and 3.

____ + ____ = ____   ____ − ____ = ____

____ + ____ = ____   ____ − ____ = ____

8. Write three names for 10.

_____ _____ _____

9. The first-grade class made a list of their pets. They listed 5 dogs, 3 cats, and 2 fish. How many pets are on the list? Complete the table to solve.

____ in all

Pets	
Animals	**Number**
cats	
dogs	
fish	

10. Use the completed table. Write a number sentence to show how many more dogs there are than fish.

____ ◯ ____ = ____

Chapter Test

Add or subtract.

1. $\begin{array}{r} 9 \\ +2 \\ \hline \end{array}$
2. $\begin{array}{r} 4 \\ +8 \\ \hline \end{array}$
3. $\begin{array}{r} 7 \\ +5 \\ \hline \end{array}$
4. $\begin{array}{r} 5 \\ +6 \\ \hline \end{array}$
5. $\begin{array}{r} 5 \\ +4 \\ \hline \end{array}$

6. $\begin{array}{r} 12 \\ -\ 9 \\ \hline \end{array}$
7. $\begin{array}{r} 11 \\ -\ 5 \\ \hline \end{array}$
8. $\begin{array}{r} 12 \\ -\ 6 \\ \hline \end{array}$
9. $\begin{array}{r} 11 \\ -\ 3 \\ \hline \end{array}$
10. $\begin{array}{r} 12 \\ -\ 7 \\ \hline \end{array}$

11. $12 - 4 = \underline{\quad}$
12. $5 + 7 = \underline{\quad}$

13. $11 - 8 = \underline{\quad}$
14. $10 - 4 = \underline{\quad}$

Write the missing addends.

15. $\boxed{} + 4 = 12$
16. $5 + \boxed{} = 11$

17. Write a fact family using the numbers 11, 5, and 6.

$\underline{\quad} + \underline{\quad} = \underline{\quad}$ $\underline{\quad} - \underline{\quad} = \underline{\quad}$

$\underline{\quad} + \underline{\quad} = \underline{\quad}$ $\underline{\quad} - \underline{\quad} = \underline{\quad}$

18. Add or subtract. Then circle the names for 9.

$\begin{array}{r} 4 \\ +5 \\ \hline \end{array}$
$\begin{array}{r} 7 \\ -2 \\ \hline \end{array}$
$\begin{array}{r} 5 \\ +6 \\ \hline \end{array}$
$\begin{array}{r} 12 \\ -\ 3 \\ \hline \end{array}$
$\begin{array}{r} 6 \\ -3 \\ \hline \end{array}$
$\begin{array}{r} 11 \\ -\ 2 \\ \hline \end{array}$

Add.

19. $4 + 4 + 3 =$ _____

20. $2 + 4 + 6 =$ _____

21. Circle the related subtraction fact for $7 + 5 = 12$.

$7 + 4 = 11$ $12 - 7 = 5$

Use the table for Exercises 22 and 23.

22. A class list of favorite toys included 6 games, 5 cars, 4 balls. The number of robots is 2 less than the number of cars. Complete the table.

23. How many more children chose games than balls?

_____ children

Favorite Toys	Number
Balls	
Cars	
Games	
Robots	

24. Shelby sees 9 bunnies. Then 6 hop away. How many bunnies are left?

_____ bunnies

25. There are 4 puppies on a farm. Then 5 more puppies are born. Now how many puppies are there?

_____ puppies

Write About It

If you know the fact $8 + 4 = 12$, what other facts do you know? **Explain** why.

_____

_____

_____

Name _____

Rolling for Numbers

What You Need

number cube with 6, 7, 8, 9, 11, 12

2 crayons

How to Play

① Choose ⬤ or ⬤ .

② Roll to get an answer.

③ Find a box below in which to write that answer. Lose a turn if you can't find the correct box.

④ The player who has the most boxes with correct answers wins.

1 2 − 3	1 1 − 4	1 1 − 5	7 +4	1 2 − 5	9 +2
1 1 − 2	1 2 − 6	9 −3	1 1 − 3	8 +4	1 2 − 4

Enrichment

Mental Math

Fill in the numbers on the path.
Add or subtract

Accessing Prior Knowledge

This story will help you review

- Identifying pennies, nickels, and dimes

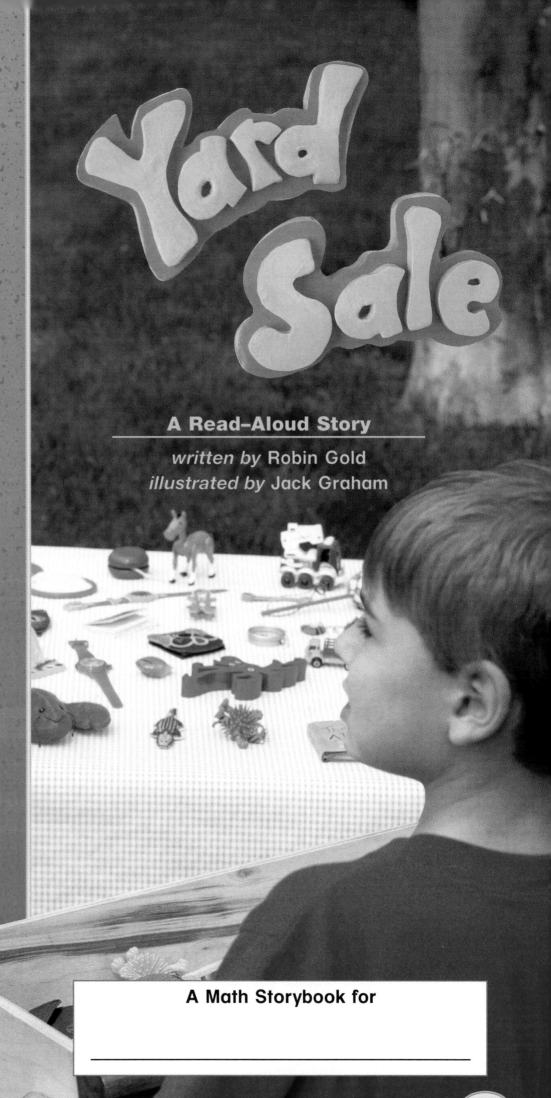

Yard Sale

A Read-Aloud Story

written by Robin Gold
illustrated by Jack Graham

A Math Storybook for

_____

I'm having fun cleaning out
And finding things I'd forgotten about.
I need items for my sale.
I see a penny and a nail.

Circle the penny.

As I look inside the drawer,
I spy a rock, a ball, and more.
I touch a feather and get a tickle.
Can you help me find the nickel?

Circle the nickel.

I spot a block that can be sold.

I also spot a pen to hold.

I see something that tells the time.

Do you see a brand-new dime?

Circle the dime.

I see cards that I can sell.
I also see a key and a bell.
I see pennies just for me.
How many pennies do you see?

_____ pennies

I spot a chain, a car, and a game.
And there is something with my name.
I can sell the little book.
I see more coins. Take a look!

How many pennies and nickels are there?

_____ pennies   _____ nickels

I view a clip, a pad, and a pin.

My sale is ready to begin.

I can use the dimes I see

As change when people buy from me.

How many dimes are there?

_____ dimes

Family Letter

Dear Family,

During the next few weeks, our math class will be learning about money.

You can expect to see work that provides practice with counting money amounts, using pennies, nickels, dimes, and quarters.

As we learn about money, you may wish to use the following samples as a guide.

Vocabulary

penny A coin worth 1 cent.

nickel A coin worth 5 cents.

dime A coin worth 10 cents.

quarter A coin worth 25 cents.

Money

| 1 penny | 1 nickel | 1 dime | 1 quarter |
| 1¢ | 5¢ | 10¢ | 25¢ |

Knowing how to count money can help children with real-life skills.

Sincerely,
Your child's teacher

Name _____

	Standards
	NS **1.5**, MR **2.0**

LESSON 1 Value of Coins

New
Vocabulary

penny
cent
nickel
dime

Learn About It

Coins have different values.

A **penny** equals 1¢, or one **cent.**

A **nickel** equals 5 pennies, or five cents.

 =

A **dime** equals 10 pennies, or ten cents.

2 nickels = 1 dime

 =

Guided Practice

Circle the coins to match each price.

1.

2.

Explain Your Thinking Would you rather have 10¢ in pennies or nickels? Why?

three hundred three **303**

Independent Practice

Circle the coins to match each price.

1.

10¢

2.

10¢

3.

10¢

4.

5¢

Problem Solving·Reasoning

Write About It

5. Look at the picture. Kevin has 2 nickels and 4 pennies. Which toy can he buy? Explain.

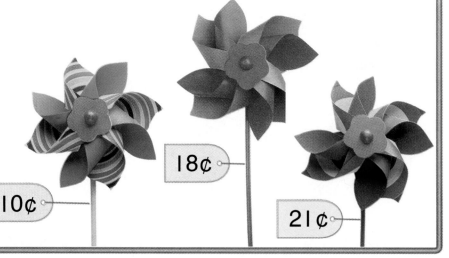

10¢

18¢

21¢

304 three hundred four

At Home Show your child some dimes, nickels, and pennies. Ask him or her to identify each coin and tell you its value.

Name _____

LESSON 2 **Nickels**

Learn About It

You can count **nickels**.

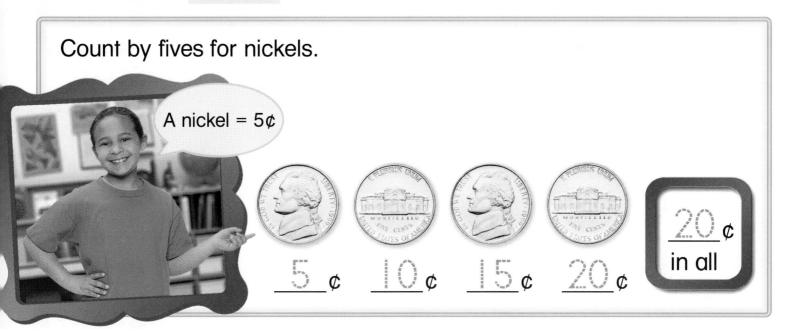

Count by fives for nickels.

A nickel = 5¢

__5__¢   _10_¢   _15_¢   _20_¢

_20_¢
in all

Guided Practice

Count by fives.
Write how much in all.

1.
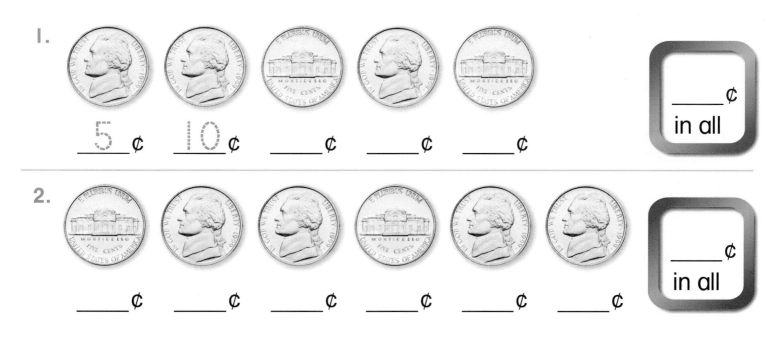

__5__¢   _10_¢   ____¢   ____¢   ____¢

____¢
in all

2.

____¢   ____¢   ____¢   ____¢   ____¢   ____¢

____¢
in all

Explain Your Thinking Why does skip counting
by fives help you count nickels?

Independent Practice

Count by fives. Write how much in all.

1.

5 ¢   10 ¢   15 ¢

15 ¢
in all

2.

____ ¢   ____ ¢   ____ ¢   ____ ¢

____ ¢
in all

3.

____ ¢   ____ ¢   ____ ¢   ____ ¢   ____ ¢

____ ¢
in all

4.

____ ¢   ____ ¢   ____ ¢   ____ ¢   ____ ¢   ____ ¢

____ ¢
in all

Problem Solving • Reasoning

5. Grace counted her nickels.
She has 40¢.
How many nickels does
she have?

_____ nickels

Draw or write to explain.

At Home Show your child groups of nickels totaling 95¢ or less. Have him or her write how much money in all.

LESSON 3 Nickels and Pennies

Learn About It

You can count nickels and pennies.

Always start with the coins of the greatest value.

How much in all?
Count by fives for nickels.
Count by ones for pennies.

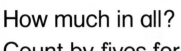

__5__ ¢   __10__ ¢   __15__ ¢   __16__ ¢   __17__ ¢   __18__ ¢

__18__ ¢
in all

Guided Practice

Count by fives. Then count by ones.
Write how much in all.

1.

 __5__ ¢   __10__ ¢   ____ ¢   ____ ¢   ____ ¢ ____ ¢

____ ¢
in all

2.

 ____ ¢   ____ ¢   ____ ¢ ____ ¢ ____ ¢ ____ ¢

____ ¢
in all

Explain Your Thinking Would you rather have
1 nickel or 4 pennies? Why?

Independent Practice

Circle the coins to match the price.

1.

2.

3.

4.

5.

6.

At Home Show your child some nickels and pennies. Have him or her write how much in all.

Standards
NS **1.5, 2.4,** AF **1.1**
SDP **2.1**

Dimes

Learn About It

You can count **dimes.**

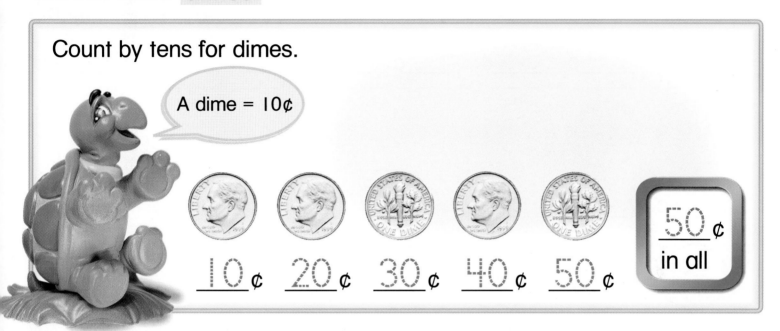

Count by tens for dimes.

A dime = 10¢

_10_¢ _20_¢ _30_¢ _40_¢ _50_¢

_50_¢
in all

Guided Practice

Count by tens.
Write how much in all.

1.
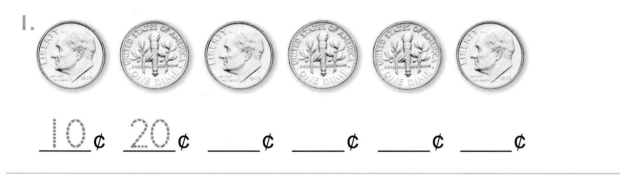

_10_¢ _20_¢ ____¢ ____¢ ____¢ ____¢

____¢
in all

2.

____¢ ____¢ ____¢ ____¢ ____¢ ____¢ ____¢

____¢
in all

Explain Your Thinking Would you rather have
30 pennies or 3 dimes? Why?

Independent Practice

Count by tens.
Write how much in all.

1.

   <u>10</u>¢ <u>20</u>¢ <u>30</u>¢ <u>40</u>¢ <u>50</u>¢

   <u>50</u>¢
   in all

2.

   _____¢ _____¢ _____¢

   _____¢
   in all

3.

   _____¢ _____¢ _____¢ _____¢

   _____¢
   in all

4.

   _____¢ _____¢ _____¢ _____¢ _____¢ _____¢

   _____¢
   in all

Problem Solving • Reasoning

Algebra Readiness · Missing Addends

5. Lara had 40¢.
   Her aunt gave her some dimes.
   Now she has 90¢. How much
   money did her aunt give her?

   $40¢ + \underline{\quad}¢ = 90¢$

   Draw or write to explain.

At Home Ask your child how many dimes he or she would need for the following amounts: 50¢, 90¢, 20¢, and 80¢.

Name _____

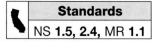

	Standards
	NS **1.5**, **2.4**, MR **1.1**

 Dimes and Pennies

Learn About It

You can count dimes and pennies.

How much in all?

Count by tens for dimes and
by ones for pennies.

<u>10</u>¢ <u>20</u>¢ <u>30</u>¢ <u>31</u>¢ <u>32</u>¢ <u>33</u>¢

<u>33</u>¢
in all

Guided Practice

Count by tens. Then count by ones.
Write how much in all.

1.

<u>10</u>¢ <u>20</u>¢ ___¢ ___¢ ___¢ ___¢ ___¢

___¢
in all

2.

___¢ ___¢ ___¢ ___¢ ___¢ ___¢ ___¢

___¢
in all

Explain Your Thinking Would you rather have 4 nickels
or 3 dimes? Why?

Independent Practice

Circle the coins that match each price.

> Count the coins with the greatest value first.

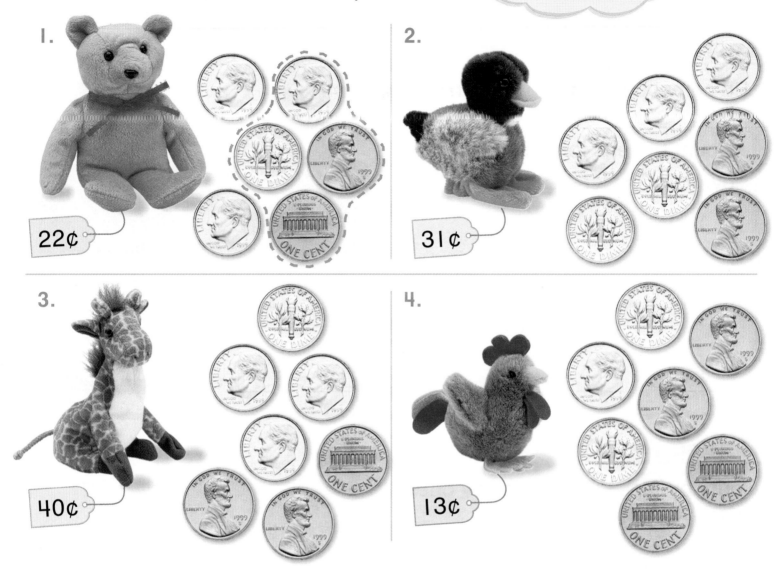

1. 22¢

2. 31¢

3. 40¢

4. 13¢

Problem Solving • Reasoning

5. Each boy has 12¢.

Write the number of coins each boy has.

Ramon has 3 coins.
_____ pennies
_____ nickels
_____ dimes

Luis has 12 coins.
_____ pennies
_____ nickels
_____ dimes

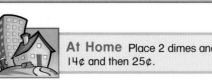

At Home Place 2 dimes and 5 pennies on a table. Ask your child to show you 14¢ and then 25¢.

Quick ✓ Check

Check Your Understanding of Lessons 1–5

Circle the coins that match each price.

1.

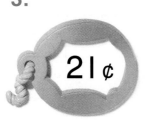 

2.

3.

4.

Write how much in all.

5.

____¢   ____¢   ____¢   ____¢   ____¢   ____¢

____¢
in all

6.

____¢   ____¢   ____¢   ____¢   ____¢   ____¢

____¢
in all

Name_____

Test Prep • Cumulative Review
Maintaining the Standards

Fill in the ○ for the correct answer.

1 Which two numbers have a 2 in the ones place?

○ 25, 27   ○ 42, 28
○ 12, 52   ○ 26, 32

2 What is the value of these coins?

50¢   32¢   17¢   5¢
○   ○   ○   ○

3 Which number sentence is in the same fact family as 5 + 5 = 10?

○ 5 + 6 = 11

○ 4 + 6 = 10

○ 10 − 5 = 5

○ 5 − 5 = 0

4 Which number is 10 more than 46?

36   47   56   66
○   ○   ○   ○

Use the graph for Exercises 5 and 6.

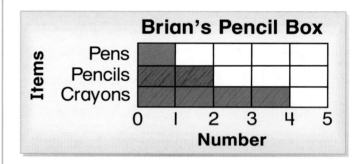

5 How many crayons and pencils in all?

6   5   3   2
○   ○   ○   ○

6 **Explain** what will happen to the graph if Brian puts in another pen and takes out a crayon.

_____

_____

Safe Site

Internet Test Prep
Visit **www.eduplace.com/kids/mhm**
for more *Test Prep Practice.*

LESSON 6 Count Coins

Learn About It

You can count **dimes**, **nickels**, and **pennies**.

How much in all?

Count by tens for dimes.
Count by fives for nickels.
Count by ones for pennies.

<u>10</u> ¢ <u>20</u> ¢ <u>25</u> ¢ <u>30</u> ¢ <u>31</u> ¢

$\dfrac{31}{\text{in all}}$ ¢

Guided Practice

Write how much in all.

1.

<u>10</u> ¢ <u>20</u> ¢ _____ ¢ _____ ¢ _____ ¢ _____ ¢

_____ ¢
in all

2.

_____ ¢ _____ ¢ _____ ¢ _____ ¢ _____ ¢ _____ ¢ _____ ¢

_____ ¢
in all

Explain Your Thinking You have 4 pennies, 2 dimes, and 5 nickels. How would you count them?

Independent Practice

Write each amount.

Remember:
Start with the coins
of the greatest value.

1.
_40_ ¢

2.
_____ ¢

3.
_____ ¢

4.
_____ ¢

5.
_____ ¢

6.
_____ ¢

Problem Solving • Reasoning

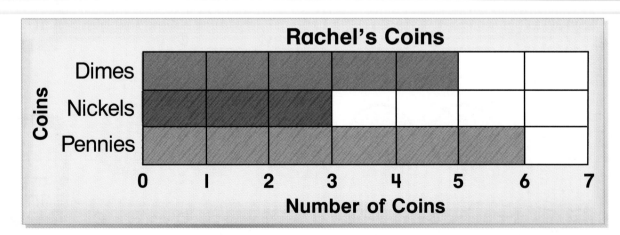

Rachel's Coins

Coins								
Dimes								
Nickels								
Pennies								
	0	1	2	3	4	5	6	7

Number of Coins

 7. Write Your Own Use this graph to write a word problem.

At Home Place a handful of dimes, nickels, and pennies on a table. Ask your child to count them for you.

Name_____

LESSON 7

Equal Amounts

Standards
NS 1.5, MR 1.2, 2.1

Learn About It

You can use different coins
to show the same amount.

I can show
21¢ another way.

Both ways show 21¢.

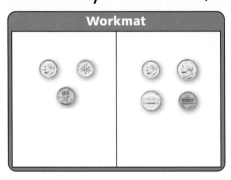

Guided Practice

Use Workmat 2 and coins.

Show these coins.	Write the amount.	Show another way.
1.	__13__¢	10¢ 1¢ 1¢ 1¢
2.	____¢	

Explain Your Thinking Why can you use only pennies to make 4¢?

three hundred seventeen **317**

Independent Practice

Use Workmat 2 and coins.

Draw 2 ways to show each amount.

1.

2.

3.

4.

Problem Solving · Reasoning

Write About It

5. Draw 32¢, using 5 coins.

6. Draw 32¢, using 7 coins.

Explain how you found your answers.

At Home Ask your child to show 42¢ in several different ways.

Name_____

| Standards |
| NS **1.5**, MR **1.0, 1.1,** |
| **1.2, 2.2, 3.0** |

LESSON 8

Problem Solving: Use Models to Act It Out

You can use models to act out problems.

Christine buys two cards with 5 dimes. One card costs 10¢ more than the other card. How much does each card cost?

Understand

What do you already know?

Two cards cost _____ dimes.

One card costs _____ more than the other card.

Plan

Circle what you would use to act out this problem.

Coins

Counters

Solve

Put 5 dimes in 2 groups. Draw circles to show your answer.

Look Back

Explain why your answer makes sense.

Guided Practice

Solve.
Use coins if you want.

Remember to use the 4 steps.

① Peggy buys a yo-yo for 15¢. She pays for it with 2 nickels and some pennies. How many pennies does she use?

Think:
What do I already know?

_5_ pennies

Draw or write to explain.

② A puzzle costs 10¢. How many different ways can you show 10¢?

Think:
What coins can I use to show 10¢?

_____ ways

③ Zeb has 1 dime, 3 nickels, and 4 pennies. Can he buy a toy truck for 27¢? Explain.

Think:
How much money does he have?

_____

④ Kim wants to buy a book for 18¢. What is the least number of coins that make 18¢?

Think:
How can I solve the problem?

_____ coins

At Home Help your child make price tags and then use coins to show the prices.

Name_____

Check Your Understanding of Lessons 6–8

Write each amount.

1.

_____ ¢

2.

_____ ¢

Draw at least two ways to show each amount.
Use coins if you want.

3.

27¢

4.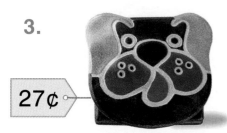

34¢

5.

41¢

6. Roland wants to buy a game for 23¢. What is the least number of coins he can use?

_____ coins

Draw or write to explain.

Name _____

Test Prep • Cumulative Review

Maintaining the Standards

Fill in the ○ for the correct answer.

1 What is the missing addend?

$$8 + \blacksquare = 12$$

3	4	5	6
○	○	○	○

2 What two numbers are likely to come next?

35, 40, 45, ___, ___

46, 47	50, 60
○	○

50, 55	55, 65
○	○

3 Grant had 10 toys. He lost four of them. How many are left?

6	5	4	3
○	○	○	○

4 Which number is the same as 11 − 7?

18	6	5	4
○	○	○	○

5 What is the value of these coins?

18¢	28¢	33¢	40¢
○	○	○	○

6 Sue has 3 dimes, 4 nickels, and 6 pennies. Can she buy a game for 52¢?
Explain how you know.

_____

_____

_____

Safe Site

Internet Test Prep
Visit **www.eduplace.com/kids/mhm**
for more *Test Prep Practice*.

LESSON 9 Quarters

New
Vocabulary
quarter

Learn About It

A **quarter** is equal to 25¢.

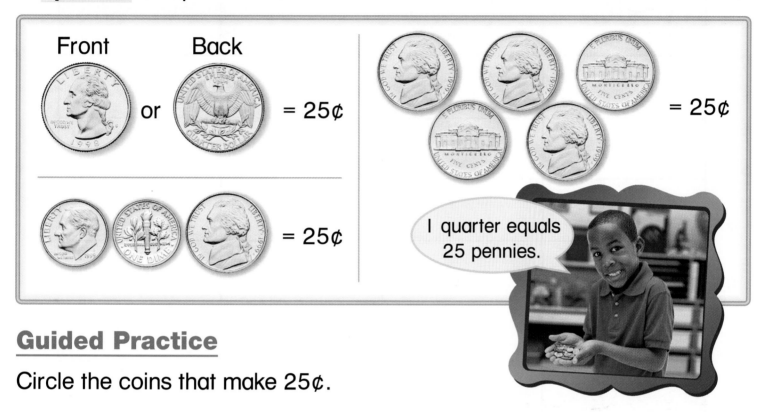

Front   Back

or   = 25¢

= 25¢

= 25¢

I quarter equals 25 pennies.

Guided Practice

Circle the coins that make 25¢.

1.

2.

3.

4.

Explain Your Thinking Why can't you make 25¢ with only dimes?

Independent Practice

Write how many of each coin you need to make 25¢.

1.	1	0	0	0
2.				
3.				
4.				
5.				
6.				

Problem Solving • Reasoning

7. Jason has 22¢.

Draw 22¢ with fewer coins than Jason has.	Draw 22¢ with more coins than Jason has.

At Home Find items under 99¢ in an advertisement. Have your child tell you the coins needed to buy each item.

Count With Quarters

Learn About It

You can count quarters, dimes, nickels, and pennies.

How much in all?

Start with 25¢.
Then count by tens.

25 ¢   35 ¢   45 ¢   55 ¢

55 ¢
in all

Guided Practice

Write how much in all.

1.

25 ¢   30 ¢   ___ ¢   ___ ¢   ___ ¢   ___ ¢

____ ¢
in all

2.

____ ¢   ____ ¢   ____ ¢   ____ ¢   ____ ¢

____ ¢
in all

Explain Your Thinking Would you rather have
1 quarter or 3 dimes or 5 nickels? Why?

Independent Practice

Circle the coins that match each price.

Remember:
Start with the coins
of the greatest value.

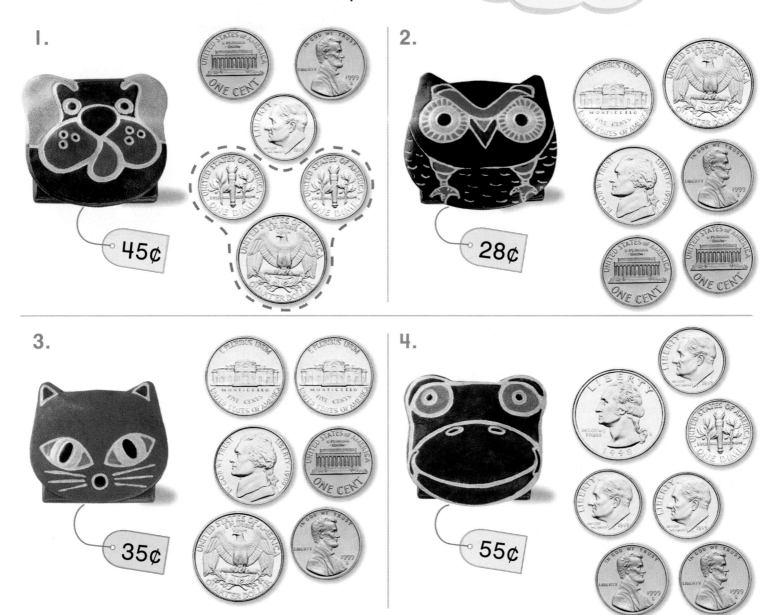

1. 45¢

2. 28¢

3. 35¢

4. 55¢

Problem Solving•Reasoning

Using Vocabulary

5. You have 1 quarter,
   2 dimes, and 3 nickels.
   You find 1 penny.
   How much do you have in all?

   _____ ¢

Draw or write to explain.

At Home Show your child 1 quarter and 2 other coins of the same type—
2 nickels, for example. Ask how much there is in all.

Name_____

Problem Solving:
Use Data From a Picture

Standards
NS **1.5**, SDP **1.2**
MR **1.0**, **1.1**, **3.0**

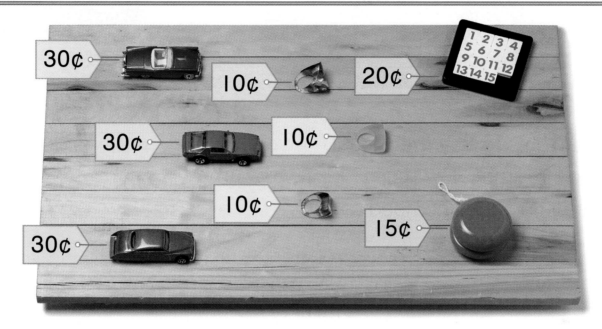

At this yard sale, you can buy cars, rings, and other toys.

Using a picture can help you decide how much money you need.

Joey wants to buy a toy car. He has a quarter and 3 pennies. What other coins does he need?

> **Think:** I need to find out how much he has now.

_____

Using a picture can help you decide how many you can buy.

Lila uses her money to buy rings. She has 2 dimes and 2 nickels. How many rings can she buy?

> **Think:** Use the picture to find the cost of a ring.

_____ rings

Guided Practice

Solve. Use coins if you want.

40¢   30¢   32¢

① Jared wants to buy the clip.
He has 1 dime. How many
more dimes does he need?

___3___ dimes

Think:
Can you count
by tens?

Draw or write to explain.

② Ashley wants to use her nickels
to buy the pen. How many
nickels does she need?

_____ nickels

Think:
Can you count
by fives?

③ Brett wants to buy the truck.
He has 28¢. What other
coins does he need?

_____

Think:
How much more
does he need?

At Home Ask your child to make up a story problem using a picture from a magazine or a newspaper.

Name_____

Choose a Strategy

Solve. Use coins if you want.

1 Ethan has 2 coins.
He has enough money to
buy the whistle.
What 2 coins does Ethan have?

_____ and _____

Draw or write to explain.

30¢
whistle

2 Megan has 45¢.
One of her coins is
a quarter. Can she
buy the drum? Explain.

_____

40¢
drum

3 Gina has 20¢. Her dad gave
her 10¢ more. Can she
buy the recorder? Explain.

_____

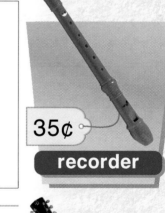
35¢
recorder

4 Alex has 4 dimes, 2 nickels,
and 5 pennies. He buys a
guitar. How much money
does he have now?

_____ ¢

50¢
guitar

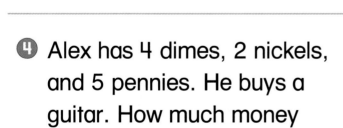

Mixed Practice

Memorize Your Facts

Add or subtract.

1. $11 - 4 = $ ___   2. $6 + 6 = $ ___   3. $2 + 9 = $ ___

4. $12 - 5 = $ ___   5. $9 - 1 = $ ___   6. $10 + 0 = $ ___

7. $\begin{array}{r} 3 \\ +8 \\ \hline \end{array}$ 8. $\begin{array}{r} 8 \\ -6 \\ \hline \end{array}$ 9. $\begin{array}{r} 11 \\ -\ 6 \\ \hline \end{array}$ 10. $\begin{array}{r} 1 \\ +9 \\ \hline \end{array}$ 11. $\begin{array}{r} 5 \\ +3 \\ \hline \end{array}$ 12. $\begin{array}{r} 9 \\ -4 \\ \hline \end{array}$

13. $\begin{array}{r} 12 \\ -\ 4 \\ \hline \end{array}$ 14. $\begin{array}{r} 7 \\ +4 \\ \hline \end{array}$ 15. $\begin{array}{r} 3 \\ +6 \\ \hline \end{array}$ 16. $\begin{array}{r} 2 \\ -0 \\ \hline \end{array}$ 17. $\begin{array}{r} 10 \\ -\ 5 \\ \hline \end{array}$ 18. $\begin{array}{r} 3 \\ +9 \\ \hline \end{array}$

19. $\begin{array}{r} 5 \\ +7 \\ \hline \end{array}$ 20. $\begin{array}{r} 11 \\ -\ 5 \\ \hline \end{array}$ 21. $\begin{array}{r} 4 \\ +5 \\ \hline \end{array}$ 22. $\begin{array}{r} 12 \\ -\ 3 \\ \hline \end{array}$ 23. $\begin{array}{r} 8 \\ +2 \\ \hline \end{array}$ 24. $\begin{array}{r} 12 \\ -\ 7 \\ \hline \end{array}$

 Brain Teaser Which Coins?

Jay has 36¢.
He doesn't have any dimes.
He has no more than two of
any coin. How many of each
coin does he have?

Draw or write to explain.

Safe Site

Internet Brain Teasers
Visit **www.eduplace.com/kids/mhm**
for more *Brain Teasers*.

Quick ✔ Check

Check Your Understanding of Lessons 9–11

Circle the coins that make 25¢.

1.

2.

Circle the coins that match each price.

3.

31¢

4.

47¢

Use the picture to solve.

5. Ally wants to buy this toy. She has 2 dimes. What other coins does she need?

Ally needs _____.

24¢

Test Prep • Cumulative Review

Maintaining the Standards

Fill in the ○ for the correct answer.

1 How many are shown?

30	40	60	70
○	○	○	○

2 Where is the green bug in the line?

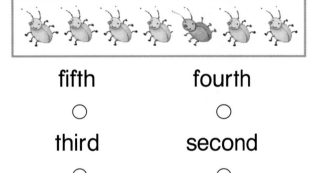

fifth   fourth
  ○   ○

third   second
  ○   ○

3 How many more 🐞 than 🐞?

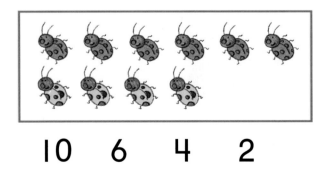

10	6	4	2
○	○	○	○

4 Subtract.

$$\begin{array}{r} 1\,2 \\ -\ \ 5 \\ \hline \end{array}$$

9	8	7	6
○	○	○	○

5 What is the value of these coins?

45¢	35¢	27¢	25¢
○	○	○	○

6 **Explain** three different ways to make 45¢.

_____

_____

_____

_____

Safe Site

Internet Test Prep
Visit **www.eduplace.com/kids/mhm**
for more *Test Prep Practice.*

Chapter Review

Match each coin to its name.

| 1. **dime** | 2. **nickel** | 3. **penny** | 4. **quarter** |

Write how much in all.

5.

____¢   ____¢   ____¢   ____¢   ____¢   ____¢ in all

6.

____¢   ____¢   ____¢   ____¢   ____¢   ____¢ in all

Circle the coins that match each price.

7.

15¢

8.

11¢

Draw two ways to show 42¢.
Use coins if you want.

1.

Circle the coins that make 25¢

2.

3.

4. Write how much in all.

_____¢   _____¢   _____¢   _____¢

_____¢
in all

5. Erin buys a game for 43¢.
   She pays for it with 4 dimes
   and some pennies. How many
   pennies does she use?

   _____ pennies

Draw or write to explain.

6. How much is 1 quarter,
   1 dime, and 1 penny?
   Circle what you can buy.

   _____¢

35¢

38¢

Name_____

Chapter Test

Write how much in all.

1.

   ____¢   ____¢   ____¢   ____¢   ____¢

   | ____¢ |
   | in all |

2.

   ____¢   ____¢   ____¢

   | ____¢ |
   | in all |

3.

   ____¢ ____¢ ____¢ ____¢ ____¢ ____¢ ____¢ ____¢

   in all

Circle the coins that match each price.

4.

5.

Write each amount.

6.

_____ ¢

7.

_____ ¢

Circle the coins that make 25¢.

8.

9.

10. Dina wants to buy this toy. She uses 7 pennies and some dimes. How many dimes does she use?

37¢

_____ dimes

 Write About It Dylan counted these coins. He says the total value is 63¢. **Explain** what he did wrong.

_____

_____

_____

Money Madness

What You Need

 coins

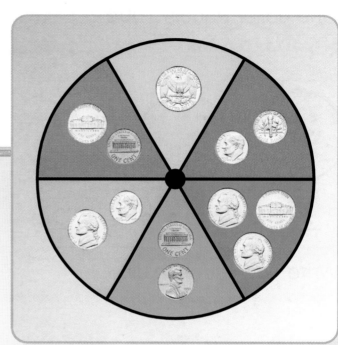

How to Play

① In turn, spin and take coins that match the coins where the spinner landed.

② Exchange pennies, nickels, or dimes for coins of greater value.

③ The first player to get 60¢ with the least number of coins wins.

Name_____

Enrichment

Dollar

One dollar equals 100¢.      or

2̲5̲¢   5̲0̲¢   7̲5̲¢   1̲0̲0̲¢

> 4 quarters equals 100¢ or one dollar.

Write how much in all.

1.

_____¢ _____¢ _____¢ _____¢ _____¢ _____¢ _____¢

2.

_____¢ _____¢ _____¢ _____¢ _____¢ _____¢ _____¢ _____¢

3.

_____¢ _____¢ _____¢ _____¢ _____¢ _____¢

Geometry,
Fractions,
and Probability

Accessing Prior Knowledge

This story will
help you review
• Shapes
• Direction
  words
• Patterns

A Picnic in Space

A Read-Aloud Story

written by Meish Goldish
illustrated by Russell Benfanti

A Math Storybook for

_____

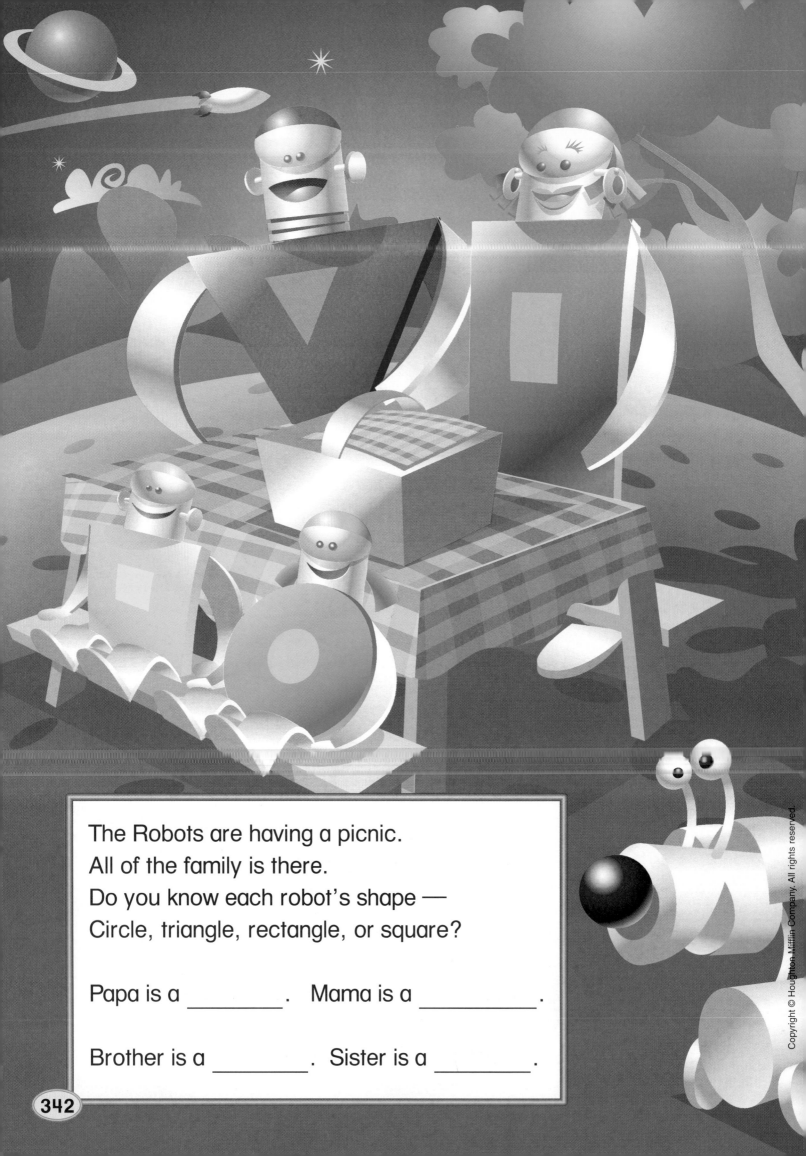

The Robots are having a picnic.
All of the family is there.
Do you know each robot's shape —
Circle, triangle, rectangle, or square?

Papa is a _____. Mama is a _____.

Brother is a _____. Sister is a _____.

342

More family has come to the picnic.
Such colorful cousins, you see!
Brother asks Sister, "Who is who?"
Help them to know their family.

What color is Ricky Rectangle? _____

What color is Tina Triangle? _____

Aunt Circle and Uncle Square are here.
They've brought good things to eat.
Each one has its very own shape.
I bet they all taste sweet!

Match each food to its shape.

circle   rectangle   triangle

Mama is ready to serve,
But why is she wearing a frown?
She can't find the sandwiches or lemonade.
Should she look left, right, up, or down?

For the sandwiches, she should look _____.

For the lemonade, she should look _____.

Time for a family picture!
The cousins line up side by side.
Who should stand next in their pattern?
You help them to decide!

Look at the two robots by the tree.
Circle the one who should line up next.

The picnic is almost over!
Papa thanks everyone who came.
How many robots do you see?
Count the shapes that are the same.

How many circles? _____ squares? _____

triangles? _____ rectangles? _____

Family Letter

Vocabulary

corner The point where sides meet.

solid shape A three-dimensional figure.

plane shape A two-dimensional figure.

symmetry If a figure can be folded in half and the two parts match, it has a line of symmetry.

Dear Family,

During the next few weeks, our math class will be learning about geometry and fractions.

You can expect to see work that provides practice in identifying spheres, cylinders, cubes, rectangular prisms, cones, pyramids, triangles, circles, squares, and rectangles as well as $\frac{1}{2}$, $\frac{1}{3}$, and $\frac{1}{4}$. You may wish to use the following as a guide.

Solid Shapes

sphere   cylinder   rectangular prism   cube   cone   pyramid

Plane Shapes

circle   square   rectangle   triangle

Fractions

$\frac{1}{4}$ is blue. $\frac{1}{2}$ is blue. $\frac{1}{3}$ is blue.

Recognizing shapes can help children solve spatial problems.

Sincerely,

Your child's teacher

LESSON 1 Position Words

Learn About It

Some words tell where objects are.

New Vocabulary

above	left
between	right
below	

above the bridge

to the **left** of the purple flowers

between the red flowers

to the **right** of the purple flowers

below the bridge

Guided Practice

Follow your teacher's directions.

Explain Your Thinking Describe something to the left of you and something to the right of you.

Independent Practice

Draw each object.

1. ☼ above the 🪐

2. ☆ to the right of the 🪐

3. 🪐 below the 🪐

4. ☁ to the left of the 🪐

5. Circle what is between the ☁ and the ☆.

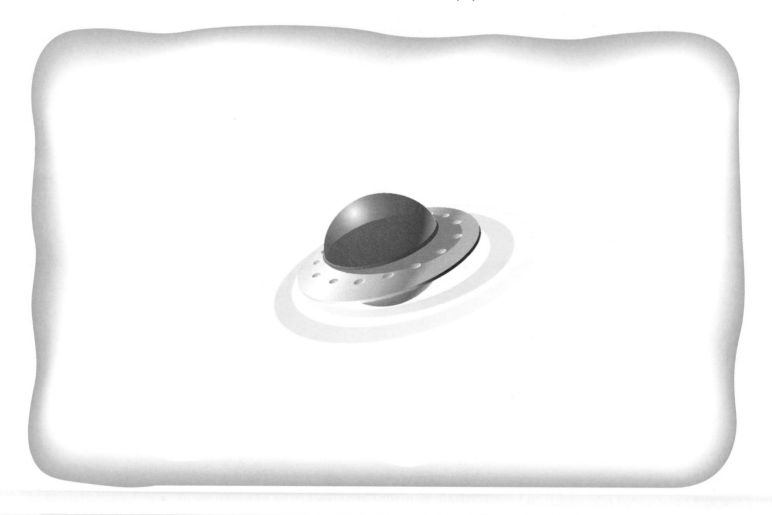

Problem Solving·Reasoning

Logical Thinking

6. Use the clues to
   label each rocket.
   S is between B and N.
   T is to the right of B.

____   ____   B___   ____

 At Home Use the words *above, below, between, left,* and *right* to have your child locate something.

LESSON 2 **More Position Words**

New Vocabulary

behind	**next to**
in front	**up**
far	**down**
near	

Learn About It

You can use words to tell where objects are.

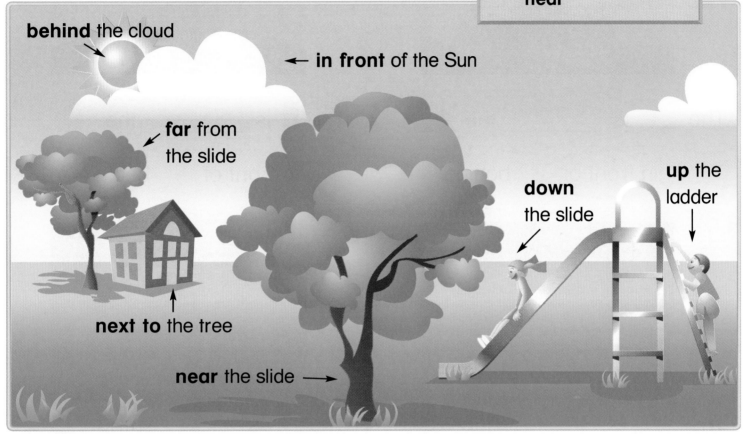

behind the cloud

← **in front** of the Sun

far from the slide

up the ladder

down the slide

next to the tree

near the slide ⟶

Guided Practice

Listen to the teacher. Follow the directions.

Explain Your Thinking Use the words **in front** and **behind** to tell where you sit in the classroom.

Independent Practice

Circle the correct words.

1.

The 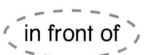 is _____ the 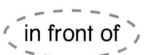 .

(**in front of**) behind

2.

The 🚀 is _____ the 🤖 .

in front of behind

3.

The  is _____ the 🐦 .

far from near

4.

The is _____ the .

far from near

5.

The is _____ the .

next to far from

6.

You go _____ the to the top.

up down

 At Home Have your child use words from this lesson to tell about his or her room.

Standards
MG **2.0, 2.1**

Plane Shapes

Learn About It

Some plane shapes have **corners** and **sides**.

New Vocabulary	
corner	side
circle	square
rectangle	triangle

Sides are straight. They don't curve.

Corners are where the sides meet.

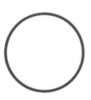    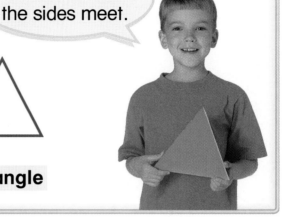

circle　　**square**　　**rectangle**　　**triangle**

Guided Practice

Trace each shape.
Write how many corners and sides.

1. rectangle

____4____ corners

____4____ sides

2. square

____ corners

____ sides

3. triangle

____ corners

____ sides

4. circle

____ corners

____ sides

Explain Your Thinking Compare the number of corners
and the number of sides for each shape. What do you see?

Independent Practice

Use at least one of each shape ◯ ◻ △ ▭ to draw a rocket.

1. Color circles ▭ .

2. Color rectangles ▭ .

3. Color triangles ▭ .

4. Color squares ▭ .

Problem Solving • Reasoning

Visual Thinking

5. Circle the puzzle piece that fits.

At Home Ask your child to draw a shape with 4 sides and 4 corners.

LESSON 4 Sorting Shapes

Learn About It

You can sort shapes in many ways.

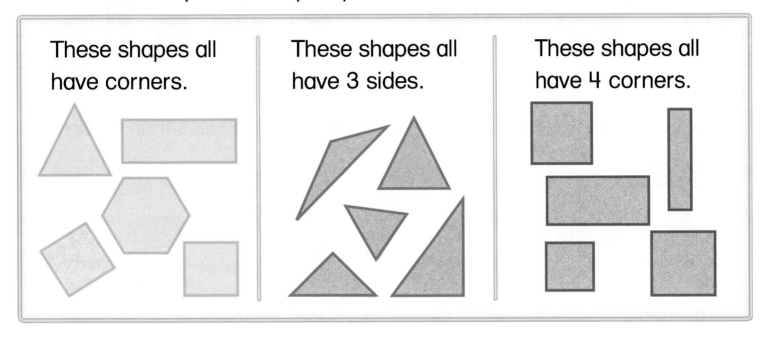

These shapes all have corners.

These shapes all have 3 sides.

These shapes all have 4 corners.

Guided Practice

Circle all the shapes that belong in each group.

1. Shapes with no sides

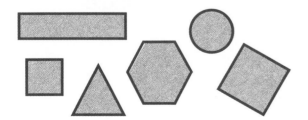

2. Shapes with 3 corners

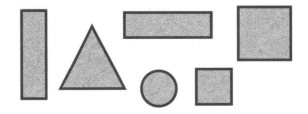

3. Shapes with more than 3 sides

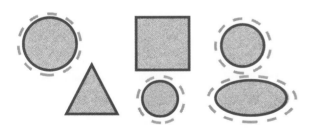

4. Shapes with 4 corners

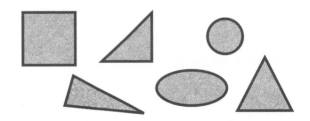

Explain Your Thinking What are other ways to sort shapes?

Independent Practice

Circle all the shapes that belong in each group.

1. Shapes with more than 2 sides

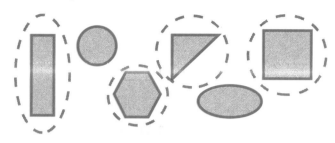

2. Round shapes

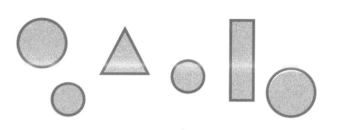

3. Shapes with 4 sides

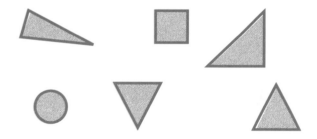

4. Shapes with less than 4 corners

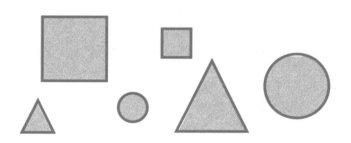

5. Triangles

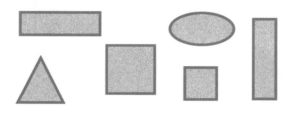

6. Small shapes

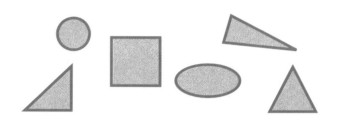

Problem Solving·Reasoning

Using Vocabulary

7. Match each name to the correct shape.

circle	square	triangle	rectangle

 At Home Gather some toys. Ask your child to sort them by shape.

Quick ✓ Check

Check Your Understanding of Lessons 1–4

Circle the correct words.

1.

The is _____ the .

in front of   behind

2.

The is _____ the .

far from   near

3.

The is _____ the  .

far from   next to

4.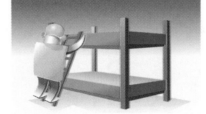

You go _____ the / to the top.

up   down

Write how many corners and sides.

5. rectangle

_____ corners

_____ sides

6. circle

_____ corners

_____ sides

Circle the shapes that belong in each group.

7. Triangles

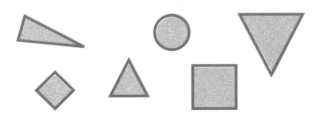

8. Shapes with more than 2 sides

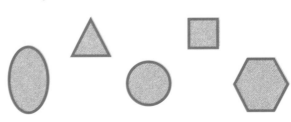

Test Prep • Cumulative Review

Maintaining the Standards

Fill in the ○ for the correct answer. NH means Not Here.

① How many bugs are there?

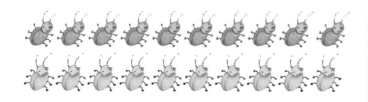

20	21	22	23
○	○	○	○

② Add. $\begin{array}{r} 8 \\ +3 \\ \hline \end{array}$

10	11	12	13
○	○	○	○

③ What is the value of the coins?

29¢	33¢	38¢	65¢
○	○	○	○

④ Subtract. $\begin{array}{r} 9 \\ -3 \\ \hline \end{array}$

12	6	3	NH
○	○	○	○

⑤ What number is likely to come next in this pattern?

4, 5, 6, 4, 5, 6, 4, 5, ____

4	5	6	7
○	○	○	○

⑥ I have 6 ones and 9 tens.
What number am I?
Explain how you know.

_____

_____

_____

Safe Site

Internet Test Prep
Visit **www.eduplace.com/kids/mhm**
for more *Test Prep Practice.*

Standards
MG **2.0, 2.2,** MR **2.1**

LESSON 5 Solid Shapes

Learn About It

Solid shapes have special names.

New Vocabulary

cube   pyramid
cone   sphere
cylinder
rectangular prism

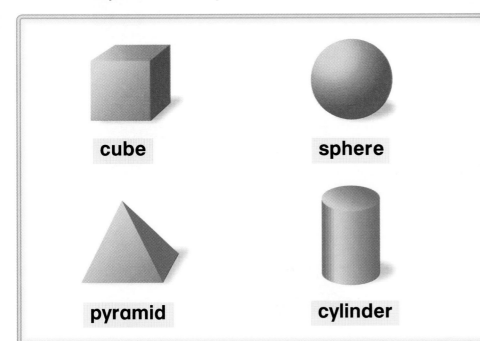

cube

sphere

rectangular prism

pyramid

cylinder

cone

Guided Practice

Circle each object that has the same shape as the solid shape.

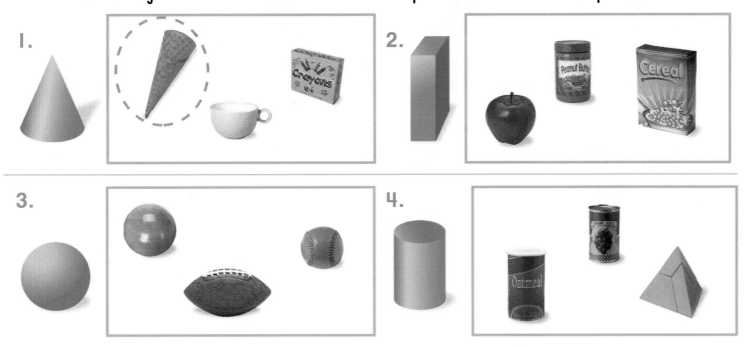

1.

2.

3.

4.

Explain Your Thinking How are a cube and a rectangular prism the same and different?

Independent Practice

Circle the objects that have the same shape.

1.

2.

3.

4.

Problem Solving•Reasoning

5. Sort the shapes into two groups.
   Color one group 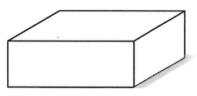 and
   the other group .
   Explain your sorting rule.

  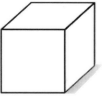

At Home Have your child choose a solid
shape and find three things in your home that are that same shape.

LESSON **6**

Identify Faces of a Solid Shape

Learn About It

A solid has flat faces. You can trace around a **face** to draw a plane shape.

New
Vocabulary

face

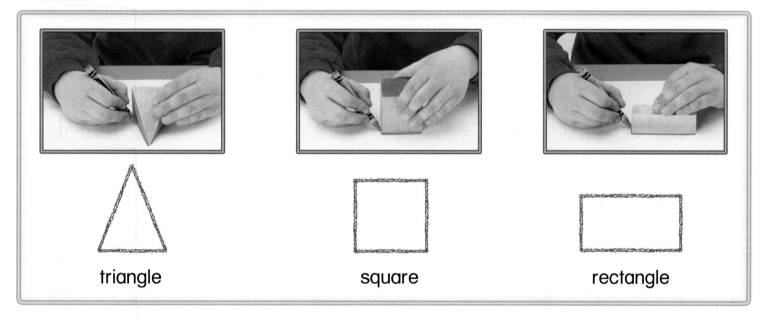

triangle   square   rectangle

Guided Practice

Circle the shape you would make if you traced around the blue face of each solid.

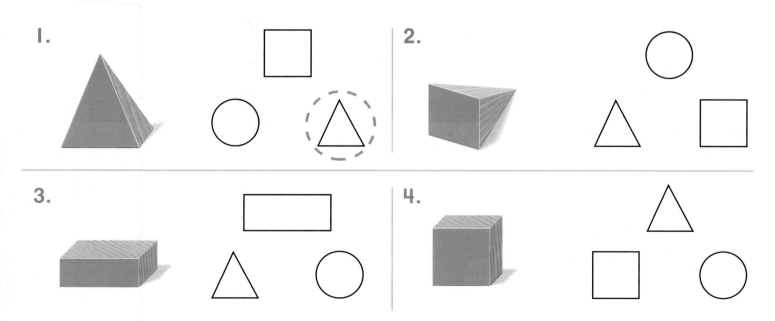

1.

2.

3.

4.

Explain Your Thinking What shape can you make when you trace around a cylinder or cone?

Independent Practice

Circle the solid with a face that matches the plane shape.

1.

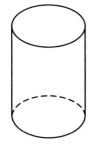 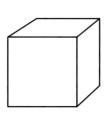 

2.

3.

4.

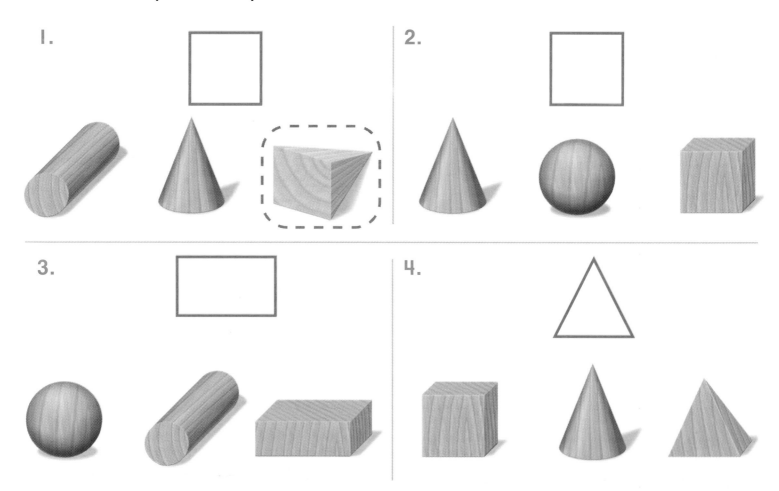

Problem Solving•Reasoning

5. Think about the plane shapes you can see on each solid.
   Make a rule to sort them into two groups.
   Color one group  and the other 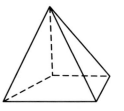 .

 6. **Write About It** Explain how you sorted your groups.

At Home Give your child some boxes. Have him or her trace around a face of each and tell you what shape was drawn.

Name_____

Problem Solving: Find a Pattern

Standards
SDP **2.0, 2.1**
MR **1.0, 1.1, 2.2**

Sometimes you need to look for a pattern to solve a problem.

Linda saw this pattern on a sheet. What picture is likely to come next?

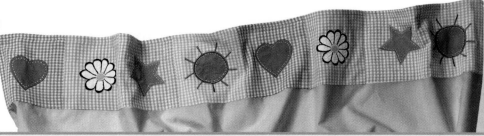

Understand

Circle what you need to find out.

How many shapes are there?

What comes next?

Plan

Circle how you would solve the problem.

Describe the pattern.

Count the shapes.

Solve

Circle the picture that is likely to come next.

Look Back

Say the pattern.
Does your answer make sense?

Guided Practice

Circle the picture that is
likely to come next in the pattern.

Remember:
► Understand
► Plan
► Solve
► Look Back

Remember to
use the 4 steps.

1 Lindsey saw this pattern on a hat.

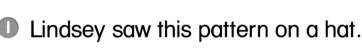

Think: Does the moon or
the star come next?

2 Jaime saw this pattern on a ribbon.

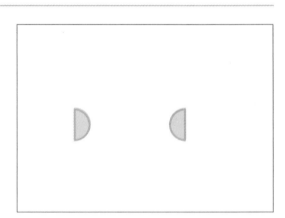

Think: Which half of the
moon should come next?

3 Ray saw this pattern on a T-shirt.

Think:
Should the next arrow be
big or small?

4 Mika saw this pattern on a backpack.

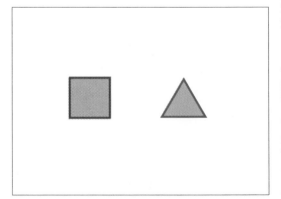

Think: Does the square or
the triangle come next?

At Home Create a pattern using dishes or silverware and ask
your child to decide what comes next.

Choose a Strategy

Solve.

① Rick wants to put this pattern on a toy box. Circle the picture that is likely to come next.

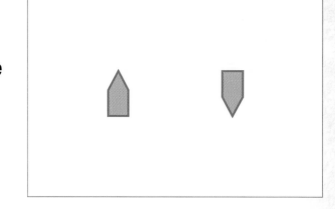

② Janell wants to put this pattern on a sweatshirt. Circle the picture that is likely to come next.

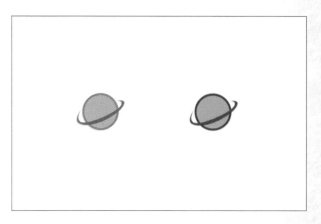

③ Juan has 11 moon stickers. Nancy has 5 more stickers than Juan. Paco has 2 less than Nancy. Who has the most?

_____

Draw or write to explain.

moon

④ Tanya drew 6 rockets and Henry drew 4. How many rockets in all did they draw?

_____ rockets

rocket

Mixed Practice

Find each sum or difference.

1. $6 + 5 = $ ____ 2. $12 - 7 = $ ____ 3. $7 + 3 = $ ____

4. $10 - 8 = $ ____ 5. $11 - 2 = $ ____ 6. $2 + 7 = $ ____

| 7. $\begin{array}{r} 7 \\ +5 \\ \hline \end{array}$ | 8. $\begin{array}{r} 12 \\ -\ 9 \\ \hline \end{array}$ | 9. $\begin{array}{r} 9 \\ -8 \\ \hline \end{array}$ | 10. $\begin{array}{r} 3 \\ +5 \\ \hline \end{array}$ | 11. $\begin{array}{r} 6 \\ +3 \\ \hline \end{array}$ | 12. $\begin{array}{r} 7 \\ -2 \\ \hline \end{array}$ |

| 13. $\begin{array}{r} 11 \\ -\ 8 \\ \hline \end{array}$ | 14. $\begin{array}{r} 9 \\ +2 \\ \hline \end{array}$ | 15. $\begin{array}{r} 7 \\ +0 \\ \hline \end{array}$ | 16. $\begin{array}{r} 8 \\ -3 \\ \hline \end{array}$ | 17. $\begin{array}{r} 10 \\ -\ 6 \\ \hline \end{array}$ | 18. $\begin{array}{r} 6 \\ +6 \\ \hline \end{array}$ |

| 19. $\begin{array}{r} 8 \\ +2 \\ \hline \end{array}$ | 20. $\begin{array}{r} 9 \\ -4 \\ \hline \end{array}$ | 21. $\begin{array}{r} 5 \\ +3 \\ \hline \end{array}$ | 22. $\begin{array}{r} 8 \\ -8 \\ \hline \end{array}$ | 23. $\begin{array}{r} 0 \\ +9 \\ \hline \end{array}$ | 24. $\begin{array}{r} 5 \\ -2 \\ \hline \end{array}$ |

 Brain Teaser How Many Triangles?

How many triangles do you see?

____ triangles

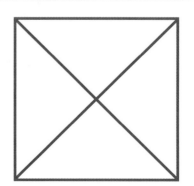

Internet Brain Teasers
Visit **www.eduplace.com/kids/mhm**
for more *Brain Teasers*.

Check Your Understanding of Lessons 5–7

1. Circle the objects that have the same shape.

Circle the shape you would make if you
traced around the blue face of each solid.

2.

3.

Circle the picture that is likely to come
next in each pattern.

4.

       |

5.

       |

Name_____

Test Prep • Cumulative Review

Maintaining the Standards

Fill in the ○ for the correct answer.

1 What number is shown?

58   67   68   78
○   ○   ○   ○

2 Which fact does **not** belong in this fact family?

$$5 + 2 = 7$$

$2 + 5 = 7$ $7 - 2 = 5$
○   ○

$7 - 5 = 2$ $7 + 2 = 9$
○   ○

3 Which one is correct?

$43 > 46$ $54 < 45$
○   ○

$43 < 46$ $54 = 45$
○   ○

Use this graph for Exercises 4 and 5.

Favorite Fruit

4 How many more than 🍎 are there?

4   3   2   1
○   ○   ○   ○

5 **Explain** how you can find out how many 🍓 and) there are in all.

_____

_____

_____

368 three hundred sixty-eight

Safe Site

Internet Test Prep
Visit **www.eduplace.com/kids/mhm**
for more *Test Prep Practice.*

Standards

Extending Grade 1
Standards

Symmetry

LESSON 8

Learn About It

Shapes with **symmetry** have matching parts.

This shape has 2 matching parts.

This shape does not have matching parts.

Guided Practice

Circle the shapes with matching parts.

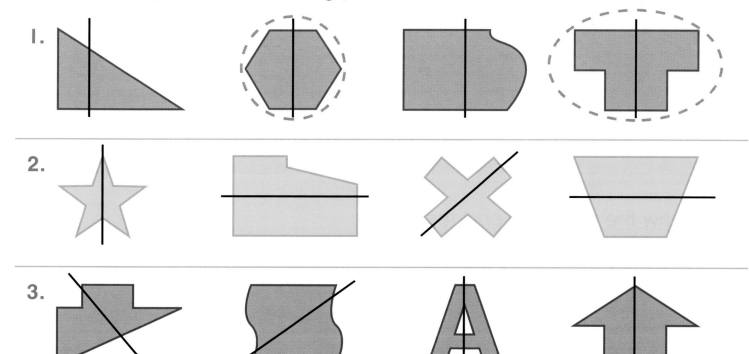

1.

2.

3.

Explain Your Thinking How would you fold a sheet of paper to show matching parts?

Independent Practice

Circle the shapes that show two matching parts.

1.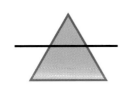

2.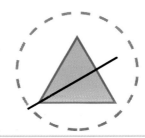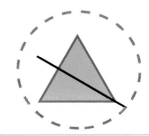

3.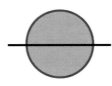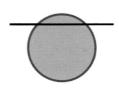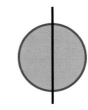

4.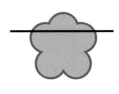

Problem Solving • Reasoning

Visual Thinking

5. Draw the matching part for each.

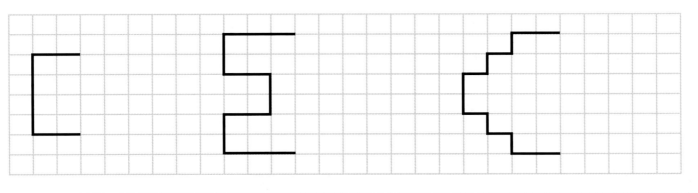

At Home Have your child fold a piece of paper and then cut a design. (Be sure he or she does not cut the fold.) Unfold to see matching parts.

Copyright © Houghton Mifflin Company. All rights reserved.

Equal Parts

New
Vocabulary
equal parts

Learn About It

Some shapes can be folded into **equal parts**.

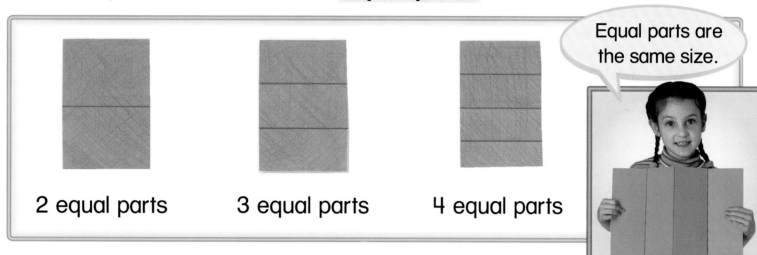

2 equal parts   3 equal parts   4 equal parts

Equal parts are
the same size.

Guided Practice

Circle the shape that shows equal parts.
Color 1 of the equal parts.

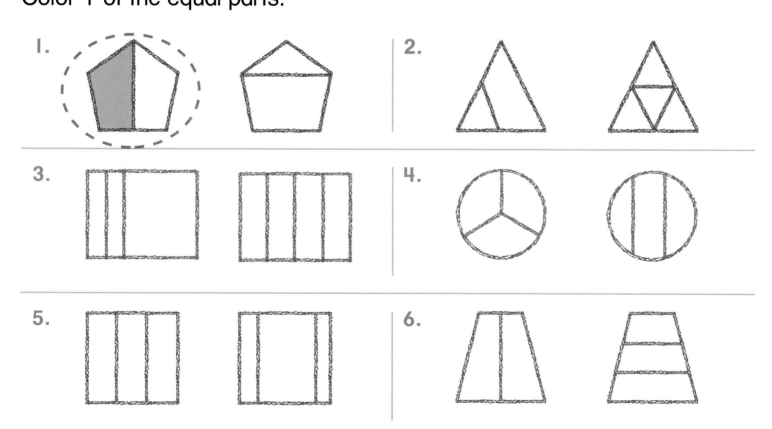

1.

2.

3.

4.

5.

6.

Explain Your Thinking Why might you want to
cut something into equal parts?

Independent Practice

Write how many equal parts.

1.

__2__ equal parts

2.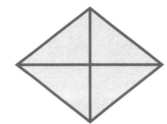

____ equal parts

3.

____ equal parts

4.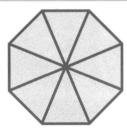

____ equal parts

5.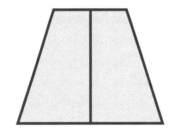

____ equal parts

6.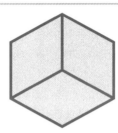

____ equal parts

7.

____ equal parts

8.

____ equal parts

9.

____ equal parts

Problem Solving·Reasoning

Visual Thinking

10. Draw 4 equal parts in 4 different ways.

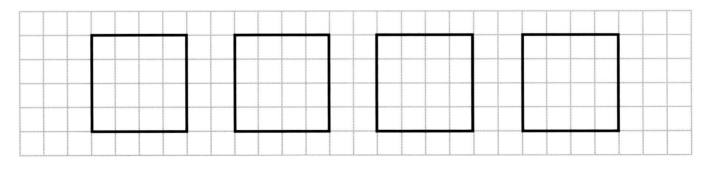

At Home During a meal, ask your child to name foods that can be divided into equal parts.

One Half

New
Vocabulary

fraction
one half

Learn About It

You can use a **fraction** to
name parts of a whole.

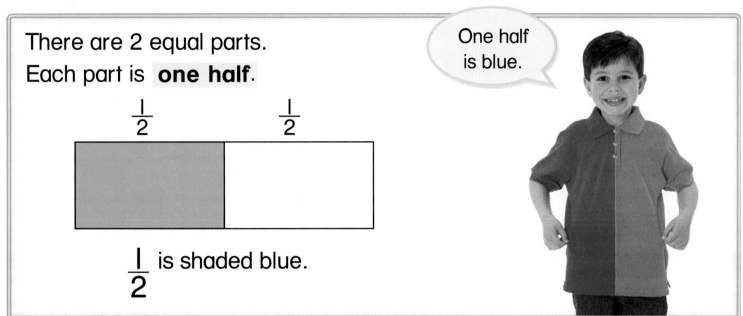

There are 2 equal parts.
Each part is **one half**.

$\frac{1}{2}$ $\frac{1}{2}$

$\frac{1}{2}$ is shaded blue.

One half
is blue.

Guided Practice

Circle the shapes that have one half shaded.

1.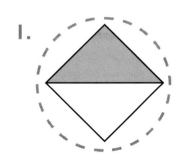

2.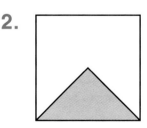

3.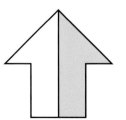

4.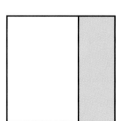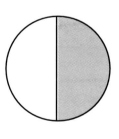

Explain Your Thinking You eat one half of an apple.
What part of the apple is left?

Independent Practice

Color $\frac{1}{2}$ of each shape.

1.

2.

3.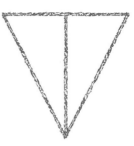

4.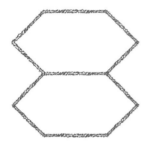

5.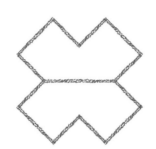

6.

7.

8.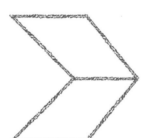

9.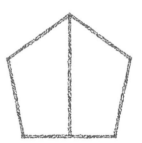

Problem Solving•Reasoning

Patterns

10. Draw the shape that is likely to come next. Explain why.

11. Write Your Own Describe a pattern you can make by clapping your hands and stamping your feet.

 **At Home** Draw a shape for your child. Have him or her color one half of the shape.

One Third and One Fourth

LESSON 11

Learn About It

One third and **one fourth** are fractions that name parts of a whole.

There are 3 equal parts.
Each part is one third.

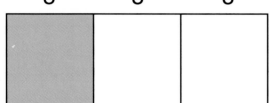

$\frac{1}{3}$ is shaded blue.

There are 4 equal parts.
Each part is one fourth.

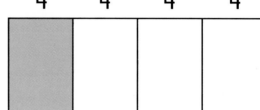

$\frac{1}{4}$ is shaded blue.

Guided Practice

Circle the shapes that have one third shaded.

1.

2.

Circle the shapes that have one fourth shaded.

3.

4.

Explain Your Thinking $\frac{1}{3}$ means 1 of 3 equal parts.
What does $\frac{1}{6}$ mean?

Independent Practice

Color 1 part. Circle each fraction.

1.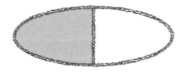

$\frac{1}{2}$ $\frac{1}{3}$ $\frac{1}{4}$

2.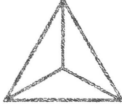

$\frac{1}{2}$ $\frac{1}{3}$ $\frac{1}{4}$

3.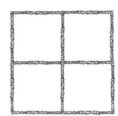

$\frac{1}{2}$ $\frac{1}{3}$ $\frac{1}{4}$

4.

$\frac{1}{2}$ $\frac{1}{3}$ $\frac{1}{4}$

5.

$\frac{1}{2}$ $\frac{1}{3}$ $\frac{1}{4}$

6.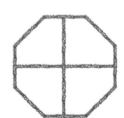

$\frac{1}{2}$ $\frac{1}{3}$ $\frac{1}{4}$

7.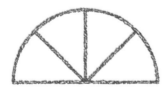

$\frac{1}{2}$ $\frac{1}{3}$ $\frac{1}{4}$

8.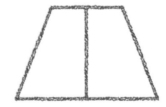

$\frac{1}{2}$ $\frac{1}{3}$ $\frac{1}{4}$

9.

$\frac{1}{2}$ $\frac{1}{3}$ $\frac{1}{4}$

Problem Solving•Reasoning

10. Circle the container that is about $\frac{1}{2}$ full.

 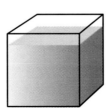 

At Home Draw two squares. Have your child color $\frac{1}{3}$ of one square and $\frac{1}{4}$ of the other square.

Hands-On Activity
LESSON 12

Spinners and Probability

Learn About It

Spinner A

You can predict what will happen.

1. On which spinner will a spin

   always land on blue?_____A_____

   sometimes land on blue?_____

   never land on blue? _____

Spinner B

2. Predict which color you will land on more often when using Spinner C.

   _____

Spinner C

3. Use Spinner C, a paper clip, and a pencil. Spin 10 times. Record your spins.

Color	Tally	Total
Red		
Blue		

4. Which color on Spinner C did you land on more often? _____

Explain Your Thinking Which color do you think you will land on more often on Spinner B? Why?

Try It Out

Use a paper clip and pencil.
Spin 10 times. Record.

1.
Spinner D
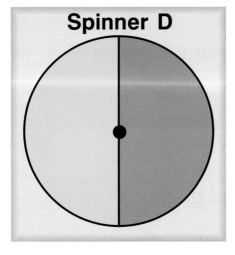

2.
Spinner E
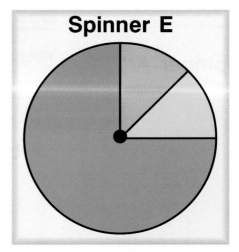

Spinner D		
Color	Tally	Total
Yellow		
Green		

Spinner E		
Color	Tally	Total
Green		
Yellow		
Orange		

3. On which spinner did you land on

   green more often? _____   yellow more often? _____

4. If you never want to land on orange,
   which spinner should you use? _____

Problem Solving • Reasoning

Write About It

5. Tim has these coins.

40¢

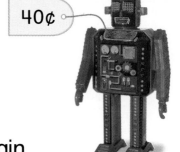

Does he have enough money to buy this toy? Explain.

At Home Have your child make a red-and-blue spinner that will land on red most often.

Name_____

Problem Solving:
Use Data From a Picture

LESSON 13

You can use a picture to
help you solve a problem.

Children enjoy climbing on the playground. There
are many shapes to be found.

**You can use a picture to
solve a problem.**

Where do you see a shape
like a pyramid?

_____

> **Think:**
> Look for triangles.

**You can use a picture to
count and solve a problem.**

How many more triangles do
you see than circles?

_____

> **Think:**
> Count the triangles.
> Then count the circles.

Guided Practice

Solve.

Use data from the picture.

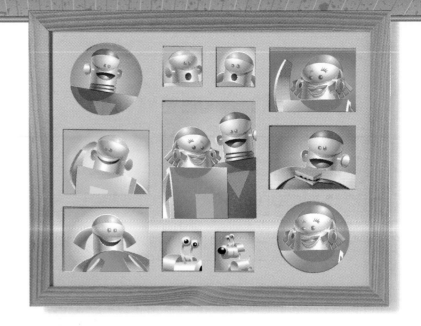

1 How many round pictures are there?

___2___

Think: Do round shapes have corners?

Draw or write to explain.

---

2 How many pictures have 4 corners?

____ shapes

Think: Which shapes have 4 corners?

---

3 Which shape is shown the most?

_____

Think: How many of each shape are there?

---

4 How many more square pictures are there than circle pictures?

____ more square pictures

Think: How many circle pictures are there?

At Home Using pictures that you have at home, create problems for your child to solve.

Choose a Strategy

Solve.

① Which food shows fourths?

_____

② The pancake was cut into
equal parts. It was cut twice.
Was it cut into halves
or fourths?

_____

③ Which food has triangle shapes?

_____

④ The chef has 8 slices
of cheese and 12 crackers.
How many more crackers does
she have than slices of cheese?

_____ more crackers

sandwich

pancake

cracker

cheese

Name _____

Mixed Practice

Memorize Your Facts

Add or subtract.

1. 6 − 4 = ___   2. 2 + 8 = ___   3. 1 + 5 = ___

4. 12 − 3 = ___   5. 7 − 7 = ___   6. 5 + 6 = ___

7. 5
  +4

8. 7
  −2

9. 11
  − 7

10. 7
   +4

11. 9
   +3

12. 9
   −7

13. 10
   − 3

14. 3
   +8

15. 8
   +4

16. 12
   − 4

17. 9
   −3

18. 4
   +6

19. 5
   +7

20. 11
   − 5

21. 10
   − 5

22. 8
   −6

23. 4
   +4

24. 4
   +3

Brain Teaser   Color the Flag

Color the flag.
Follow the clues.

$\frac{1}{2}$ is blue.

$\frac{1}{4}$ is green.

$\frac{1}{4}$ is red.

Safe Site

Internet Brain Teasers
Visit **www.eduplace.com/kids/mhm**
for more *Brain Teasers*.

Name_____

Check Your Understanding of Lessons 8–13

1. Circle the shapes with matching parts.

2. Circle the shapes that show one half.

   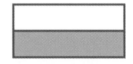

3. Circle the shapes that show one third.

4. Circle the shapes that show one fourth.

  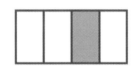

5. Which color will you land on most often if you use this spinner?

_____

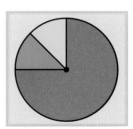

6. Circle the food that shows equal parts.

Name_____

Test Prep • Cumulative Review

Maintaining the Standards

Fill in the ○ for the correct answer.

1 Which number is 10 more than 53?

63   54   52   43
○   ○   ○   ○

2 Which bug is between the flowers?

○   ○   ○   ○

3 Which shape is a square?

○   ○

○   ○

4 Add.

$7 + 4 = $ ■

8   9   10   11
○   ○   ○   ○

5 Which shape is likely to come next in this pattern?

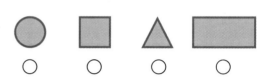
○   ○   ○   ○

6 Subtract.

$10 - 3 = $ ■

6   7   8   13
○   ○   ○   ○

7 Hannah has 3 dimes and 6 pennies. Does she have enough money to buy a pin that costs 35¢? **Explain** how you can find out.

_____

_____

_____

Safe Site

Internet Test Prep
Visit **www.eduplace.com/kids/mhm**
for more *Test Prep Practice.*

Chapter Review

1. Draw a **circle between** a **triangle** and a **square**.

2. Circle the shape that shows **equal parts**.

3. Write how many **sides** and **corners** a **rectangle** has.

_____ sides

_____ corners

4. Circle the object with a **face** that matches the **plane shape**.

5. Circle the objects that have the same shape.

6. Circle all the shapes with 3 corners.

7. Circle the shapes with matching parts.

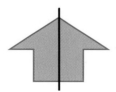

1. Circle the shapes that show one half.

2. Circle the shapes that show one third.

3. Circle the shapes that show one fourth.

4. Circle the spinner you would use to land on blue more often.

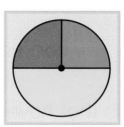 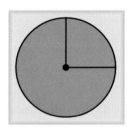

5. Circle the picture that is likely to come next in the pattern.

6. How many round pictures are there?

Chapter Test

1. Circle the correct words.

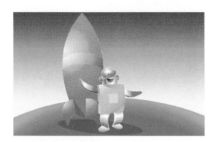

The  is _____ the .

in front of   behind

2. Circle the objects that have the same shape.

3. Circle the object with a face that matches the plane shape.

4. Circle all the shapes with less than 4 corners.

5. Circle the shapes with matching parts.

 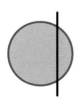 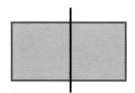 

6. Circle the shapes that show one half.

7. Circle the shapes that show one fourth.

 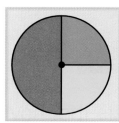

8. Circle the spinner on which you would never land on yellow.

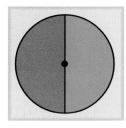

9. Circle the picture that is likely to come next in the pattern.

10. How many bugs are there in all?

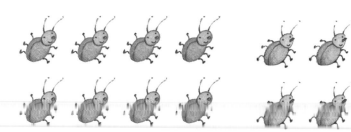

 _____ bugs

 **Write About It**

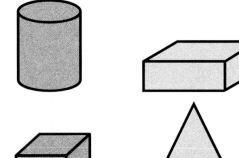

Explain how you can sort these shapes in two different ways.

_____

_____

_____

_____

Name _____

Design a Pattern

What You Need

    pattern blocks

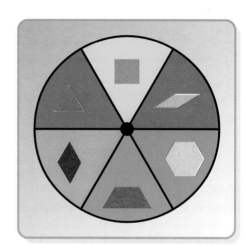

How to Play

1. Spin the spinner 3 times.

2. With the shapes you landed on, make a pattern that repeats 3 times.

3. Your partner continues the pattern by placing the 2 shapes likely to come next.

4. If your partner gets it right, it becomes his or her turn to spin and make a pattern.

Standards
MG **2.1, 2.2, 2.4**

Enrichment

Sorting by Position

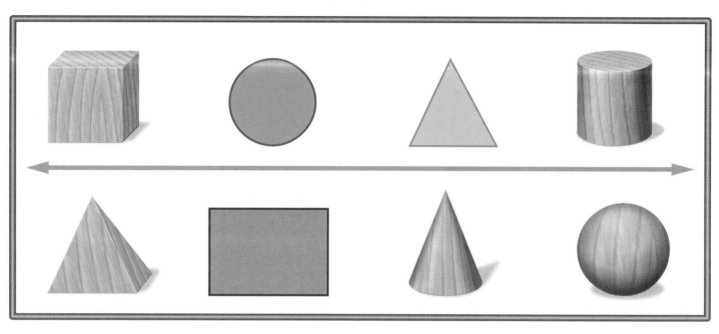

Circle the correct word.

1. Which shape is above the line?

   cube   cone

2. Which shape is below the line?

   cylinder   rectangle

3. Which shape is to the right of the rectangle?

   cone   pyramid

4. Which shape is above the cone?

   sphere   triangle

5. Which shape is next to the triangle?

   cylinder   pyramid

6. Which shape is to the left of the circle?

   triangle   cube

CHAPTER
9

Addition
and
Subtraction
Facts
to 20

Accessing Prior Knowledge

This story will help you review
• Addition facts

Play Ball!

A Read-Aloud Story

written by Sarah Curran
illustrated by Rusty Fletcher

A Math Storybook for

_____

"Can we have some footballs?
We want to play a game."

"I have some footballs you can share.
Some are here and some are there."

How many footballs are there in all?

2 + 3 = _____ footballs

"Can we have some softballs?
We want to play a game."

"I have some softballs you can share.
Some are here and some are there."

How many softballs are there in all?

6 + 4 = _____ softballs

"Can we have some volleyballs?
We want to play a game."

"I have some volleyballs you can share.
Some are here and some are there."

How many volleyballs are there in all?

5 + 7 = _____ volleyballs

"Can we have some basketballs?
We want to play a game."

"I have some basketballs you can share.
Some are here and some are there."

How many basketballs are there in all?

3 + 3 = _____ basketballs

"Can we have some soccer balls?
We want to play a game."

"I have some soccer balls you can share.
Some are here and some are there."

How many soccer balls are there in all?

5 + 3 = _____ soccer balls

Go, go, go!

Let's play, let's play, let's play.

We'll kick and throw and bounce and catch.

Then we'll put the balls away!

How many balls are there in all?

_____ footballs + _____ softballs + _____ soccer balls = _____ balls in all

Family Letter

addend Each of the numbers added in an addition problem.

difference The answer to a subtraction problem.

Dear Family,

During the next few weeks, our math class will be learning and practicing addition and subtraction facts to 20.

You can expect to see work that provides practice with addition and subtraction facts to 20.

As we learn about related facts and fact families, you may wish to use the following sample as a guide.

Related facts

$7 + 5 = 12$ $12 - 5 = 7$

Fact family

$7 + 5 = 12$ $12 - 7 = 5$

$5 + 7 = 12$ $12 - 5 = 7$

Knowing addition facts can help children learn the related subtraction facts.

Sincerely,

Your child's teacher

LESSON 1

Add Doubles

Learn About It

A double fact has two **addends** that are the same.

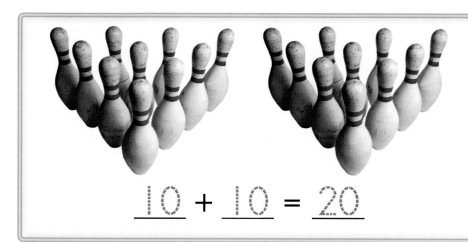

10 + 10 is a double fact.

$$\underline{10} + \underline{10} = \underline{20}$$

Guided Practice

Write the addends. Then write the sum.

1. How many bowling balls in all?

$$\underline{7} + \underline{7} = \underline{14}$$

2. How many shoes in all?

$$\underline{} + \underline{} = \underline{}$$

Write each sum.

3. $\begin{array}{r} 5 \\ +5 \\ \hline \end{array}$ 4. $\begin{array}{r} 6 \\ +6 \\ \hline \end{array}$ 5. $\begin{array}{r} 7 \\ +7 \\ \hline \end{array}$ 6. $\begin{array}{r} 8 \\ +8 \\ \hline \end{array}$ 7. $\begin{array}{r} 9 \\ +9 \\ \hline \end{array}$ 8. $\begin{array}{r} 10 \\ +10 \\ \hline \end{array}$

Explain Your Thinking Some children think double facts are the easiest to learn. Why might they think this?

Independent Practice

Remember: Both addends are the same in a double fact.

Write each sum.
Circle the double facts.

1. $\begin{array}{r} 4 \\ +4 \\ \hline 8 \end{array}$

2. $\begin{array}{r} 5 \\ +7 \\ \hline \end{array}$

3. $\begin{array}{r} 9 \\ +9 \\ \hline \end{array}$

4. $\begin{array}{r} 0 \\ +9 \\ \hline \end{array}$

5. $\begin{array}{r} 2 \\ +9 \\ \hline \end{array}$

6. $\begin{array}{r} 5 \\ +4 \\ \hline \end{array}$

7. $\begin{array}{r} 1 \\ +1 \\ \hline \end{array}$

8. $\begin{array}{r} 4 \\ +8 \\ \hline \end{array}$

9. $\begin{array}{r} 1 \\ +9 \\ \hline \end{array}$

10. $\begin{array}{r} 7 \\ +7 \\ \hline \end{array}$

11. $\begin{array}{r} 8 \\ +2 \\ \hline \end{array}$

12. $\begin{array}{r} 5 \\ +5 \\ \hline \end{array}$

13. $\begin{array}{r} 6 \\ +6 \\ \hline \end{array}$

14. $\begin{array}{r} 8 \\ +8 \\ \hline \end{array}$

15. $\begin{array}{r} 4 \\ +7 \\ \hline \end{array}$

16. $\begin{array}{r} 10 \\ +10 \\ \hline \end{array}$

17. $5 + 5 =$ ___

18. $3 + 8 =$ ___

19. $10 + 10 =$ ___

20. $9 + 9 =$ ___

21. $5 + 6 =$ ___

22. $3 + 9 =$ ___

Problem Solving • Reasoning

Write About It

23. Catherine wants to put these coins into equal groups. Explain the different ways that she can do this.

At Home Ask your child to give you the sums for $5 + 5$, $6 + 6$, $7 + 7$, $8 + 8$, $9 + 9$, and $10 + 10$.

LESSON 2 # Doubles Plus One

Learn About It

You can use a double fact to help you find other sums.

7 + 7

7 + 7 = __14__

7 + 7 and 1 more

7 + 8 = __15__

8 + 7 = __15__

Guided Practice

Write each sum.

1.

8 + 8 = __16__

8 + 9 = __17__

9 + 8 = __17__

2.

6 + 6 = ___

6 + 7 = ___

7 + 6 = ___

3.
```
   5        5        6
  +5       +6       +5
  ___      ___      ___
```

4.
```
   4        4        5
  +4       +5       +4
  ___      ___      ___
```

Explain Your Thinking How can you find the sum of 9 + 8?

Independent Practice

Write each sum.

Use ![crayon] to circle each double fact.

Use ![crayon] to circle each double plus one.

9 + 8 is the same as
8 + 8 and 1 more.

1.
```
  9
 +8
 ‾‾
 17
```

2.
```
  5
 +5
 ‾‾
```

3.
```
  6
 +7
 ‾‾
```

4.
```
  8
 +8
 ‾‾
```

5.
```
  8
 +4
 ‾‾
```

6.
```
  7
 +7
 ‾‾
```

7.
```
  6
 +5
 ‾‾
```

8.
```
  9
 +3
 ‾‾
```

9.
```
  4
 +5
 ‾‾
```

10.
```
  7
 +5
 ‾‾
```

11.
```
  8
 +9
 ‾‾
```

12.
```
  3
 +3
 ‾‾
```

13.
```
  6
 +6
 ‾‾
```

14.
```
  7
 +8
 ‾‾
```

15.
```
  6
 +4
 ‾‾
```

16.
```
  7
 +6
 ‾‾
```

17. 9 + 9 = ___

18. 8 + 7 = ___

19. 5 + 4 = ___

20. 6 + 7 = ___

21. 8 + 9 = ___

22. 6 + 8 = ___

23. 2 + 9 = ___

24. 5 + 6 = ___

25. 9 + 8 = ___

Problem Solving•Reasoning

Compare. Circle >, <, or =.

26. 18 >/</= 81

27. 65 >/</= 65

28. 96 >/</= 69

At Home Ask your child to tell you the sums for 5 + 4, 5 + 6, 6 + 7, 7 + 8, and 8 + 9.

LESSON 3

Add With Ten

Learn About It

You can use a ten frame to add a number to 10.

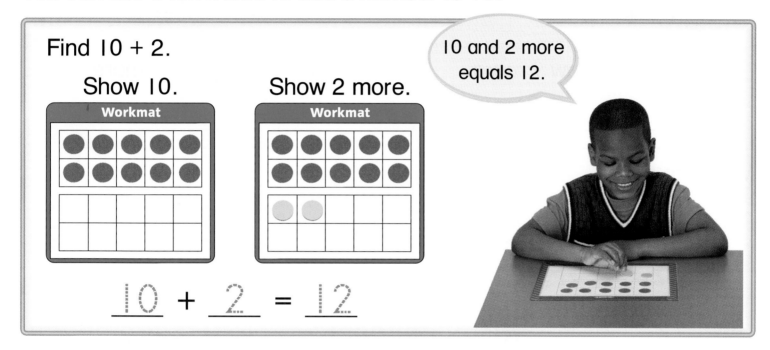

Find 10 + 2.

Show 10.   Show 2 more.

10 and 2 more
equals 12.

Workmat   Workmat

$$\underline{10} + \underline{2} = \underline{12}$$

Guided Practice

Use Workmat 6 and counters.
Show each number. Write the number sentence.

1. Show 10. Show 4 more.

   $$\underline{10} + \underline{4} = \underline{14}$$

2. Show 10. Show 5 more.

   $$\underline{} + \underline{} = \underline{}$$

3. Show 10. Show 6 more.

   $$\underline{} + \underline{} = \underline{}$$

4. Show 10. Show 8 more.

   $$\underline{} + \underline{} = \underline{}$$

5. Show 10. Show 2 more.

   $$\underline{} + \underline{} = \underline{}$$

6. Show 10. Show 1 more.

   $$\underline{} + \underline{} = \underline{}$$

Explain Your Thinking Why is adding a number
to 10 like showing a number with tens and ones?

Independent Practice

Use Workmat 6 and counters.
Show each number. Write the number sentence.

1. Show 10. Show 7 more.

   $\underline{10} + \underline{7} = \underline{17}$

2. Show 10. Show 3 more.

   $\underline{} + \underline{} = \underline{}$

3. Show 10. Show 9 more.

   $\underline{} + \underline{} = \underline{}$

4. Show 10. Show 10 more.

   $\underline{} + \underline{} = \underline{}$

Write the sum.

5. $\begin{array}{r} 10 \\ +\ 6 \\ \hline \end{array}$

6. $\begin{array}{r} 3 \\ +10 \\ \hline \end{array}$

7. $\begin{array}{r} 10 \\ +\ 4 \\ \hline \end{array}$

8. $\begin{array}{r} 9 \\ +10 \\ \hline \end{array}$

9. $\begin{array}{r} 10 \\ +\ 7 \\ \hline \end{array}$

10. $\begin{array}{r} 10 \\ +10 \\ \hline \end{array}$

11. $\begin{array}{r} 2 \\ +10 \\ \hline \end{array}$

12. $\begin{array}{r} 10 \\ +\ 5 \\ \hline \end{array}$

13. $\begin{array}{r} 10 \\ +\ 8 \\ \hline \end{array}$

14. $\begin{array}{r} 1 \\ +10 \\ \hline \end{array}$

15. $\begin{array}{r} 10 \\ +\ 9 \\ \hline \end{array}$

16. $\begin{array}{r} 10 \\ +\ 3 \\ \hline \end{array}$

17. $\begin{array}{r} 10 \\ +\ 1 \\ \hline \end{array}$

18. $\begin{array}{r} 10 \\ +10 \\ \hline \end{array}$

19. $\begin{array}{r} 10 \\ +\ 5 \\ \hline \end{array}$

Problem Solving • Reasoning

Algebra Readiness • Number Sentences

Write a related subtraction fact for each.

20. $5 + 6 = 11$

$\underline{} - \underline{} = \underline{}$

21. $7 + 5 = 12$

$\underline{} - \underline{} = \underline{}$

At Home Ask your child to add 10 to any number less than 11.

Hands-On Activity

LESSON **4**

Make a Ten to Add

Learn About It

You can make a 10 to help you add with 7, 8, and 9.

Think: 8 + 4 is the same as 10 + 2.
10 + 2 = 12

Find 8 + 4.

Show 8 and 4 more.

8 + 4

Move 2 counters to make 10.

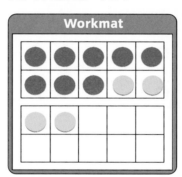

10 + 2

8 + 4 = 12

Guided Practice

Use Workmat 6 and counters.
Show the numbers. Then add.

1. Show 9 and 4 more.

    9 + 4 = 13

2. Show 7 and 4 more.

    7 + 4 = ___

3. Show 8 and 5 more.

    8 + 5 = ___

4. Show 7 and 5 more.

    7 + 5 = ___

Explain Your Thinking How does thinking about 10 help you find the sum of 9 + 5?

Independent Practice

Use Workmat 6 and counters.
Show the numbers. Then add.

1. Show 9 and 6 more.

   $9 + 6 = \underline{15}$

2. Show 8 and 6 more.

   $8 + 6 = \underline{}$

3. Show 9 and 7 more.

   $9 + 7 = \underline{}$

4. Show 8 and 7 more.

   $8 + 7 = \underline{}$

Add. Use counters if you want.

5. $\begin{array}{r} 9 \\ +4 \\ \hline \end{array}$
6. $\begin{array}{r} 9 \\ +5 \\ \hline \end{array}$
7. $\begin{array}{r} 9 \\ +6 \\ \hline \end{array}$
8. $\begin{array}{r} 9 \\ +7 \\ \hline \end{array}$
9. $\begin{array}{r} 9 \\ +8 \\ \hline \end{array}$
10. $\begin{array}{r} 9 \\ +9 \\ \hline \end{array}$

11. $\begin{array}{r} 8 \\ +4 \\ \hline \end{array}$
12. $\begin{array}{r} 8 \\ +5 \\ \hline \end{array}$
13. $\begin{array}{r} 8 \\ +6 \\ \hline \end{array}$
14. $\begin{array}{r} 8 \\ +7 \\ \hline \end{array}$
15. $\begin{array}{r} 8 \\ +8 \\ \hline \end{array}$
16. $\begin{array}{r} 8 \\ +9 \\ \hline \end{array}$

17. $\begin{array}{r} 7 \\ +4 \\ \hline \end{array}$
18. $\begin{array}{r} 7 \\ +5 \\ \hline \end{array}$
19. $\begin{array}{r} 7 \\ +6 \\ \hline \end{array}$
20. $\begin{array}{r} 7 \\ +7 \\ \hline \end{array}$
21. $\begin{array}{r} 7 \\ +8 \\ \hline \end{array}$
22. $\begin{array}{r} 7 \\ +9 \\ \hline \end{array}$

Problem Solving • Reasoning

23. Raja scored 9 points. Then he scored 5 more. How many points does he have now?

    _____ points

    Draw or write to explain.

At Home Have your child tell you the sums for 8 + 6, 9 + 6, 7 + 5, 8 + 5, 9 + 5, 7 + 4, 8 + 4, and 9 + 4.

LESSON 5

Add Three Numbers

Learn About It

Looking for facts you know can help you add 3 numbers.

Find doubles.

$$\begin{array}{r} 7 \\ 4 \\ + 3 \\ \hline 14 \end{array} \qquad \begin{array}{r} 7 \\ +7 \\ \hline \end{array}$$

Think:
7 + 7

Make a 10.

$$\begin{array}{r} 7 \\ 4 \\ + 3 \\ \hline 14 \end{array} \qquad \begin{array}{r} 10 \\ + 4 \\ \hline \end{array}$$

Think:
10 + 4

Add in any order.

$$\begin{array}{r} 7 \\ 4 \\ + 3 \\ \hline 14 \end{array} \qquad \begin{array}{r} 11 \\ + 3 \\ \hline \end{array}$$

Think:
11 + 3

Guided Practice

Add. Look for a fact you know.

1.
$$\begin{array}{r} 8 \\ 2 \\ + 3 \\ \hline \end{array} \qquad \begin{array}{r} 10 \\ + 3 \\ \hline 13 \end{array}$$

2.
$$\begin{array}{r} 2 \\ 6 \\ + 6 \\ \hline \end{array} \qquad \begin{array}{r} \\ + \\ \hline \end{array}$$

3.
$$\begin{array}{r} 9 \\ 5 \\ + 1 \\ \hline \end{array} \qquad \begin{array}{r} \\ + \\ \hline \end{array}$$

4.
$$\begin{array}{r} 7 \\ 8 \\ + 2 \\ \hline \end{array} \qquad \begin{array}{r} \\ + \\ \hline \end{array}$$

5.
$$\begin{array}{r} 9 \\ 4 \\ + 5 \\ \hline \end{array} \qquad \begin{array}{r} \\ + \\ \hline \end{array}$$

6.
$$\begin{array}{r} 6 \\ 7 \\ + 4 \\ \hline \end{array} \qquad \begin{array}{r} \\ + \\ \hline \end{array}$$

7. $2 + 9 + 8 =$ ___

8. $6 + 5 + 4 =$ ___

Explain Your Thinking Describe two ways you could find the sum of $8 + 6 + 2$.

Independent Practice

Add.

1. 6
    8
  + 1

    ¦5

2. 3
    7
  + 7
  ------

3. 9
    6
  + 1
  ------

4. 6
    6
  + 4
  ------

5. 10
    1
  + 3
  ------

6. 9
    9
  + 1
  ------

7. 8
    7
  + 3
  ------

8. 8
    4
  + 4
  ------

9. 6
    3
  + 4
  ------

10. 7
     2
   + 7
   ------

11. 1
     9
   + 7
   ------

12. 3
     3
   + 6
   ------

13. 2 + 8 + 2 = ___

14. 3 + 5 + 8 = ___

15. 8 + 0 + 4 = ___

16. 4 + 9 + 6 = ___

17. 5 + 5 + 5 = ___

18. 3 + 9 + 7 = ___

Problem Solving • Reasoning

Using Data

19. Kobe scored 5 points in the second half of the game. What is his final score?

____ points

20. **Write Your Own** Write a story problem about the points scored by Chris and Lea.

Points Scored in First Half

At Home Give your child three numbers less than 10. Ask him or her to give you the sum of those numbers.

Name_____

Check Your Understanding of Lessons 1–5

Write each sum. Circle the double facts.

1.   5
    +4

2.   4
    +4

3.   4
    +8

4.   5
    +5

5.   7
    +7

6.   8
    +6

7. $9 + 9 =$ ___   8. $3 + 9 =$ ___   9. $8 + 8 =$ ___

Write each sum.

Use [crayon] to circle each double fact.

Use [crayon] to circle each double-plus-one fact.

10.   7
     +8

11.   6
     +3

12.   9
     +8

13.   8
     +8

14.   4
     +4

15.   6
     +7

16. $4 + 3 =$ ___   17. $10 + 9 =$ ___   18. $6 + 4 =$ ___

Write each sum. Use counters if you want.

19.   10
     + 7

20.   1
     +10

21.   4
     +10

22.   10
     +10

23.   9
     +6

24.   8
     +7

Add.

25.   6
      8
     +1

26.   3
      3
     +4

27.   6
      4
     +6

28.   1
      9
     +7

29.   7
      2
     +7

30.   3
      3
     +6

Test Prep • Cumulative Review

Maintaining the Standards

Name_____

Fill in the ○ for the correct answer.

1 Ann saw 3 birds. Craig saw 8 birds. How many birds did they see in all?

13   12   11   5
○   ○   ○   ○

2 Which number is 2 tens 3 ones?

6   23   32   50
○   ○   ○   ○

3 Which number sentence is a related **subtraction** fact for 6 + 3 = 9?

○ 6 − 3 = 3
○ 9 − 6 = 3
○ 6 + 9 = 15
○ 9 + 3 = 12

4 What is the value of these coins?

56¢ 61¢ 66¢ 80¢
○   ○   ○   ○

5 What is the sum?

7 + 2 + 0 = ■

10   9   7   5
○   ○   ○   ○

6 **Explain** how making a 10 can help you find the sum of 9 + 8.

_____

_____

_____

Safe Site

Internet Test Prep
Visit **www.eduplace.com/kids/mhm**
for more *Test Prep Practice*.

LESSON 6

Use Doubles to Subtract

Learn About It

Think about addition doubles to help you subtract.

Find 14 − 7.

You know **7 + 7 = 14.** So **14 − 7 = _7_ .**

Guided Practice

Add. Then subtract.

1.

$$9 + 9 = \underline{18}$$

$$18 - 9 = \underline{9}$$

2.

$$10 + 10 = \underline{}$$

$$20 - 10 = \underline{}$$

3.
$$\begin{array}{r} 8 \\ +8 \\ \hline \end{array} \qquad \begin{array}{r} 16 \\ -\ 8 \\ \hline \end{array}$$

4.
$$\begin{array}{r} 6 \\ +6 \\ \hline \end{array} \qquad \begin{array}{r} 12 \\ -\ 6 \\ \hline \end{array}$$

5.
$$\begin{array}{r} 5 \\ +5 \\ \hline \end{array} \qquad \begin{array}{r} 10 \\ -\ 5 \\ \hline \end{array}$$

Explain Your Thinking Why are 5 + 5 = 10 and 10 − 5 = 5 related?

Independent Practice

Add. Then subtract.

1. $1 + 1 = \underline{2}$
    $2 - 1 = \underline{1}$

2. $2 + 2 = \underline{}$
    $4 - 2 = \underline{}$

3. $3 + 3 = \underline{}$
    $6 - 3 = \underline{}$

4. $4 + 4 = \underline{}$
    $8 - 4 = \underline{}$

5. $5 + 5 = \underline{}$
    $10 - 5 = \underline{}$

6. $6 + 6 = \underline{}$
    $12 - 6 = \underline{}$

7. $7 + 7 = \underline{}$
    $14 - 7 = \underline{}$

8. $8 + 8 = \underline{}$
    $16 - 8 = \underline{}$

9. $9 + 9 = \underline{}$
    $18 - 9 = \underline{}$

10. $\begin{array}{r} 5 \\ +5 \\ \hline \end{array}$ $\begin{array}{r} 10 \\ -\ 5 \\ \hline \end{array}$

11. $\begin{array}{r} 6 \\ +6 \\ \hline \end{array}$ $\begin{array}{r} 12 \\ -\ 6 \\ \hline \end{array}$

12. $\begin{array}{r} 7 \\ +7 \\ \hline \end{array}$ $\begin{array}{r} 14 \\ -\ 7 \\ \hline \end{array}$

13. $\begin{array}{r} 8 \\ +8 \\ \hline \end{array}$ $\begin{array}{r} 16 \\ -\ 8 \\ \hline \end{array}$

14. $\begin{array}{r} 9 \\ +9 \\ \hline \end{array}$ $\begin{array}{r} 18 \\ -\ 9 \\ \hline \end{array}$

15. $\begin{array}{r} 10 \\ +10 \\ \hline \end{array}$ $\begin{array}{r} 20 \\ -10 \\ \hline \end{array}$

Problem Solving • Reasoning

Write About It

16. Bonnie has these coins. What other coins does she need to have 41¢?

412 four hundred twelve

At Home Ask your child to name a double fact and give the related subtraction fact.

Standards
NS 1.1, 2.1, 2.6
AF 1.1

LESSON 7 Subtract From 13 and 14

Learn About It

A related fact can help you find the **difference**.

The numbers 8, 5, and 13 are used for all three facts.

$$\begin{array}{r} 8 \\ +5 \\ \hline 13 \end{array}$$

$$\begin{array}{r} 13 \\ -5 \\ \hline 8 \end{array}$$

$$\begin{array}{r} 13 \\ -8 \\ \hline 5 \end{array}$$

Guided Practice

Add. Then write each difference.

1. $$\begin{array}{r} 8 \\ +6 \\ \hline 14 \end{array}$$
$$\begin{array}{r} 14 \\ -6 \\ \hline 8 \end{array}$$
$$\begin{array}{r} 14 \\ -8 \\ \hline 6 \end{array}$$

2. $$\begin{array}{r} 7 \\ +6 \end{array}$$
$$\begin{array}{r} 13 \\ -6 \end{array}$$
$$\begin{array}{r} 13 \\ -7 \end{array}$$

3. $$\begin{array}{r} 9 \\ +4 \end{array}$$
$$\begin{array}{r} 13 \\ -4 \end{array}$$
$$\begin{array}{r} 13 \\ -9 \end{array}$$

4. $$\begin{array}{r} 9 \\ +5 \end{array}$$
$$\begin{array}{r} 14 \\ -5 \end{array}$$
$$\begin{array}{r} 14 \\ -9 \end{array}$$

Explain Your Thinking What addition fact can help you find 13 − 3?

Independent Practice

Add. Then write each difference.
Use counters if you want.

1.
```
   6        13       13
  +7       - 7      - 6
  ----     ----     ----
  13        6        7
```

2.
```
   6        14       14
  +8       - 8      - 6
  ----     ----     ----
```

3.
```
   5        14       14
  +9       - 9      - 5
  ----     ----     ----
```

4.
```
   5        13       13
  +8       - 8      - 5
  ----     ----     ----
```

5.
```
   4        13       13
  +9       - 9      - 4
  ----     ----     ----
```

6.
```
  10        13       13
  + 3      - 3      -10
  ----     ----     ----
```

7.
```
   4        12       12
  +8       - 8      - 4
  ----     ----     ----
```

8.
```
   7        12       12
  +5       - 5      - 7
  ----     ----     ----
```

Problem Solving • Reasoning

Write an addition sentence to match the picture.
Write 2 subtraction sentences.

9.

____ + ____ = ____

____ − ____ = ____

____ − ____ = ____

At Home Ask your child to subtract 5 and 6 from 10, 11, 12, 13, and 14.

LESSON 8

Subtract From 15 and 16

Learn About It

You can use an addition fact to help you subtract.

$$\begin{array}{r} 8 \\ +7 \\ \hline 15 \end{array}$$

$$\begin{array}{r} 15 \\ -\ 7 \\ \hline 8 \end{array}$$

$$\begin{array}{r} 15 \\ -\ 8 \\ \hline 7 \end{array}$$

Guided Practice

Add. Then subtract.

1.
$$\begin{array}{r} 9 \\ +7 \\ \hline 16 \end{array}$$
$$\begin{array}{r} 16 \\ -\ 7 \\ \hline 9 \end{array}$$
$$\begin{array}{r} 16 \\ -\ 9 \\ \hline 7 \end{array}$$

2.
$$\begin{array}{r} 9 \\ +6 \\ \hline \end{array}$$
$$\begin{array}{r} 15 \\ -\ 6 \\ \hline \end{array}$$
$$\begin{array}{r} 15 \\ -\ 9 \\ \hline \end{array}$$

3.
$$\begin{array}{r} 10 \\ +\ 5 \\ \hline \end{array}$$
$$\begin{array}{r} 15 \\ -\ 5 \\ \hline \end{array}$$
$$\begin{array}{r} 15 \\ -10 \\ \hline \end{array}$$

4.
$$\begin{array}{r} 10 \\ +\ 6 \\ \hline \end{array}$$
$$\begin{array}{r} 16 \\ -\ 6 \\ \hline \end{array}$$
$$\begin{array}{r} 16 \\ -10 \\ \hline \end{array}$$

Explain Your Thinking If you know 7 + 9 = 16, what 2 related subtraction facts do you know?

Independent Practice

Add. Then subtract.
Use counters if you want.

1.
$$\begin{array}{r} 7 \\ +9 \\ \hline 16 \end{array} \qquad \begin{array}{r} 16 \\ -\ 9 \\ \hline 7 \end{array} \qquad \begin{array}{r} 16 \\ -\ 7 \\ \hline 9 \end{array}$$

2.
$$\begin{array}{r} 7 \\ +8 \\ \hline \end{array} \qquad \begin{array}{r} 15 \\ -\ 8 \\ \hline \end{array} \qquad \begin{array}{r} 15 \\ -\ 7 \\ \hline \end{array}$$

3.
$$\begin{array}{r} 6 \\ +10 \\ \hline \end{array} \qquad \begin{array}{r} 16 \\ -10 \\ \hline \end{array} \qquad \begin{array}{r} 16 \\ -\ 6 \\ \hline \end{array}$$

4.
$$\begin{array}{r} 6 \\ +9 \\ \hline \end{array} \qquad \begin{array}{r} 15 \\ -\ 9 \\ \hline \end{array} \qquad \begin{array}{r} 15 \\ -\ 6 \\ \hline \end{array}$$

5.
$$\begin{array}{r} 5 \\ +10 \\ \hline \end{array} \qquad \begin{array}{r} 15 \\ -10 \\ \hline \end{array} \qquad \begin{array}{r} 15 \\ -\ 5 \\ \hline \end{array}$$

6.
$$\begin{array}{r} 5 \\ +9 \\ \hline \end{array} \qquad \begin{array}{r} 14 \\ -\ 9 \\ \hline \end{array} \qquad \begin{array}{r} 14 \\ -\ 5 \\ \hline \end{array}$$

7.
$$\begin{array}{r} 5 \\ +8 \\ \hline \end{array} \qquad \begin{array}{r} 13 \\ -\ 8 \\ \hline \end{array} \qquad \begin{array}{r} 13 \\ -\ 5 \\ \hline \end{array}$$

8.
$$\begin{array}{r} 5 \\ +7 \\ \hline \end{array} \qquad \begin{array}{r} 12 \\ -\ 7 \\ \hline \end{array} \qquad \begin{array}{r} 12 \\ -\ 5 \\ \hline \end{array}$$

Problem Solving·Reasoning

Using Vocabulary

9. Write the word name for the number that completes the sentence.

   Fifteen minus seven equals _____.

   Sixteen minus nine equals _____.

At Home Ask your child what addition facts can help him or her solve these subtraction facts: $15 - 6$, $15 - 7$, and $16 - 9$.

LESSON 9 Subtract From 17 Through 20

Learn About It

Knowing an addition fact can help you subtract.

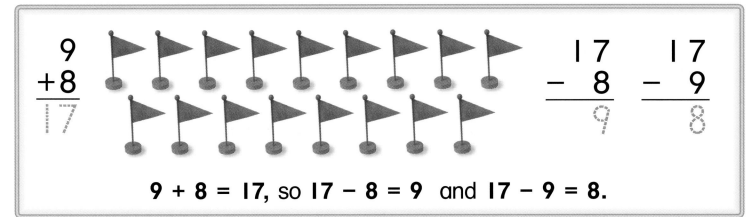

$$9 + 8 = 17, \text{ so } 17 - 8 = 9 \text{ and } 17 - 9 = 8.$$

Guided Practice

Add. Then subtract.

1.
$$\begin{array}{r} 9 \\ +9 \\ \hline 18 \end{array}$$

$$\begin{array}{r} 18 \\ -\ 9 \\ \hline \end{array}$$

2.
$$\begin{array}{r} 10 \\ +10 \\ \hline \end{array}$$

$$\begin{array}{r} 20 \\ -10 \\ \hline \end{array}$$

3.
$$\begin{array}{r} 9 \\ +10 \\ \hline \end{array}$$

$$\begin{array}{r} 19 \\ -10 \\ \hline \end{array}$$
$$\begin{array}{r} 19 \\ -\ 9 \\ \hline \end{array}$$

Explain Your Thinking Why is it easy to add
and subtract with 10?

Independent Practice

Subtract.

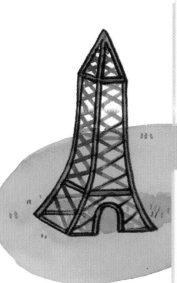

$$\begin{array}{r} 13 \\ -9 \\ \hline 4 \end{array}$$

$$\begin{array}{r} 14 \\ -9 \\ \hline \end{array}$$

$$\begin{array}{r} 15 \\ -9 \\ \hline \end{array}$$

$$\begin{array}{r} 16 \\ -9 \\ \hline \end{array}$$

$$\begin{array}{r} 17 \\ -9 \\ \hline \end{array}$$

$$\begin{array}{r} 18 \\ -9 \\ \hline \end{array}$$

$$\begin{array}{r} 19 \\ -9 \\ \hline \end{array}$$

$$\begin{array}{r} 14 \\ -8 \\ \hline \end{array}$$

$$\begin{array}{r} 15 \\ -8 \\ \hline \end{array}$$

$$\begin{array}{r} 16 \\ -8 \\ \hline \end{array}$$

$$\begin{array}{r} 17 \\ -8 \\ \hline \end{array}$$

$$\begin{array}{r} 18 \\ -8 \\ \hline \end{array}$$

$$\begin{array}{r} 13 \\ -7 \\ \hline \end{array}$$

$$\begin{array}{r} 14 \\ -7 \\ \hline \end{array}$$

$$\begin{array}{r} 15 \\ -7 \\ \hline \end{array}$$

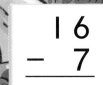

$$\begin{array}{r} 16 \\ -7 \\ \hline \end{array}$$

$$\begin{array}{r} 17 \\ -7 \\ \hline \end{array}$$

$$\begin{array}{r} 20 \\ -10 \\ \hline \end{array}$$

At Home Ask your child to subtract 8 and 9 from any number between 10 and 18.

Name_____

LESSON 10

Problem Solving: Write a Number Sentence

Standards
NS **2.1, 2.6,** AF **1.1**
MR **1.0, 1.1, 2.2**

You can write a number sentence to help you solve problems.

The Bluebirds and the Cardinals are playing baseball. Each team has 9 players. How many players are there in all?

Understand

What do you already know?

_____ Bluebirds

_____ Cardinals

Plan

Circle how you would solve this problem.

add

subtract

Solve

Write a number sentence.

_____ ◯ _____ = _____ players in all

Look Back

Did you answer the question? Explain how you know.

Guided Practice

Solve.
Write a number sentence.

Remember to use the 4 steps.

1 The Cardinals score 2 runs. The Bluebirds score 2 runs. Then the Bluebirds score 1 more run. How many runs are scored in all?

Think: Do I add or subtract?

Draw or write to explain.

__2__ ⊕ __2__ ⊕ __1__ = ____ runs

2 The Bluebirds scored 10 runs. The Cardinals scored 5 runs. How many more runs did the Bluebirds score than the Cardinals?

Think: How can I find out how many more?

____ ◯ ____ = ____ more runs

3 6 Cardinals bat in the first inning.
3 Cardinals bat in the second inning.
3 Cardinals bat in the third inning. How many Cardinals bat in all?

Think: What do I need to find out?

____ ◯ ____ ◯ ____ = ____ in all

At Home Write some addition problems using doubles, such as 6 + 6 and 7 + 7, for your child to solve.

Name_____

Choose a Strategy

Solve.

① The pitcher throws 6 fastballs. Then he throws 6 curve balls. How many balls does he throw in all?

_____ balls

Draw or write to explain.

pitcher

② A fielder throws 9 balls to the catcher and 10 balls to the shortstop. How many balls does she throw?

_____ balls

fielder

③ Ari is at bat 8 times. He gets on base 4 times. How many times does he not get on base?

_____ times

batter

④ Harry catches 8 balls. Tara catches 9 balls. How many balls do they catch in all?

_____ balls in all

catcher

Name _____

Mixed Practice

Find each sum or difference.

1. $8 + 3 =$ ___

2. $13 - 3 =$ ___

3. $7 + 7 =$

4. $9 - 5 =$ ___

5. $18 - 9 =$ ___

6. $4 + 8 =$ ___

7.
$$\begin{array}{r} 7 \\ +6 \\ \hline \end{array}$$

8.
$$\begin{array}{r} 14 \\ -5 \\ \hline \end{array}$$

9.
$$\begin{array}{r} 15 \\ -9 \\ \hline \end{array}$$

10.
$$\begin{array}{r} 8 \\ +8 \\ \hline \end{array}$$

11.
$$\begin{array}{r} 10 \\ +2 \\ \hline \end{array}$$

12.
$$\begin{array}{r} 17 \\ -8 \\ \hline \end{array}$$

13.
$$\begin{array}{r} 12 \\ -3 \\ \hline \end{array}$$

14.
$$\begin{array}{r} 4 \\ +9 \\ \hline \end{array}$$

15.
$$\begin{array}{r} 7 \\ +8 \\ \hline \end{array}$$

16.
$$\begin{array}{r} 16 \\ -7 \\ \hline \end{array}$$

17.
$$\begin{array}{r} 11 \\ -4 \\ \hline \end{array}$$

18.
$$\begin{array}{r} 8 \\ +5 \\ \hline \end{array}$$

19.
$$\begin{array}{r} 7 \\ +10 \\ \hline \end{array}$$

20.
$$\begin{array}{r} 15 \\ -8 \\ \hline \end{array}$$

21.
$$\begin{array}{r} 9 \\ +6 \\ \hline \end{array}$$

22.
$$\begin{array}{r} 18 \\ -9 \\ \hline \end{array}$$

23.
$$\begin{array}{r} 20 \\ -10 \\ \hline \end{array}$$

24.
$$\begin{array}{r} 17 \\ -7 \\ \hline \end{array}$$

 Brain Teaser Number Search

Add across and down.
Circle two or more numbers
next to each other that have
a sum of 13.

2	5	8	7	4
10	3	1	6	9
8	4	9	1	8
5	7	6	5	3
4	3	6	8	10

Internet Brain Teasers
Visit **www.eduplace.com/kids/mhm**
for more *Brain Teasers*.

Name_____

Check Your Understanding of Lessons 6–10

Add. Then subtract.

1. $2 + 2 =$ ___ 2. $8 + 8 =$ ___ 3. $9 + 9 =$ ___
   $4 - 2 =$ ___ $16 - 8 =$ ___ $18 - 9 =$ ___

Write each sum or difference.

4. $10 + 10 =$ ___ | 5. $20 - 10 =$ ___

Add. Then write each difference.

6. $\begin{array}{r} 7 \\ +6 \\ \hline \end{array}$ $\begin{array}{r} 13 \\ -\ 6 \\ \hline \end{array}$ $\begin{array}{r} 13 \\ -\ 7 \\ \hline \end{array}$ | 7. $\begin{array}{r} 6 \\ +8 \\ \hline \end{array}$ $\begin{array}{r} 14 \\ -\ 8 \\ \hline \end{array}$ $\begin{array}{r} 14 \\ -\ 6 \\ \hline \end{array}$

8. $\begin{array}{r} 9 \\ +6 \\ \hline \end{array}$ $\begin{array}{r} 15 \\ -\ 6 \\ \hline \end{array}$ $\begin{array}{r} 15 \\ -\ 9 \\ \hline \end{array}$ | 9. $\begin{array}{r} 10 \\ +\ 6 \\ \hline \end{array}$ $\begin{array}{r} 16 \\ -\ 6 \\ \hline \end{array}$ $\begin{array}{r} 16 \\ -10 \\ \hline \end{array}$

10. $\begin{array}{r} 9 \\ +8 \\ \hline \end{array}$ $\begin{array}{r} 17 \\ -\ 8 \\ \hline \end{array}$ $\begin{array}{r} 17 \\ -\ 9 \\ \hline \end{array}$ | 11. $\begin{array}{r} 9 \\ +10 \\ \hline \end{array}$ $\begin{array}{r} 19 \\ -10 \\ \hline \end{array}$ $\begin{array}{r} 19 \\ -\ 9 \\ \hline \end{array}$

12. Carla scored 3 runs on Monday, 5 runs on Friday, and 7 runs on Saturday. How many runs did she score in all?

Draw or write to explain.

 ____ ◯ ____ ◯ ____ = ____ runs in all

Test Prep • Cumulative Review

Maintaining the Standards

Fill in the ○ for the correct answer. NH means Not Here.

1 Which addition sentence describes this picture?

- ○ 1 + 2 = 3
- ○ 2 + 2 = 4
- ○ 3 + 1 = 4
- ○ NH

2 Kelly picked 7 pears. Noah picked 5 pears. How many more pears did Kelly pick than Noah?

   12   7   3   2
   ○   ○   ○   ○

3 How many of these shapes have 4 corners?

   1   2   3   4
   ○   ○   ○   ○

4 What is the missing addend?

$$3 + \blacksquare = 12$$

   3   6   8   NH
   ○   ○   ○   ○

5 What number is likely to come next in this pattern?

20 25 30 ____

   31   32   35   40
   ○   ○   ○   ○

6 What number can you add to 9 to get 14?

Explain how knowing a related **subtraction** fact can help you find the answer.

_____

_____

_____

Safe Site

Internet Test Prep
Visit **www.eduplace.com/kids/mhm**
for more *Test Prep Practice.*

LESSON 11

Algebra Readiness: Fact Families

A fact family uses the same numbers.

Learn About It

You can make a fact family by writing related facts.

These four related facts make a fact family.

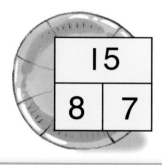

15	
8	7

$$\begin{array}{r} 8 \\ +7 \\ \hline 15 \end{array}$$

$$\begin{array}{r} 7 \\ 8 \\ \hline 15 \end{array}$$

$$\begin{array}{r} 15 \\ -\ 7 \\ \hline 8 \end{array}$$

$$\begin{array}{r} 15 \\ 8 \\ \hline 7 \end{array}$$

Guided Practice

Complete each fact family.

1.
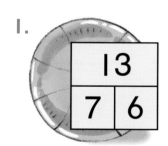

13	
7	6

$$\begin{array}{r} 7 \\ +6 \\ \hline 13 \end{array}$$

$$\begin{array}{r} 6 \\ 7 \\ \hline 13 \end{array}$$

$$\begin{array}{r} 13 \\ -\ 6 \\ \hline 7 \end{array}$$

$$\begin{array}{r} 13 \\ 6 \\ \hline 7 \end{array}$$

2.
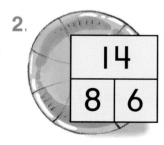

14	
8	6

$$\begin{array}{r} 8 \\ +6 \\ \hline \end{array}$$

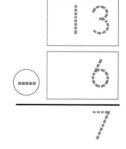

$$\begin{array}{r} 14 \\ -\ 6 \\ \hline \end{array}$$

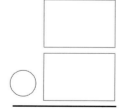

Explain Your Thinking   What is the fact family for 8 + 9 = 17?

Independent Practice

Write each fact family.

1.

9	8	17	17
8	9	8	9

17   17   9   8

2.

3.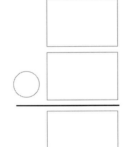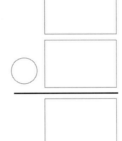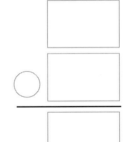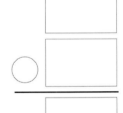

Problem Solving•Reasoning

Logical Thinking

4. Use the code. Complete each number sentence.

Code

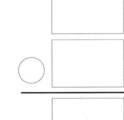 = 8    = 9

 + = ____   + = ____

 At Home Ask your child to write a fact family by using the numbers 7, 4, and 11.

LESSON 12

Algebra Readiness:
Relate Addition and Subtraction

Learn About It

Addition and subtraction are related. You can use addition to help you subtract.

Find 13 − 9.

$$9 + 4 = 13,$$

so

$$13 − 9 = 4.$$

Think: What number plus 9 equals 13?

Guided Practice

Write the missing numbers.

1. $15 − 7 = \underline{8}$

    Think: What number can I add to 7 to get 15?

    $7 + \underline{8} = 15$

2. $13 − 8 = \underline{}$

    Think: What number can I add to 8 to get 13?

    $8 + \underline{} = 13$

3. $16 − 9 = \underline{}$

    $9 + \underline{} = 16$

4. $16 − 8 = \underline{}$

    $8 + \underline{} = 16$

5. $15 − 9 = \underline{}$

    $9 + \underline{} = 15$

Explain Your Thinking What number can you add to 7 to get 13? Name a related subtraction fact.

Independent Practice

Write the missing numbers.

1. $18 - 9 = \underline{9}$

   $9 + \underline{9} = 18$

2. $17 - 8 = \underline{}$

   $8 + \underline{} = 17$

3. $16 - 7 = \underline{}$

   $7 + \underline{} = 16$

4. $15 - 8 = \underline{}$

   $8 + \underline{} = 15$

5. $14 - 9 = \underline{}$

   $9 + \underline{} = 14$

6. $13 - 7 = \underline{}$

   $7 + \underline{} = 13$

7. $11 - 7 = \underline{}$

   $7 + \underline{} = 11$

8. $12 - 6 = \underline{}$

   $6 + \underline{} = 12$

9. $12 - 4 = \underline{}$

   $4 + \underline{} = 12$

10. $20 - 10 = \underline{}$

    $10 + \underline{} = 20$

11. $15 - 5 = \underline{}$

    $5 + \underline{} = 15$

12. $12 - 9 = \underline{}$

    $9 + \underline{} = 12$

Problem Solving • Reasoning

Visual Thinking

13. Write a fact family by using the numbers outside the circle but inside the square.

    $\underline{} + \underline{} = \underline{}$

    $\underline{} + \underline{} = \underline{}$

    $\underline{} - \underline{} = \underline{}$

    $\underline{} - \underline{} = \underline{}$

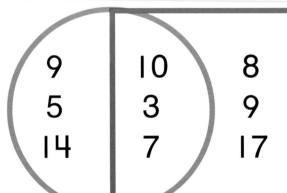

9 5 14   10 3 7   8 9 17

At Home Ask your child to write related addition and subtraction sentences using 7, 9, and 16.

Standards
NS **2.1, 2.6**
MR **1.1, 2.0, 2.1**

LESSON 13 ## Different Ways to Subtract

Learn About It

You can subtract in different ways.

Use doubles.

$$\begin{array}{r} 16 \\ -8 \\ \hline 8 \end{array}$$

Think:
8 + 8 = 16

Use an addition fact.

$$\begin{array}{r} 14 \\ -8 \\ \hline 6 \end{array}$$

Think:
8 + 6 = 14

Guided Practice

Write each difference.

1.
$$\begin{array}{r} 13 \\ -7 \\ \hline 6 \end{array}$$

2.
$$\begin{array}{r} 14 \\ -6 \\ \hline \end{array}$$

3.
$$\begin{array}{r} 16 \\ -7 \\ \hline \end{array}$$

4.
$$\begin{array}{r} 15 \\ -8 \\ \hline \end{array}$$

5.
$$\begin{array}{r} 13 \\ -8 \\ \hline \end{array}$$

6.
$$\begin{array}{r} 15 \\ -9 \\ \hline \end{array}$$

7.
$$\begin{array}{r} 13 \\ -5 \\ \hline \end{array}$$

8.
$$\begin{array}{r} 17 \\ -10 \\ \hline \end{array}$$

9.
$$\begin{array}{r} 18 \\ -9 \\ \hline \end{array}$$

10.
$$\begin{array}{r} 14 \\ -7 \\ \hline \end{array}$$

11.
$$\begin{array}{r} 17 \\ -8 \\ \hline \end{array}$$

12.
$$\begin{array}{r} 16 \\ -9 \\ \hline \end{array}$$

13.
$$\begin{array}{r} 13 \\ -3 \\ \hline \end{array}$$

14.
$$\begin{array}{r} 18 \\ -10 \\ \hline \end{array}$$

15.
$$\begin{array}{r} 14 \\ -5 \\ \hline \end{array}$$

Explain Your Thinking Describe a way to find 20 − 10.

four hundred twenty-nine **429**

Independent Practice

Write each difference.

1. 13
    − 4
    ——
     9

2. 14
    − 4
    ——

3. 16
    − 8
    ——

4. 17
    − 9
    ——

5. 15
    −10
    ——

6. 16
    − 9
    ——

7. 13
    −10
    ——

8. 14
    − 9
    ——

9. 18
    −10
    ——

10. 16
     −10
     ——

11. 16
     − 7
     ——

12. 19
     − 9
     ——

13. 15
     − 7
     ——

14. 17
     − 7
     ——

15. 13
     − 6
     ——

16. 14
     −10
     ——

17. 18
     − 9
     ——

18. 13
     − 9
     ——

19. 19
     −10
     ——

20. 15
     − 6
     ——

21. 14
     − 8
     ——

22. 16
     − 6
     ——

23. 15
     − 9
     ——

24. 17
     − 8
     ——

25. 18
     − 8
     ——

Problem Solving•Reasoning

Write About It

26. Half the marbles are John's.
Half the marbles are Mary's.
How many are John's? _____

Explain how you know you
are right.

At Home Ask your child how he or she found the answer
to some of the subtraction exercises on this page.

Name _____

LESSON 14

Problem Solving: Choose the Operation

Standards
NS **2.1, 2.6**
MR **1.0, 1.1, 3.0**

Ice hockey is an exciting game. Each team tries to score by shooting at the other team's goal.

You can use addition to help you solve problems.

Chad shoots at the goal 7 times in the first game. He shoots 6 times in the next game. How many times does he shoot in all?

◯ ☐ times
☐ times
_____
☐ times in all

Think:
Find the numbers in the problem. Add to find the total.

You can use subtraction to help you solve problems.

The Wings shoot at the goal 11 times. The Flyers shoot at the goal 7 times. How many more times do the Wings shoot at the goal?

◯ ☐ times
☐ times
_____
☐ times

Think:
Find the numbers in the problem. Subtract to find the difference.

Guided Practice

Write the number sentence.
Add or subtract to solve.

1 The Wings play 9 games. They win
5 games. How many games do they lose?

> **Think:**
> How can I solve
> the problem?

_4_ games

2 The Flyers play 10 games in December.
They play 5 games in January. How many
games do they play in all?

> **Think:**
> What do I need
> to find out?

_____ games

3 The Flyers play 17 games. They lose
8 games. How many games do they win?

> **Think:**
> What do I
> already know?

_____ games

4 The Wings scored 8 goals. The Flyers
scored 6 goals. How many goals did
they score altogether?

> **Think:**
> Do I add or
> subtract?

_____ goals

At Home Ask your child how he or she decided to solve each problem.

Name_____

Choose a Strategy

Solve.

1 There are 12 gloves on the hockey shelf. Barb puts 4 gloves on the shelf. How many gloves are on the shelf now?

Draw or write to explain.

gloves

_____ gloves

2 The team has 18 helmets. There are nine blue helmets. The rest are white. How many helmets are white?

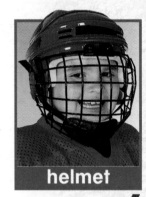
helmet

_____ white helmets

3 4 sticks have black tape. 6 have red tape. How many more sticks have red tape?

stick

_____ more sticks

4 There are 4 skates with red stripes, 2 with white stripes, and 6 with green stripes. How many skates are there in all?

skates

_____ skates

Name _____

Mixed Practice

Memorize Your Facts

Add or subtract.

1. $12 - 5 =$ ___   2. $6 + 8 =$ ___   3. $5 + 9 =$ ___

4. $13 - 6 =$ ___   5. $15 - 8 =$ ___   6. $8 + 6 =$ ___

7. $\begin{array}{r} 5 \\ +8 \\ \hline \end{array}$ 8. $\begin{array}{r} 11 \\ -\ 9 \\ \hline \end{array}$ 9. $\begin{array}{r} 12 \\ -\ 6 \\ \hline \end{array}$ 10. $\begin{array}{r} 6 \\ +7 \\ \hline \end{array}$ 11. $\begin{array}{r} 7 \\ +5 \\ \hline \end{array}$ 12. $\begin{array}{r} 13 \\ -\ 4 \\ \hline \end{array}$

13. $\begin{array}{r} 16 \\ -\ 8 \\ \hline \end{array}$ 14. $\begin{array}{r} 8 \\ +7 \\ \hline \end{array}$ 15. $\begin{array}{r} 7 \\ +9 \\ \hline \end{array}$ 16. $\begin{array}{r} 17 \\ -\ 9 \\ \hline \end{array}$ 17. $\begin{array}{r} 14 \\ -\ 6 \\ \hline \end{array}$ 18. $\begin{array}{r} 9 \\ +9 \\ \hline \end{array}$

 Brain Teaser Magic Triangle

This is a magic triangle.
When you add the numbers along each side, you get the same sum.

Fill in the missing numbers.

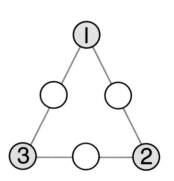

Safe Site

Internet Brain Teasers
Visit **www.eduplace.com/kids/mhm**
for more *Brain Teasers*.

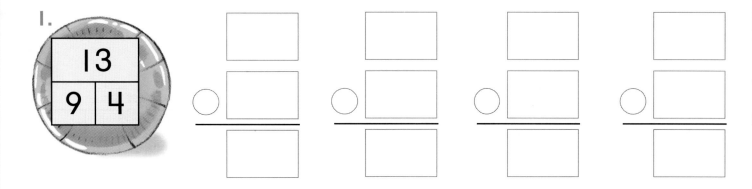

Quick ✓ Check

Check Your Understanding of Lessons 11–14

Complete each fact family.

1.

|13|
|9|4|

○ ▢ ▢ ▢ ▢
——— ——— ——— ———

Write the missing numbers.

2. 15 − 8 = ___

   8 + ___ = 15

3. 20 − 10 = ___

   10 + ___ = 20

Write each difference.

4. 13
   − 5
   ___

5. 14
   − 8
   ___

6. 17
   −10
   ___

7. 16
   − 6
   ___

8. 18
   − 9
   ___

9. Wendy reads 3 books. Miguel reads 2 more books than Wendy. Tory reads 4 more books than Wendy. How many books do they read in all?

   ____ books

   Draw or write to explain.

Name _____

Test Prep • Cumulative Review

Maintaining the Standards

Fill in the ○ for the correct answer. NH means Not Here.

1 Which number names 11 − 3?

　○　　○　　○　　○
　3　　8　　9　　11

2 Which is the missing addend?

　■ + 7 = 16

　7　　8　　9　　NH
　○　　○　　○　　○

3 Richard has been saving nickels. He wants to buy a toy that costs 45¢. How many nickels does he need to buy the toy?

　9　　8　　7　　6
　○　　○　　○　　○

4 Choose a sign to make the sentence true.

　27 ○ 17

　=　　<　　>　　¢
　○　　○　　○　　○

Use this graph for Exercises 5 and 6.

Alissa's Stickers

5 How many more ★ does Alissa have than ✿ ?

　1　　2　　3　　4
　○　　○　　○　　○

6 Alissa gives away 1 ✿ and 2 ★. How many stickers does she have left?
Explain how you would use the bar graph to find the answer.

_____

_____

_____

Safe Site

Internet Test Prep
Visit **www.eduplace.com/kids/mhm**
for more *Test Prep Practice.*

Name _____

Chapter Review

1. Write the **addends** for the double fact that has a sum of 12.

____ ____

2. The answer in a subtraction sentence is called the

_____.

3. Write two related facts.

_____   _____

Write each sum. Circle the double facts.

4. 9   5. 4   6. 1 0   7. 6   8. 5   9. 8
   +9   +8   +1 0   +6   +4   +8

Write each sum. Circle each double-plus-one fact.

10. 9   11. 5   12. 7   13. 4   14. 9   15. 7
    +8   +5   +6   +5   +3   +7

Add. Then write each difference.

16. 6   1 3   1 3   17. 5   1 4   1 4
    +7   − 7   − 6   +9   − 9   − 5

18. 9   1 7   1 7   19. 9   1 9   1 9
    +8   − 8   − 9   +1 0   −1 0   − 9

Add. Then subtract.

1. $9 + 9 = \underline{\quad}$

$18 - 9 = \underline{\quad}$

2. $\underline{\quad} = 10 + 10$

$\underline{\quad} = 20 - 10$

Add.

3.
$$\begin{array}{r} 7 \\ 4 \\ +3 \\ \hline \end{array}$$

4.
$$\begin{array}{r} 8 \\ 3 \\ +2 \\ \hline \end{array}$$

5.
$$\begin{array}{r} 6 \\ 4 \\ +2 \\ \hline \end{array}$$

6.
$$\begin{array}{r} 3 \\ 7 \\ +7 \\ \hline \end{array}$$

7.
$$\begin{array}{r} 9 \\ 6 \\ +1 \\ \hline \end{array}$$

8.
$$\begin{array}{r} 8 \\ 4 \\ +4 \\ \hline \end{array}$$

Write the missing numbers.

9. $14 - 8 = \underline{\quad}$

$8 + \underline{\quad} = \underline{\quad}$

10. $16 - 9 = \underline{\quad}$

$9 + \underline{\quad} = 16$

11. The pitcher throws 18 pitches in the first inning. Seven of the pitches are curve balls. How many are not curve balls?

$\underline{\quad} \bigcirc \underline{\quad} = \underline{\quad}$

Draw or write to explain.

12. The Wings play 2 games the first week, 4 games the second week, and 3 games the third week. How many games do they play in all?

$\underline{\quad}$ games in all

Draw or write to explain.

438 four hundred thirty-eight

Chapter Test

Write each sum.

Use ▭ to circle each double fact.

Use ▭ to circle each double-plus-one fact.

1.	2.	3.	4.	5.	6.
8 +9	6 +6	9 +3	7 +6	6 +4	4 +5

Complete each number sentence.

7. $10 + 7 = $ ___

8. $9 + 6 = $ ___

Add.

9.	10.	11.	12.	13.	14.
3 5 +8	6 5 +6	1 9 +4	7 3 +6	9 4 +5	8 0 +4

15. $4 + 9 + 6 = $ ___

16. $8 + 0 + 7 = $ ___

Add. Then write each difference.

17.			18.		
6 +9	15 - 9	15 - 6	10 + 8	18 - 8	18 -10

19. Use the numbers 16, 9, and 7 to write a fact family.

____ ◯ ____ = ____   ____ ◯ ____ = ____

____ ◯ ____ = ____   ____ ◯ ____ = ____

Write the missing numbers.

20. $17 - 8 =$ ___

___ $+ 8 = 17$

21. $15 -$ ___ $= 7$

$7 +$ ___ $= 15$

22. $20 - 10 =$ ___

$10 +$ ___ $= 20$

23. $18 - 9 =$ ___

$9 +$ ___ $= 18$

24. The Hornets had 5 runs. The Pandas had 8 runs. How many runs did they have in all?

____ ◯ ____ = ____

Draw or write to explain.

25. Andi shoots for the basket 15 times. She misses 4 times. How many baskets does she make?

____ baskets

Draw or write to explain.

✎ **Write About It**

Explain how addition and subtraction are related. Show examples.

_____

_____

_____

Name _____

Fun-Filled Facts

What You Need

number cards 1–12, 14, 16, 18, and 20

How to Play

1. Choose or .

2. Put the cards facedown in a pile.

3. Take turns picking the top card.

4. Find a box below in which to write that number as the correct answer. Lose a turn if you can't find a box.

5. The player with the most boxes with correct answers wins.

4 +7	5 +4	16 − 8	9 +3	6 +4	9 −2
10 − 7	8 +8	9 −4	8 −7	7 −5	9 +9

Enrichment

Fractions of a Group

You can use a fraction to name a part of a group.

$\dfrac{1}{4}$ ← part blue
← parts in all

Circle which part of the group is blue.

1.

$\dfrac{1}{2}$ $\dfrac{1}{3}$ $\dfrac{1}{4}$

2.

$\dfrac{1}{2}$ $\dfrac{1}{3}$ $\dfrac{1}{4}$

3.

$\dfrac{1}{2}$ $\dfrac{1}{3}$ $\dfrac{1}{4}$

4.

$\dfrac{1}{2}$ $\dfrac{1}{3}$ $\dfrac{1}{4}$

5.

$\dfrac{1}{2}$ $\dfrac{1}{3}$ $\dfrac{1}{4}$

6.

$\dfrac{1}{2}$ $\dfrac{1}{3}$ $\dfrac{1}{4}$

Let's Paint

A Read-Aloud Story

written by Laura Black
illustrated by Terry Kovalcik

Accessing Prior Knowledge

This story will
help you review:
- Comparing
  length, size,
  and weight

A Math Storybook for

_____

Here are two blank papers.
One is short and one is long.
We are going to paint them.
Won't you come along?

Circle the **longer** paper.

We will need some paint.
I will open the jar of blue.
We have a little yellow
And a lot of red, too!

Circle the jar with the **most** paint.

This can of paint is heavy,
So we poured some in a cup.
The cup is so much lighter
And easier to pick up.

Circle the **lighter** paint container.

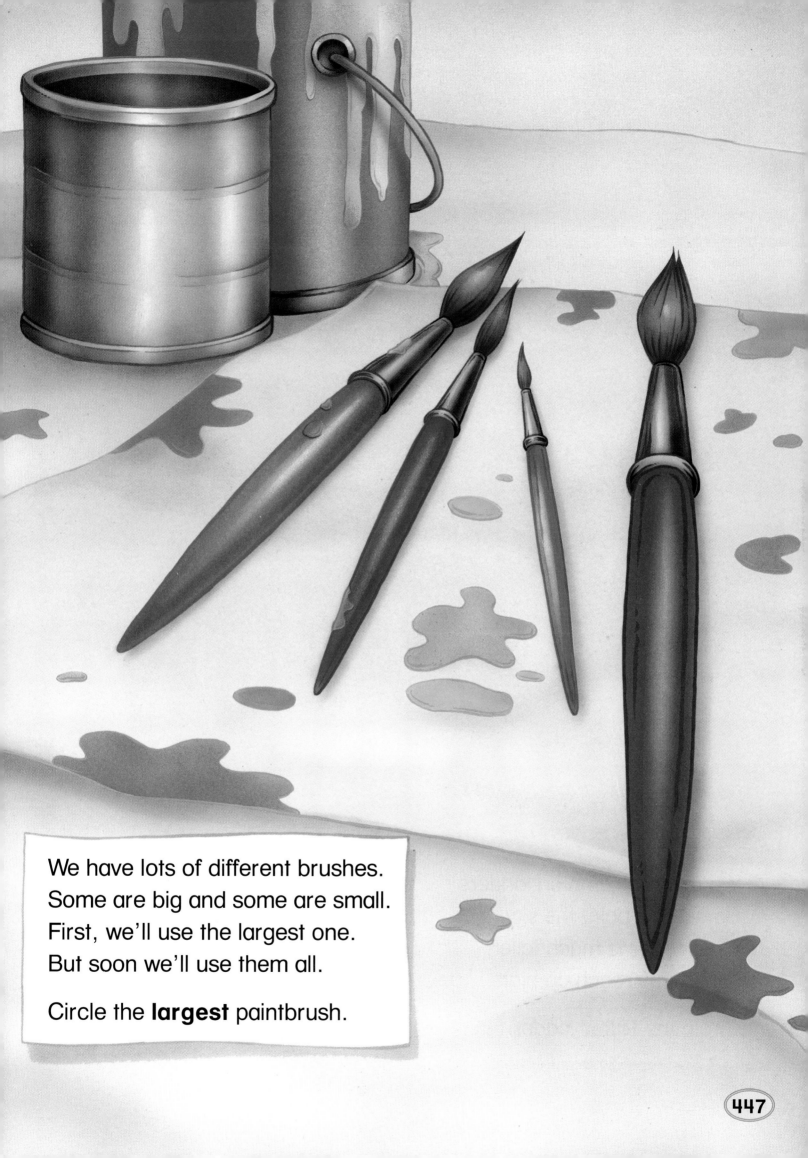

We have lots of different brushes.
Some are big and some are small.
First, we'll use the largest one.
But soon we'll use them all.

Circle the **largest** paintbrush.

We need to climb on ladders
So we can paint the sky.
One ladder is much taller,
To help us reach up high.

Circle the **taller** ladder.

Look at what we painted.
Two murals you can see.
My friend painted this tall flower.
The shorter one's by me!

Circle the **shorter** flower.

Family Letter

Dear Family,

During the next few weeks, our math class will be learning about measurement.

You can expect to see work that provides practice with measuring length and comparing weight and capacity.

As we learn about measurement, you may wish to use the following sample as a guide.

To measure capacity

cup   **pint**   **quart**   **liter**

Knowing about measurement can help children find the length, weight, and capacity of items they use in everyday life.

Sincerely,

Your child's teacher

Vocabulary

centimeter A metric unit of length.

inch A customary unit of length.

pound A unit used to measure weight.

kilogram A metric unit used to measure mass.

cup / pint / quart / liter Units used to measure capacity.

shorter / longer Words used to compare length.

shorter / taller Words used to compare height.

heavier / lighter Words used to compare weight.

450

Compare Length and Height

Learn About It

You can use words such as **longer, taller,** and **shorter** to compare lengths.

Shorter than the bookcase →

Longer than the picture →

Shorter than Tommy

← Taller than Tommy

Guided Practice

Circle the objects that are taller than you in .
Circle the objects that are shorter than you in .

1.

2.

3.

4.

5.

6.

7.

8.

Explain Your Thinking Can one object be taller than one person and shorter than another? Why or why not?

Independent Practice

 I am tall.  I am taller. I am the tallest.

Circle the tallest in 🖍.
Circle the shortest in 🖍.

1.

2.

Circle the longest in 🖍.
Circle the shortest in 🖍.

3.

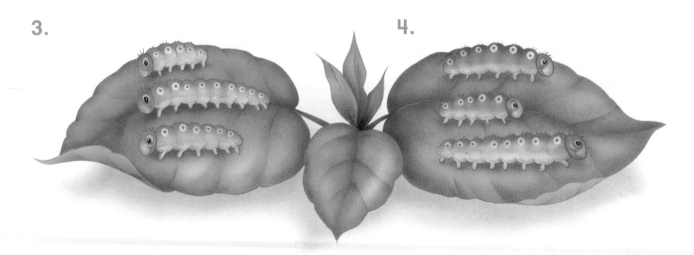

4.

Problem Solving • Reasoning

Logical Thinking

5. Use the clues to draw the letters.

A is taller than B.

C is shorter than B.

D is the tallest of all.

Draw or write to explain.

At Home Encourage your child to select three or four household objects and then put them in order from tallest to shortest.

Name _____

Standards
MG **1.0, 1.1, 2.2**
MR **1.2**

Nonstandard Units

Learn About It

You can use objects to **estimate** length.

How long is the pencil?
Line up paper clips end to end.

Make sure they touch each other.

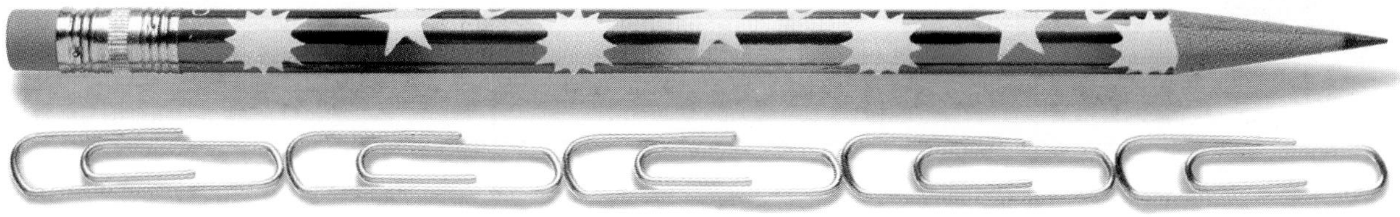

about ___5___ ⬭ long

Guided Practice

Estimate. Measure with ⬭.

	Find the object.	Estimate.	Measure.
1.		about _____ ⬭	about _____ ⬭
2.		about _____ ⬭	about _____ ⬭
3.		about _____ ⬭	about _____ ⬭
4.		about _____ ⬭	about _____ ⬭

Explain Your Thinking How would your answers change if you used larger paper clips?

Independent Practice

Estimate. Measure with ⌁.

	Find the object.	Estimate.	Measure.
1.		about _____ ⌁	about _____ ⌁
2.		about _____ ⌁	about _____ ⌁
3.		about _____ ⌁	about _____ ⌁
4.		about _____ ⌁	about _____ ⌁
5.		about _____ ⌁	about _____ ⌁

Problem Solving•Reasoning

6. Circle the objects that can roll.

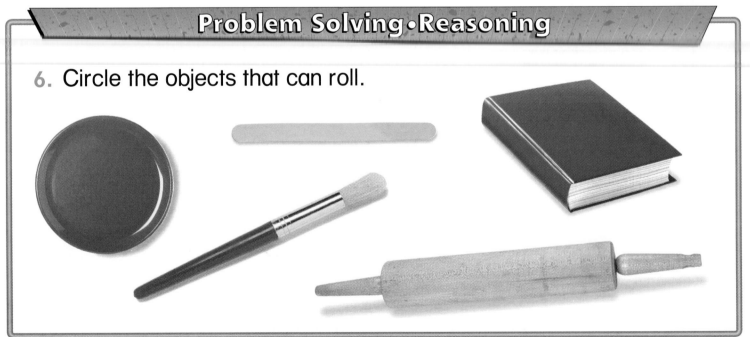

At Home Ask your child to use pennies to measure the length of something at home.

LESSON 3 Inches

New
Vocabulary
inch

Learn About It

You can measure objects with an **inch** ruler.

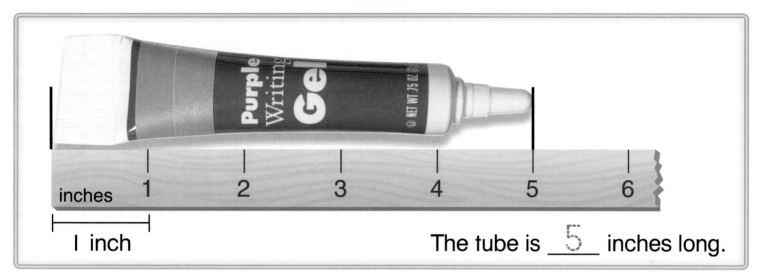

inches   1   2   3   4   5   6

I inch

The tube is __5__ inches long.

Guided Practice

Use an inch ruler.

Measure each object to the nearest inch.

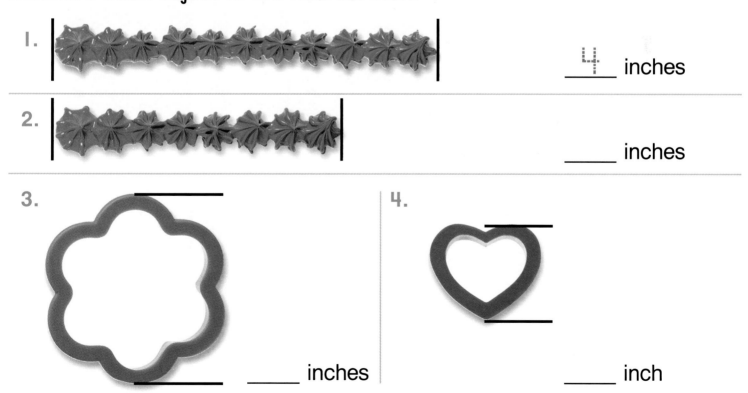

1. ___4___ inches

2. _____ inches

3. _____ inches

4. _____ inch

Explain Your Thinking List some objects that are shorter than 5 inches and some that are longer than 5 inches.

Independent Practice

Use an inch ruler.
Measure each part to the nearest inch.

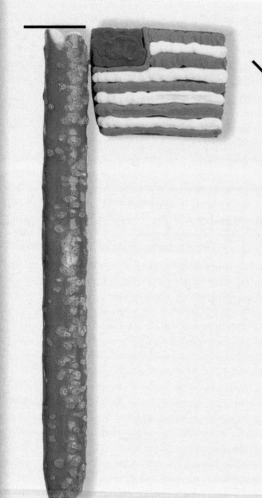

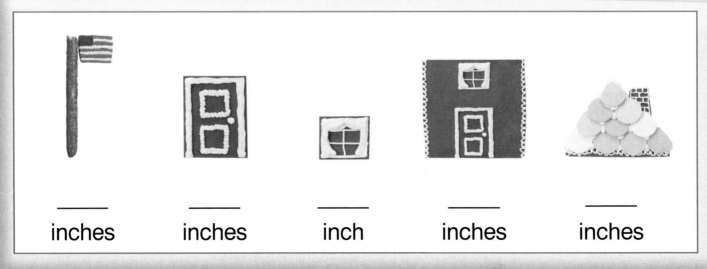

____ inches	____ inches	____ inch	____ inches	____ inches

At Home Ask your child to use an inch ruler to measure the length of a fork.

LESSON 4 Centimeters

Learn About It

You can also measure objects
with a **centimeter** ruler.

New Vocabulary
centimeter

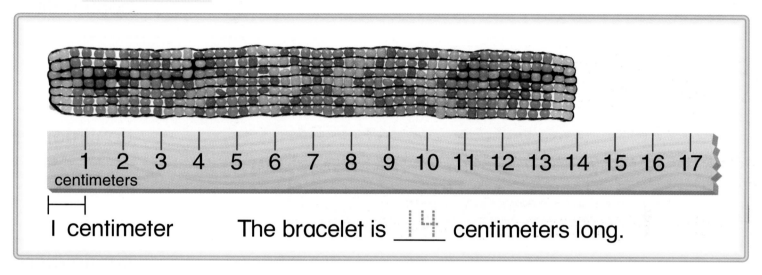

| | | | | | | | | | | | | | | | | |
| 1 | 2 | 3 | 4 | 5 | 6 | 7 | 8 | 9 | 10 | 11 | 12 | 13 | 14 | 15 | 16 | 17 |

centimeters

1 centimeter   The bracelet is __14__ centimeters long.

Guided Practice

Use a centimeter ruler.
Measure each object to the nearest centimeter.

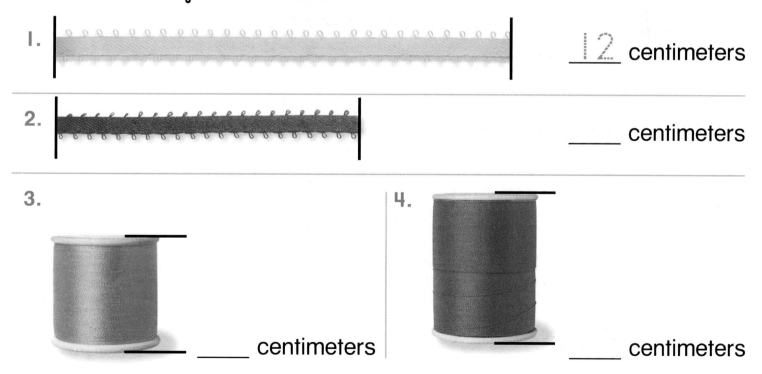

1. ___12___ centimeters

2. _____ centimeters

3. _____ centimeters

4. _____ centimeters

Explain Your Thinking List some objects that are
shorter than 10 centimeters.

Independent Practice

Use a centimeter ruler.
Measure each object.

Remember to line up your ruler on the left.

1. _____ centimeters

2. _____ centimeters

3. _____ centimeters

4.
_____ centimeters

5. _____ centimeters

Problem Solving • Reasoning

Using Vocabulary

6. Color the **shortest** feather 🖍 .

7. Color the **longest** feather 🖍 .

8. Circle the feather that is about 8 **centimeters** long.

At Home Find five objects in your home that are more than 10 centimeters long.

Name_____

Problem Solving: Logical Thinking

	Standards
	MR **1.0, 1.1, 2.2**

You can use clues to help
you solve problems.

Noelle wants a necklace with beads. She
also wants it to be shorter than the purple
one. Which one should she choose?

Understand

Circle what you need to find out.

Which necklace Noelle
should choose.

Which necklace is shortest?

Plan

Circle how you would solve this problem.

Use clues.

Subtract.

Solve

Follow the clues. Cross out the necklaces in the picture that do not match the clues.

with beads

shorter than the purple one

Look Back

Does your answer match the clues? Explain why.

Guided Practice

Solve. Circle the picture that matches the clues.

Remember:
► Understand
► Plan
► Solve
► Look Back

Remember to use the 4 steps.

① It is shorter than the orange bracelet. It has square beads.

Think:
Which bracelets are shorter than the orange bracelet?

② It has a triangle on it. It is longer than the bracelet with a square on it.

Think:
Which one is longer than the bracelet with a square on it?

③ It is longer than the bracelet with the cats. It is made out of metal.

Think:
Which bracelets are longer than the bracelet with the cats?

④ It is not the longest one. It is made of stones.

Think:
Which bracelet is made of stones?

At Home Help your child make up a problem using clues that compare the heights of three family members.

Name_____

Choose a Strategy

Solve.

1 It can bend. It goes around your neck. What is it?

Draw or write to explain.

_____

bracelet

2 It has many colors. It goes around your wrist. What is it?

_____

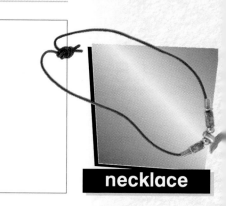

necklace

3 Amanda has 8 rings. Her aunt gives her 4 more rings. How many rings does Amanda have now?

_____ rings

ring

4 Yuki has 17 hair combs. She keeps them in 2 boxes. One box has 5 more than the other box. How many hair combs are in each box?

_____ _____

hair comb

Name _____

Mixed Practice

Memorize Your Facts

Find each sum or difference.

1. 13 − 5 = ___
2. 9 + 4 = ___
3. 5 + 7 = ___

4. 11 − 6 = ___
5. 15 − 7 = ___
6. 6 + 9 = ___

7. 12 − 5 = ___
8. 7 + 9 = ___
9. 17 − 8 = ___

10. 9
  +5

11. 16
  − 9

12. 17
  − 7

13. 8
  +9

14. 3
  +9

15. 14
  − 7

16. 15
  − 6

17. 9
  +7

18. 10
  + 1

19. 13
  − 7

20. 10
  − 2

21. 10
  +10

22. 9
  +9

23. 14
  − 6

24. 16
  − 8

25. 7
  +8

26. 13
  − 9

27. 7
  +7

 Brain Teaser **Which Way?**

One unit is from one dot to another.
Draw a path from to
 that is 6 units long.

Safe Site

Internet Brain Teasers
Visit **www.eduplace.com/kids/mhm**
for more *Brain Teasers*.

Quick ✓ Check

Check Your Understanding of Lessons 1–5

Circle the objects taller than you .
Circle the objects shorter than you .

1.

2.

3.

4.

Circle the longest .
Circle the shortest .

5.

6.

Use an inch ruler to measure each object.

7.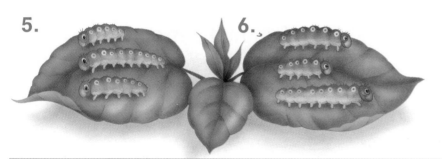

_____ inches

8.

_____ inch

Use a centimeter ruler to measure each object.

9.

_____ centimeters

10.

_____ centimeters

11. Circle the shape that matches
the clues. I have straight sides.
I have 4 corners.

Test Prep • Cumulative Review

Maintaining the Standards

Fill in the ○ for the correct answer.

1 What is the value of these coins?

   37¢   32¢   30¢   28¢
   ○   ○   ○   ○

Use this table for Exercises 2 and 3.

Trees Seen	
Ash	8
Oak	12
Maple	7

2 How many maple and ash trees were seen?

   7   8   15   16
   ○   ○   ○   ○

3 Which tree was seen the most?

   ash   oak   maple   elm
   ○   ○   ○   ○

4 Choose a sign to make the sentence true.

$$56 \quad ○ \quad 49$$

   <   >   =   ¢
   ○   ○   ○   ○

5 What number comes between?

$$26, \underline{\quad\quad}, 43$$

   17   24   39   44
   ○   ○   ○   ○

6 Which number is greater, 61 or 16?

Explain how you know.

_____

_____

_____

Safe Site

Internet Test Prep
Visit **www.eduplace.com/kids/mhm**
for more *Test Prep Practice*.

LESSON 6 Compare Weight

Learn About It

A balance scale can show you which is **heavier** and which is **lighter.**

New Vocabulary
heavier
lighter

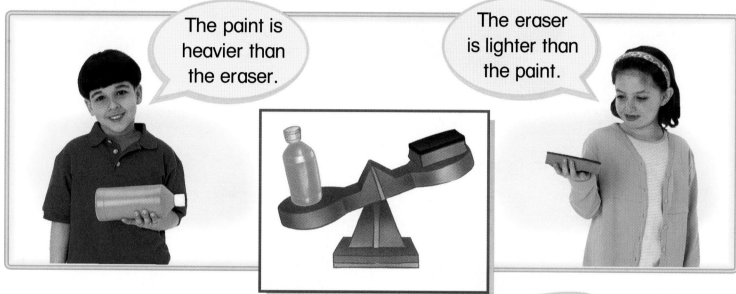

The paint is heavier than the eraser.

The eraser is lighter than the paint.

Think: heavier side lower, lighter side higher

Guided Practice

Use a balance scale and real objects.
Circle the heavier one in each.

1.   2.

Circle the lighter one in each.

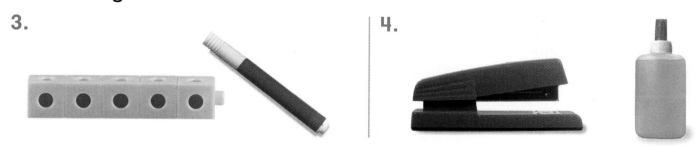

3.   4.

Explain Your Thinking Did you find two things that weighed about the same? How did you know?

Independent Practice

Use a balance scale and real objects.
Circle the heavier one in each.

1.

2.

Circle the lighter one in each.

3.

4.

Problem Solving • Reasoning

Estimation

5. Compare the weight of each item. Circle the item that weighs about 2 boxes.

At Home Choose two kitchen items. Ask your child which is heavier and which is lighter.

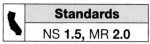

LESSON 7 Pounds

New
Vocabulary
pound

Learn About It

You can measure weight in **pounds.**

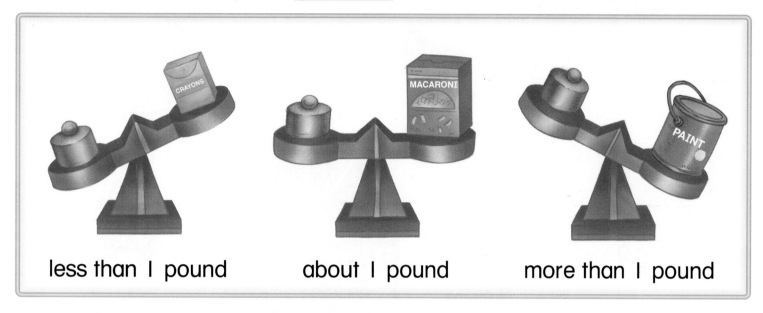

less than 1 pound | about 1 pound | more than 1 pound

Guided Practice

Does each object weigh more than or less
than 1 pound?

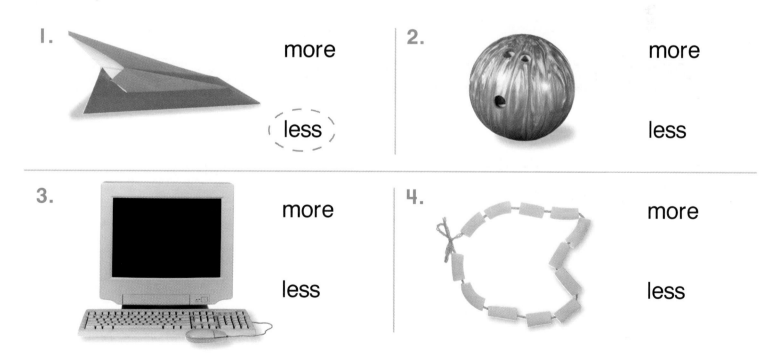

1. more
(less)

2. more
less

3. more
less

4. more
less

Explain Your Thinking Is a pound of cotton lighter
than a pound of bricks? Why or why not?

Independent Practice

Circle the objects.

1. Use for objects that weigh more than 1 pound.
2. Use for objects that weigh less than 1 pound.

Problem Solving·Reasoning

Write About It

3. Pedro has these coins. He buys a mask for 50¢. How much money does he have left? _____¢

4. Explain what coins Pedro might have left.

At Home Find foods in your kitchen that weigh about 1 pound.

Standards
Extends Grade 1
Standards

Kilograms

Learn About It

You can also measure objects in **kilograms.**

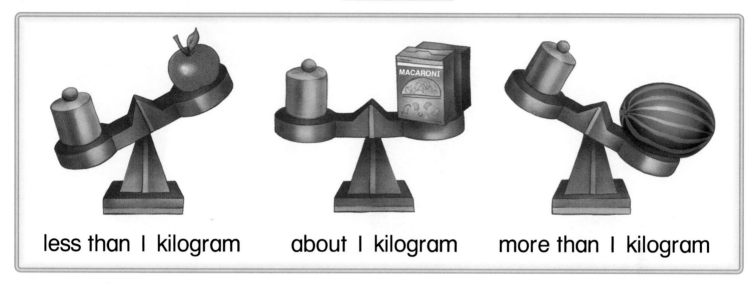

less than I kilogram   about I kilogram   more than I kilogram

Guided Practice

Is each object more than or less
than I kilogram? Circle the answer.

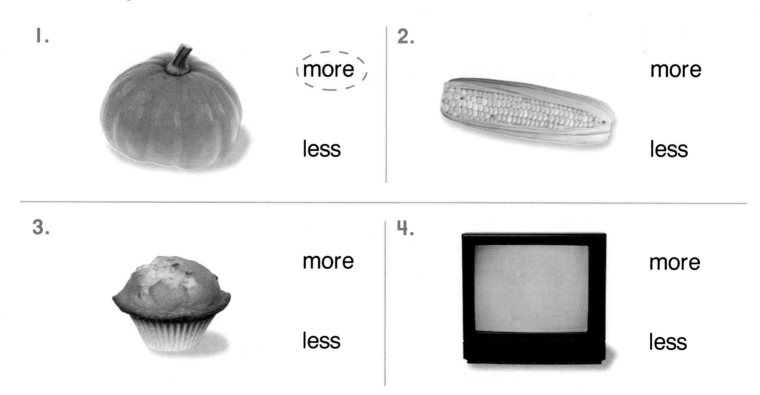

1.   more   less

2.   more   less

3.   more   less

4.   more   less

Explain Your Thinking Would you measure the
length of a straw in kilograms or centimeters? Why?

Independent Practice

Circle the objects.

1. Use  for objects that are more than 1 kilogram.

2. Use  for objects that are less than 1 kilogram.

Problem Solving·Reasoning

Visual Thinking

3. Write 9, 90, and 900 under the correct pictures.

about

_____ kilograms

about

_____ kilograms

about

_____ kilograms

470 four hundred seventy

Quick ✔ Check

Check Your Understanding of Lessons 6–8

Circle the heavier real object.

1.

2.

Circle the lighter real object.

3.

4.

Does each object weigh more than or less than 1 pound?

5.

more   less

6.

more   less

Circle the objects that are more than 1 kilogram.

7.

Name _____

Test Prep • Cumulative Review

Maintaining the Standards

Fill in the ○ for the correct answer. NH means Not Here.

1 What number is 50 + 9?

14   59   95   509
○   ○   ○   ○

2 What is the value of this coin?

1¢   5¢   10¢   25¢
○   ○   ○   ○

3 Which number sentence will help you find how many more 🐞 than 🐞?

○ 8 + 5 = ___

○ 5 + 8 = ___

○ 8 − 5 = ___

○ 13 − 5 = ___

4 Evan read 9 books. Then he read 7 more. How many books did he read in all?

18   17   16   NH
○   ○   ○   ○

5 Count by tens. What number is missing?

30, 40, 50, ___, 70

51   55   60   65
○   ○   ○   ○

6 Which feather is longer? **Explain** how you know.

_____

_____

_____

Safe Site

Internet Test Prep
Visit **www.eduplace.com/kids/mhm**
for more *Test Prep Practice.*

Compare Capacity

Learn About It

You can compare the amounts that containers hold.

Fill one container.
Pour it into the other container.

The pail is not full, so the pail holds more.

Guided Practice

Use real containers.
Circle the one that holds more.

1.

2.

Circle the one that holds less.

3.

4.

Explain Your Thinking Name three containers. Put them in order from the greatest to the least amount held.

Independent Practice

Number the containers in order from the least to the greatest amount held.

The one that holds the least is 1. The one that holds the most is 3.

1.

_1_   _3_   _2_

2.

_____   _____   _____

3.

_____   _____   _____

4.

_____   _____   _____

Problem Solving • Reasoning

Visual Thinking

5. Circle the smallest box that can hold all of these buttons.

At Home Show your child two different bowls. Ask him or her which bowl holds more.

LESSON 10 Cups, Pints, and Quarts

Learn About It

You can use **cups, pints,** and **quarts** to tell how much a container holds.

New
Vocabulary
cup
pint
quart

Guided Practice

Circle the ones that hold the same amount.

1.

2.

3.

4.

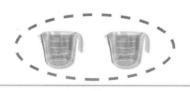  

Explain Your Thinking How many cups of milk
will fill a quart container? How do you know?

Independent Practice

Help Keisha make fruit punch. Use the recipe card. Circle the amounts she needs.

Fruit Punch

2 cups grape juice

1 quart mango juice

1 pint cranberry juice

> **Remember:**
> 2 cups = I pint
> 2 pints = I quart

1. grape

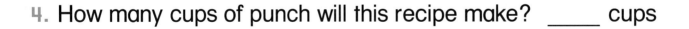

2. mango

3. cranberry

4. How many cups of punch will this recipe make? _____ cups

Problem Solving·Reasoning

Using Data

5. The vase holds _____ more cups than the mug.

6. **Write Your Own**
   Write a question you can answer by using the graph.

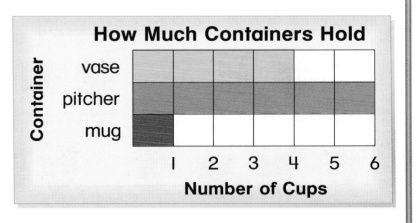

How Much Containers Hold

Container	1	2	3	4	5	6
vase						
pitcher						
mug						

Number of Cups

At Home Ask your child to find things that hold about I cup.

Name_____

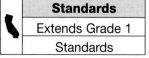
 **Liters**

Learn About It

New
Vocabulary
liter

You can also use **liters** to tell how much a container holds.

less than 1 liter

1 liter

more than 1 liter

Guided Practice

Circle the objects.

1. Use ⬤ for objects that hold more than 1 liter.
2. Use ◯ for objects that hold less than 1 liter.

Explain Your Thinking Would you use a liter container to fill a swimming pool? Why or why not?

Independent Practice

Remember this is 1 liter.

1. Circle the containers that hold more than 1 liter.

Problem Solving • Reasoning

Using Vocabulary

2. Underline the words that tell you how much a container holds.

3. Circle the words that tell you how long an object is.

cup	liter
centimeter	quart
pint	inch

At Home Ask your child to find items in your house that could hold about 1 liter.

Name_____

Standards
MR **1.0, 1.1, 3.0**

LESSON
12

Problem Solving: Use Measurement

Dawn and Tanya put pebbles, soil, and plants into jars. They are making terrariums.

Sometimes you need to decide which measurement tool to use.

Dawn needs to find out if a plant will fit in her terrarium. What should she use to measure the plant?

a ruler   a balance scale

Think:
A ruler measures length. A balance scale measures weight.

Sometimes you need to add or subtract to solve a measurement problem.

Tanya uses a jar that is 12 inches tall. Dawn uses a jar that is 10 inches tall. How much taller is Tanya's jar than Dawn's jar?

Think:
You need to compare the jars. Subtract to find the difference.

_____ ◯ _____ = _____

_____ inches taller

Guided Practice

Use measurement to solve each problem.

1 Jimmy wants to know how long the side of his picture frame is. What can he use to find out?

_____

Think:
Do I use a ruler or a balance scale?

Draw or write to explain.

2 Becky's pencil holder is 12 inches tall. Taylor's is 7 inches tall. How much taller is Becky's pencil holder?

_____ inches taller

Think:
Do I add or subtract?

3 Asia has seeds and cubes. What can she use to find out which is heavier?

_____

Think:
Do I use a ruler or a balance scale?

4 Matthew fills a pint container with paint. How many cups of paint does the container hold?

_____ cups

Think:
How many cups are in a pint?

480 four hundred eighty

Name_____

Choose a Strategy

Solve each problem.

1 Paige's vase is 11 inches tall. Michele's vase is 7 inches tall. How much taller is Paige's vase?

_____ inches taller

Draw or write to explain.

vase

2 Each ball of clay weighs 1 pound. Nick uses 1 ball. Ella uses 2 balls. How much clay does Ella use for her clay bird?

_____ pounds

clay bird

3 Marco put a sponge animal into water. It grew 4 inches. It is now 6 inches long. How long was the sponge animal before he put it in the water?

_____ inches long

sponge animal

4 Ian fills a jar with 4 cups of blue sand, 1 cup of yellow, and 2 cups of red. How much sand is in his sand art?

_____ cups

sand art

Mixed Practice

Memorize Your Facts

Add or subtract.

1. $14 - 9 =$ ___   2. $9 + 6 =$ ___   3. $4 + 9 =$ ___

4. $13 - 8 =$ ___   5. $12 - 8 =$ ___   6. $10 + 5 =$ ___

7. $\begin{array}{r} 9 \\ +8 \\ \hline \end{array}$ 8. $\begin{array}{r} 15 \\ -\ 7 \\ \hline \end{array}$ 9. $\begin{array}{r} 20 \\ -10 \\ \hline \end{array}$ 10. $\begin{array}{r} 9 \\ +0 \\ \hline \end{array}$ 11. $\begin{array}{r} 3 \\ +7 \\ \hline \end{array}$ 12. $\begin{array}{r} 13 \\ -\ 9 \\ \hline \end{array}$

13. $\begin{array}{r} 6 \\ +7 \\ \hline \end{array}$ 14. $\begin{array}{r} 16 \\ -\ 8 \\ \hline \end{array}$ 15. $\begin{array}{r} 11 \\ -\ 3 \\ \hline \end{array}$ 16. $\begin{array}{r} 7 \\ +7 \\ \hline \end{array}$ 17. $\begin{array}{r} 7 \\ +9 \\ \hline \end{array}$ 18. $\begin{array}{r} 14 \\ -\ 8 \\ \hline \end{array}$

Brain Teaser Balance It

Balance the scale. Draw the shapes on the scale so the same weight is shown on each side.

 1 pound   2 pounds

 3 pounds    4 pounds

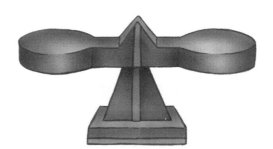

Quick ✓ Check

Check Your Understanding of Lessons 9–12

Number the containers in order from the least
to the greatest amount held.

1.

____   ____   ____

Circle the ones that hold the same amount.

2.

3.

Circle the objects that hold more than 1 liter.

4.   5.   6.

Circle the objects that hold less than 1 liter.

7.   8.   9.

10. Tami fills a quart pitcher with
    juice. How many cups of juice
    does the pitcher hold?

    Draw or write to explain.

____ cups

Name _____

Test Prep • Cumulative Review

Maintaining the Standards

Fill in the ○ for the correct answer.

1 What is another name for fifty-six?

- ○ 5 + 6
- ○ 50 + 6
- ○ 50 + 60
- ○ 500 + 6

2 What number is likely to come next?

46, 48, 50, 52, ____

51   53   54   55
○   ○   ○   ○

3 Choose a sign to make the sentence true.

48 ◯ 84

>   <   =   ¢
○   ○   ○   ○

4 Pang's rope is 17 inches long. He cuts off 5 inches. Now how long is the rope?

- ○ 22 inches
- ○ 13 inches
- ○ 14 inches
- ○ 12 inches

5 What is the value of these coins?

30¢   50¢   55¢   75¢
○   ○   ○   ○

6 Which is a related fact for 6 + 4 = 10?

- ○ 5 + 5 = 10
- ○ 10 − 4 = 6
- ○ 6 − 4 = 2
- ○ 10 + 4 = 14

7 **Explain** two different ways you could show 48¢.

_____

_____

Safe Site

Internet Test Prep
Visit **www.eduplace.com/kids/mhm**
for more *Test Prep Practice*.

Name_____

Chapter Review

Number these units in order from the
greatest to the least.

1.   **pint**   **quart**   **cup**

          _____   _____   _____

---

2. Match each word to the measurement tool used with it.

| **centimeter** | **liter** | **kilogram** |

---

3. Circle the word that shows the unit you
would use to measure a kitten's weight.   **pound**   **inches**

---

4. Use an inch ruler to measure.

                                             _____ inches

---

5. Use a centimeter ruler to measure.

                                          _____ centimeters

Is each object more or less than 1 kilogram?

| 6.  | more

less | 7. | more

less |

Circle the objects that weigh more than 1 pound.
Underline the objects that weigh less than 1 pound.

1.

2.

3.

Circle the ones that hold the same amount.

4.

Circle the objects that hold more than 1 liter.

5.

6.

7.

Circle the objects that hold less than 1 liter.

8.

9.

10.

11. Circle the one that matches the clues.
I have a square top.
I do not have diamonds.

12. Rex pours 1 pint of juice in
the bowl. Then Shane puts in
2 cups of juice. Now how many
cups of juice are in the bowl?

_____ cups

Draw or write to explain.

Name_____

Chapter Test

Use an inch ruler to measure each object.

1.

_____ inches

_____ inches

Use a centimeter ruler to measure each object.

2.

_____ centimeters

_____ centimeters

Does each object weigh more than or less than 1 pound?

3.

more

less

4.

more

less

Is each object more than or less than 1 kilogram?

5.

more

less

6.

more

less

Circle the ones that hold the same amount.

7.

8.

9. Circle the objects that hold more than 1 liter.
Underline the objects that hold less than 1 liter.

10. Circle the letter that matches the clues.
I am taller than the C.
I am shorter than the D.
I have no curves.

A B c D

 Write About It

Bill placed his ruler down like this to measure the yarn.
Does the ruler show the correct measurement? **Explain**.

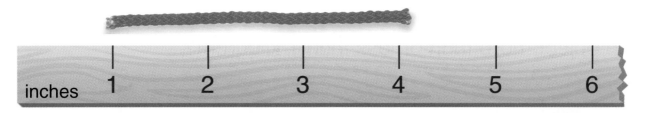

inches   1   2   3   4   5   6

_____

_____

Name _____

Measure Up!

Players
2–4

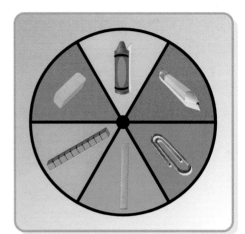

What You Need

cubes

inch ruler

How to Play

① Spin the spinner.

② Use an inch ruler to measure an object like that in your classroom.

③ Take cubes to match that number of inches.

④ Take turns.

⑤ The first player with 20 cubes wins.

Enrichment

Temperature

Circle the picture that shows something hot.

1.

2.

3.

4.

Circle the picture that shows something cold.

5.

6.

7.

8.

MY
BIG
NIGHT

A Read-Aloud Story

written by Harold Mitchell
illustrated by Michele Noiset

Accessing Prior Knowledge

This story will
help you review
• Time concepts

A Math Storybook for

_____

Tonight at 7 o'clock
I'll be acting in a play.
But it's only _____ o'clock.
It's still 6 hours away.

Tonight at 7 o'clock
I'll be singing in a play.
But it's only _____ o'clock.
It's still 5 hours away.

Tonight at 7 o'clock
I'll be dancing in a play.
But it's only _____ o'clock.
It's still 4 hours away.

Tonight at 7 o'clock
I'll be roaring in a play.
But it's only _____ o'clock.
It's still 2 hours away.

495

It's Saturday at _____ o'clock.
It's time to start the play.
I've got butterflies in my stomach.
I wish they'd go away!

It's Saturday at _____ o'clock
I just completed the play.
I smile so wide and take a bow,
While the crowd shouts out, "Hooray!"

Family Letter

Vocabulary

minute A unit of time that is 60 seconds.

hour A unit of time that is 60 minutes.

hour hand The shorter hand on a clock.

minute hand The longer hand on a clock.

Dear Family,

During the next few weeks, our math class will be learning about time.

You can expect to see work that provides practice in telling time.

As we learn about time, you may wish to use the following samples as a guide.

Time

 11:00

 11:30

minute hand

hour hand

Knowing how to tell time can help children with real-life skills.

Sincerely,

Your child's teacher

Order Events

LESSON 1

Learn About It

Some events happen **before** others.
Some events happen **after**.

We make the pizza before we bake it.

We bake the pizza.

We eat the pizza after we bake it.

1 **2** **3**

Guided Practice

Write **1, 2,** and **3** to show the correct order.

1.

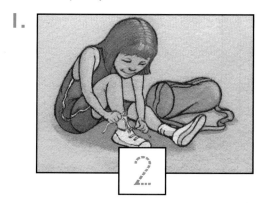

2   **1**   **3**

2.

      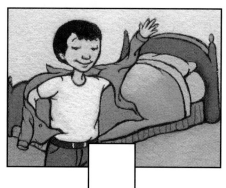

Explain Your Thinking What do you do before lunch at school? What do you do after lunch?

Independent Practice

Write **1**, **2**, and **3** to show the correct order.

1.  2  1  3

2.

3. Draw 3 pictures in order to show something you did today.

1	2	3

Problem Solving • Reasoning

Jake brushed his teeth.

Next, he read a story.

Then he went to bed.

4. What did Jake do before he read a story? _____

5. What did Jake do after he read a story? _____

At Home Discuss some daily routines with your child. Have your child use the words *before* and *after* in telling about events.

LESSON 2 Compare Time

Learn About It

New
Vocabulary

minute
hour

Some activities take about a **minute**.
Other activities take about an **hour**.

It takes about a minute to wash your hands.

A minute is short.

It takes about an hour to wash clothes.

An hour is longer.

Guided Practice

Circle the time it takes to do each activity.

1.

about a minute

about an hour

2.

about a minute

about an hour

3.

about a minute

about an hour

4.

about a minute

about an hour

Explain Your Thinking What are some things
that take more than an hour to do?

Independent Practice

Circle the activity that takes a shorter time to do.

1.

2.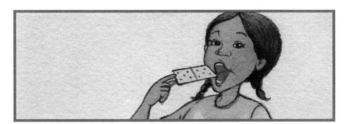

Circle the activity that takes a longer time to do.

3.

4.

Problem Solving•Reasoning

A.    B.    C.

5. Which project took the longest time to make? _____

6. Which project took the shortest time to make? _____

At Home Name two activities and discuss with your child which one takes a shorter time to do. Then discuss about how much time each one takes.

LESSON 3 Hour

Learn About It

The **hour hand** and **minute hand** show time on a clock.

New Vocabulary

hour hand
minute hand
o'clock

It is 4 **o'clock**.

The shorter hand is the hour hand.

The **minute hand** points to 12.

The **hour hand** points to 4.

Guided Practice

Draw the hour hand to show each time.

1.

8 o'clock

2.

2 o'clock

3.

9 o'clock

Write each time.

4.

_____ o'clock

5.

_____ o'clock

6.

_____ o'clock

Explain Your Thinking Where do the hands point on a clock showing 7 o'clock?

Independent Practice

Remember: The shorter hand is the hour hand.

Write each time.

1.

_____ o'clock

2.

_____ o'clock

3.

_____ o'clock

4.

_____ o'clock

5.

_____ o'clock

6.

_____ o'clock

Problem Solving • Reasoning

Using Data

7. How many children eat dinner at 5 o'clock? _____ children

8. How many more children eat dinner at 6 o'clock than at 7 o'clock? _____ children

9. **Write Your Own** Write a question about this graph.

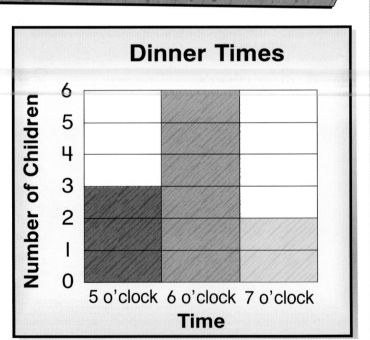

 At Home Have your child practice telling time on the hour. Use a variety of clocks.

	Standards
	MG **1.2**

Half-Hour

New Vocabulary
half-hour

Learn About It

When the minute hand points to the 6, it shows
time on the **half-hour**.

The minute
hand has gone
halfway around
the clock.

2 o'clock   half past 2

Guided Practice

Write each time.

1.

half past __6__

2.

half past _____

3.

half past _____

4.

half past _____

5.

half past _____

6.

half past _____

Explain Your Thinking If the hour hand is halfway between
4 and 5 and the minute hand points to 6, what time is it?

Independent Practice

Write each time.

I.

half past __4__

2.

half past _____

3.

half past _____

4.

half past _____

5.

half past _____

6.

half past _____

7.

half past _____

8.

half past _____

9.

half past _____

Problem Solving • Reasoning

Using Vocabulary

Circle the correct answer.

10. It takes about _____ to comb your hair.

   a minute   an hour

11. When it is 3 o'clock, the _____ points to 12.

   minute hand   hour hand

At Home Help your child practice telling time on the half-hour.

Quick ✓ Check

Check Your Understanding of Lessons 1–4

1. Write **1, 2,** and **3** to show the correct order.

Circle the time it takes to do each activity.

2.

about a minute

about an hour

3.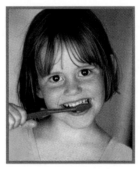

about a minute

about an hour

4. Circle the activity that takes a longer time.

Write each time.

5.

____ o'clock

6.

half past ____

7.

____ o'clock

Name_____

Test Prep • Cumulative Review
Maintaining the Standards

Fill in the ○ for the correct answer.

1 Which one is correct?

23 = 32   32 > 23
○   ○

22 > 23   32 < 23
○   ○

2 Which group of coins has the same value as this group?

○

○

○

○

3 Mark the missing number.

55, 60, ____, 70

61   62   65   69
○   ○   ○   ○

4 Which is heaviest?

○   ○

○   ○

5 **Explain** how you can use an addition fact to solve 17 − 8.

_____

_____

_____

Safe Site

Internet Test Prep
Visit **www.eduplace.com/kids/mhm**
for more *Test Prep Practice.*

Standards
MG **1.2**, SDP **2.1**

LESSON **5** # Write Time Another Way

Learn About It

You can use numbers to write the time.

Review
Vocabulary
minute

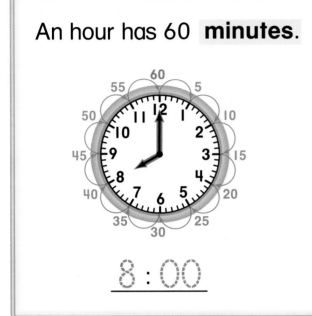

An hour has 60 **minutes**.

A half-hour has 30 minutes.

Half past 8 o'clock is 8:30.

8:00

8:30

Guided Practice

Write each time two ways.

1.

half past __2__

2:30

2.

____ o'clock

___:___

3.

half past ____

___:___

Explain Your Thinking If the minute hand is pointing to 6, is the clock showing the time on the hour or half-hour?

Independent Practice

Write each time two ways.

1.

2:00

2 o'clock

2.

___ : ___

half past ____

3.

___ : ___

half past ____

4.

___ : ___

____ o'clock

5.

___ : ___

half past ____

6.

___ : ___

____ o'clock

Problem Solving • Reasoning

Patterns

7. Write the time each clock shows.

___ : ___   ___ : ___   ___ : ___   ___ : ___

8. **Write About It** Write about the pattern you see above.

At Home Have your child tell you and then write the times shown on some of the clocks in this lesson.

LESSON
6

Digital Clocks

Learn About It

Some clocks show time in a different way.

The two kinds of clocks tell the same time.

Digital clocks have numbers but no hands.

7:00

3:30

Guided Practice

Draw lines to match the clocks.

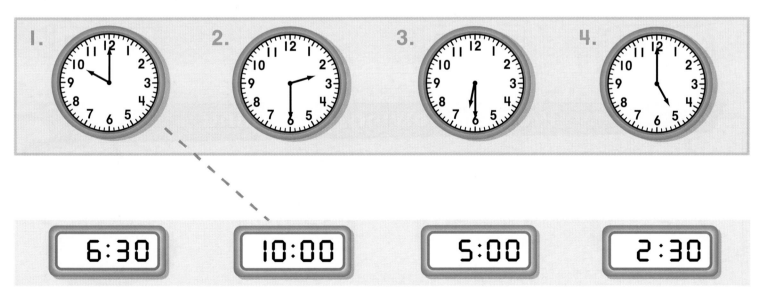

I.

2.

3.

4.

6:30

10:00

5:00

2:30

Explain Your Thinking Do you think it is easier to tell time on a digital clock? Why?

Independent Practice

Draw lines to match the clocks.

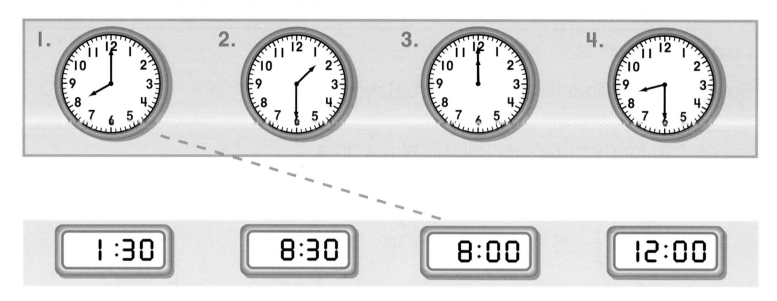

1. 2. 3. 4.

1:30   8:30   8:00   12:00

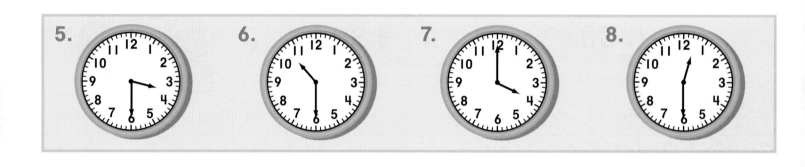

5. 6. 7. 8.

3:30   12:30   4:00   10:30

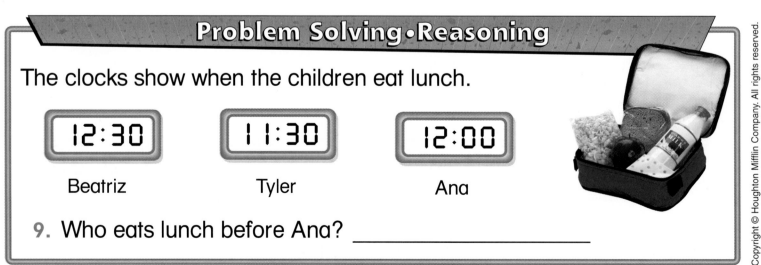

Problem Solving • Reasoning

The clocks show when the children eat lunch.

12:30   11:30   12:00

Beatriz   Tyler   Ana

9. Who eats lunch before Ana? _____

512 five hundred twelve

At Home Help your child compare different kinds of clocks (grandfather clocks, digital clocks, watches, and timers) in your home or neighborhood.

Standards
MG **1.2**, SDP **1.0**

LESSON 7 Practice Telling Time

Learn About It

You can show the same time in different ways.

You can use a clock with hands.

You can use a digital clock.

9:30

You can use words.

half past 9

Guided Practice

Show each time on the two clocks.

1. 8 o'clock

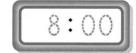
8:00

2. half past 1

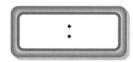

3. 11 o'clock

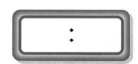

4. half past 5

Explain Your Thinking Why is it important for you to be able to tell time on different kinds of clocks?

Independent Practice

Show the time on the clock.

1. School starts at 8:30.

2. Math class starts at 9:00.

 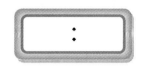

3. We read a story at 10:30.

4. We play at 11:30.

5. Lunchtime is at 12:00.

6. School is over at 3:30.

Problem Solving • Reasoning

7. Fill in the times on the schedule.

spelling	_____ : _____
music	_____ : _____
science	_____ : _____

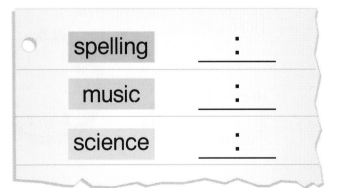

spelling   science

`1:00`

music

At Home With your child, find signs that tell when stores, libraries, and other places are open. Help your child read the times.

Hands-On Activity · LESSON 8

Name _____

Elapsed Time

Standards
NS **1.5**, MG **1.2**
MR **1.2**

Learn About It

A clock can help you find out how long an activity lasts.

Start

End

You practice for 1 hour.

Guided Practice

Use a clock. Move the hands to show each time.
Write how long the activity lasts.

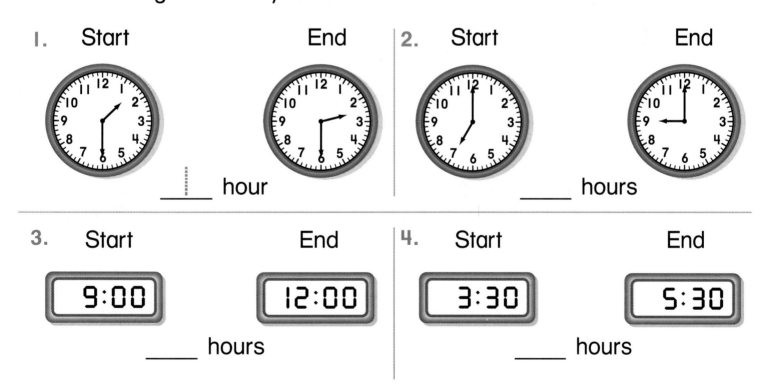

1. Start   End

_____ hour

2. Start   End

_____ hours

3. Start   End

| 9:00 | 12:00 |

_____ hours

4. Start   End

| 3:30 | 5:30 |

_____ hours

Explain Your Thinking How does moving the hands on a clock help you find out how long an activity lasts?

Independent Practice

Show when each activity started or ended.
Use a clock if you want.

	Start	How long?	End
1.		I hour swimming	
2.	⬚ : ⬚	2 hours on the boat	4:00
3.		I hour finding shells	
4.	6:30	I hour flying a kite	⬚ : ⬚

Problem Solving•Reasoning

✏️ **Write About It**

5. Susie has these coins.
   Can she buy a toy that
   costs 45¢? Explain.

 At Home Discuss with your child when activities start and end. Help your child find out how long each activity lasts.

Name_____

Standards
MG **1.2**, MR **1.0**, **1.1**, **1.2**, **2.2**, **3.0**

LESSON 9

Problem Solving: Use Models to Act It Out

You can use models to act out problems.

The children do many activities at Field Day. The sack race starts at 1:00. It lasts for 1 hour. What time does the sack race end?

Understand

What do you already know?

Race starts _____ : _____

Lasts how long? _____

Plan

Circle what you would use to act out this problem.

A clock

Counters

Solve

Start at _____ : _____ .

Move the minute hand _____ hour.

The sack race ends at _____ : _____ .

Look Back

Explain why your answer makes sense.

Guided Practice

Solve each problem.
Use a clock if you want.

Remember to use the 4 steps.

① The ball toss starts at 12:30. It lasts for 1 hour. What time does it end?

Think: Will the hour hand move one hour or one half-hour?

Draw or write to explain.

_1 : 30_

② The Wheelbarrow race starts at 9:00. It ends at 11:00. How long does the race last?

Think: How many times does the minute hand go around the clock?

_____ hours

③ The hoop contest takes 2 hours. It ends at 4:00. What time does it start?

Think: How many hours do I go back?

_____ : _____

④ Field Day starts at 12:00. It ends at 4:00. How many hours does it last?

Think: How many hours are between 12 and 4?

_____ hours

At Home Show your child a starting time on a clock and tell him or her the length of an activity. Have your child tell you the ending time.

Name_____

Choose a Strategy

Solve.

① 10 teams are in the jump-rope contest. It starts at 10:30 and ends at 11:30. How long does it last?

_____ hour

Draw or write to explain.

jump rope

② A team must sign up for the relay race one hour before it starts. The race starts at 3:00. At what time should Courtney's team sign up?

_____ : _____

relay race

③ 18 children are on 2 teams in the long jump. There are 4 more children on Team 1 than on Team 2. How many children are on each team?

_____ Team 1   _____ Team 2

long jump

④ The ring toss starts 1 hour before 10:00. It ends at 11:00. How long does the ring toss last?

_____ hours

ring toss

Mixed Practice

Memorize
Your Facts

Find each sum or difference.

1. 8 + 6 = ___
2. 13 − 7 = ___
3. 9 + 4 = ___

4. 14 − 5 = ___
5. 15 − 5 = ___
6. 10 + 7 = ___

7. 9
  +3

8. 18
  − 9

9. 14
  − 7

10. 8
  +5

11. 7
  +8

12. 17
  − 9

13. 6
  −6

14. 10
  + 9

15. 4
  +8

16. 10
  − 2

17. 12
  − 9

18. 9
  +7

19. 10
  +10

20. 16
  − 8

21. 9
  +8

22. 7
  +6

23. 12
  − 8

24. 12
  − 5

 ## Brain Teaser Movie Time

Judy has dance class at 2:00.
Class is 1 hour long.
Which movies could Judy go
to see after dance class?

Movie	Start Time
THE STAR	2:30
SCHOOL DAYS	3:30
SPRING	4:00

_____

Safe Site

Internet Brain Teasers
Visit **www.eduplace.com/kids/mhm**
for more *Brain Teasers.*

Name_____

Check Your Understanding of Lessons 5–9

Write each time two ways.

1.    ____ : ____

   ____ o'clock

2.    ____ : ____

   half past ____

Draw lines to match the clocks.

3.    4.    5.    6.

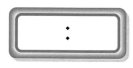         

4:00   8:30   10:00   1:30

7. Show half past 3 on two clocks.

8. Write how long the activity lasts.

   Start   End

   5:30   7:30

   ____ hours

9. The movie starts at 5:00.
   It lasts 3 hours.
   What time does it end?

   ____ : ____

   Draw or write to explain.

Name _____

Test Prep • Cumulative Review
Maintaining the Standards

Fill in the ○ for the correct answer.

1 Which shape has 4 corners?

○

○

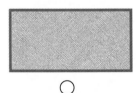
○

○

2 Which one shows 34?

○

○

○

○

3 Which number is the same as 90 + 6?

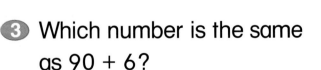
66   69   96   906
○   ○   ○   ○

4 Mark the number seventy-two.

2   72   77   82
○   ○   ○   ○

5 Which numbers are in order from least to greatest?

○ 32, 33, 34

○ 33, 32, 34

○ 34, 33, 32

○ 34, 32, 33

6 **Explain** how to find 10 less than 63.

_____

_____

_____

Safe Site

Internet Test Prep
Visit **www.eduplace.com/kids/mhm**
for more *Test Prep Practice.*

Calendar

New
Vocabulary
calendar

Learn About It

A **calendar** shows months, weeks, and days.

March

Sunday	Monday	Tuesday	Wednesday	Thursday	Friday	Saturday
	1	2	3	4	5	6
7	8	9	10	11	12	13
14	15	16	17	18	19	20
21	22	23	24	25	26	27
28	29	30	31			

Guided Practice

1. The name of the month is _____ March _____ .

2. How many days are in a week? _____

3. What day of the week is March 12? _____

4. The date of the fourth Thursday in March is _____ .

5. What is the date of the last Tuesday in March? _____

Explain Your Thinking Are there more Tuesdays
or Fridays on this calendar?

Independent Practice

Fill in the calendar for this month.
Answer the questions.

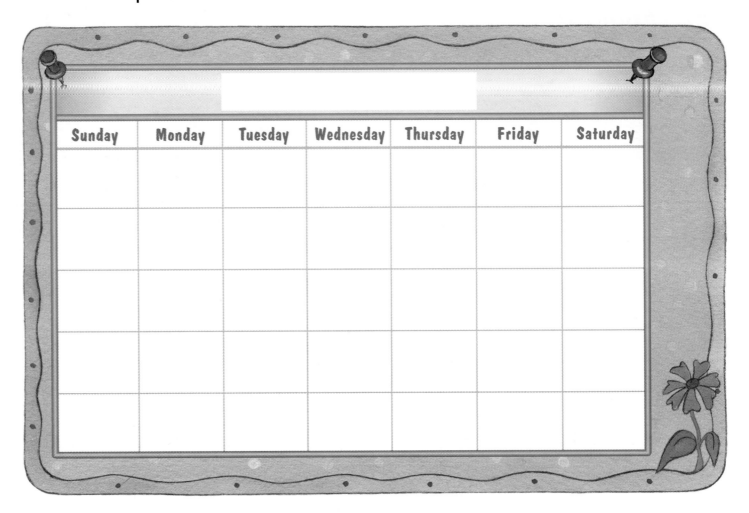

Sunday	Monday	Tuesday	Wednesday	Thursday	Friday	Saturday

1. Color today ▭ .

2. Color yesterday ▭ .

3. Color tomorrow ▭ .

4. Color the first Sunday ▭ .

5. How many Mondays are in this month? _____

6. What day of the week is the ninth? _____

7. What is the date on the second Friday? _____

8. How many days are in this month? _____

At Home Ask your child to name the dates of all the Wednesdays shown on the calendar.

Use a Calendar

Learn About It

There are 12 months in each year.

Here are the months of the year in order.

APRIL

Sunday	Monday	Tuesday	Wednesday	Thursday	Friday	Saturday
		1	2	3	4	5
6	7	8	9	10	11	12
13	14	15	16	17	18	19
20	21	22	23	24	25	26
27	28	29	30			

January
February
March
April
May
June
July
August
September
October
November
December

Guided Practice

Use the calendar and list of months.
Answer the questions.

1. What day of the week is April 11? _____Friday_____

2. How many Tuesdays are in this month? _____

3. What is the last month of the year? _____

4. What month comes before June? _____

Explain Your Thinking What months come
between August and December?

Independent Practice

Use the calendars to answer each question.

May

Sun.	Mon.	Tues.	Wed.	Thurs.	Fri.	Sat.
			1	2	3	
4	5	6	7	8	9	10
11	12	13	14	15	16	17
18	19	20	21	22	23	24
25	26	27	28	29	30	31

June

Sun.	Mon.	Tues.	Wed.	Thurs.	Fri.	Sat.
1	2	3	4	5	6	7
8	9	10	11	12	13	14
15	16	17	18	19	20	21
22	23	24	25	26	27	28
29	30					

July

Sun.	Mon.	Tues.	Wed.	Thurs.	Fri.	Sat.
			1	2	3	4	5
6	7	8	9	10	11	12
13	14	15	16	17	18	19
20	21	22	23	24	25	26
27	28	29	30	31		

1. Which of these months has the fewest days?  June

2. Which month has 5 Wednesdays? _____

3. Field Day is June 6. Color it ( ) .

4. Cinco de Mayo is May 5. Color it ✏ .

5. Color all Fridays in July ✏ .

6. Color May 26 ✏ .

Problem Solving•Reasoning

Number Sense

Use the calendar to find each sum.
Then write the addends.

7. ____ + ____ = [   ] ⟵ Second Friday in May

8. ____ + ____ = [   ] ⟵ First Wednesday in June

At Home Using your home calendar for this month and next month, help your child find your family's special days.

Name_____

Standards
MG **1.2**, MR **1.0, 1.1**

LESSON
12

Problem Solving:
Use a Table

The Wilsons are having a family reunion. People are coming from all over the country to meet and have fun.

Arrival Schedule	
Person	**Time**
Grandma	12:00
Uncle Ken	1:30
Aunt Nora	3:00
Cousin Eva	6:00

You can use a table to get information.

Dan picks up Grandma at the airport. How many hours will they have to wait to pick up Aunt Nora?

Grandma _____:_____

Aunt Nora _____:_____ _____ hours

Think: Find the times in the table. Use a clock to show the times.

You can use a table to help you solve problems.

Molly picks up Cousin Eva at the train station. It takes them 1 hour to drive to the reunion. When will they get to the reunion?

Cousin Eva _____:_____

1 hour later _____:_____

Think: Find the time on the table. Add 1 hour to that time.

Guided Practice

Use the table to solve each problem.

| Friday Schedule | |
Activity	Time
Sign in	8:00
Boat trip	9:00
Lunch	12:00
Soccer game	2:00
Dinner	6:00

1 Cathy signs in at 8:00. How much time does she have until the boat trip?

Think: What time is the boat trip?

Draw or write to explain.

_____ hour

2 What activity starts 3 hours before lunch?

Think: What time is lunch?

_____

3 How many hours are there between lunch and dinner?

Think: What time should you start with?

_____ hours

4 What activity begins 4 hours before dinner?

Think: What time is dinner?

_____

At Home Have your child make a schedule showing his or her activities for one day. Help your child use that schedule to determine the time between events.

Name_____

Choose a Strategy

Solve. Use the table if you need to.

How Family Arrived	
Airplane	8
Car	9
Bus	15
Train	12

① The Dorfs traveled by airplane. They left at 2:00. They arrived at 5:00. How long was their flight?

_____ hours

Draw or write to explain.

airplane

② Eight children traveled by train. How many adults did they travel with on the train?

_____ adults

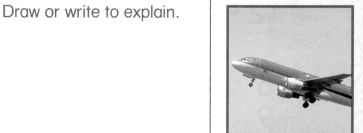
train

③ The Smiths traveled by bus. The Andersons traveled by car. How many more people traveled by bus than by car?

_____ more people

bus

④ Sue's aunt arrived before her uncle. Her cousin arrived after her uncle and before her brother. Who arrived second?

_____

car

Name

Name _____

Test Prep • Cumulative Review

Maintaining the Standards

Fill in the ○ for the correct answer.

1 Mark what is likely to come next in the pattern.

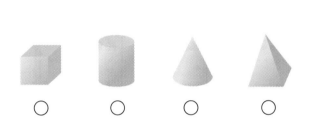

○   ○   ○   ○

---

2 Choose a sign to make this sentence true.

$$64 \bigcirc 84$$

<   >   =   –

○   ○   ○   ○

---

3 Mark the related addition fact.

$$14 - 6 = 8$$

○ $8 - 6 = 2$

○ $14 + 6 = 20$

○ $8 + 6 = 14$

○ $14 - 8 = 20$

4 Mark the one in which the circle is to the right of the square.

○

○

○

○

---

5 **Explain** how you can estimate how many frogs are shown.

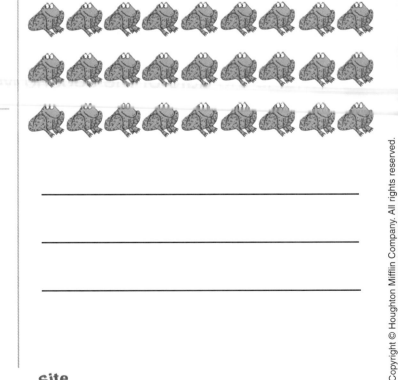

_____

_____

_____

Safe Site

Internet Test Prep
Visit **www.eduplace.com/kids/mhm**
for more *Test Prep Practice.*

Name_____

Chapter Review

1. Show 4 **o'clock**.
   Draw the **minute hand** .
   Draw the **hour hand** .

2. Circle the time it takes.

about a minute

about an hour

3. Write the time.

half past _____

4. Write **1, 2,** and **3** to show the correct order.

Write each time two ways.

5.    _____ : _____

   _____ o'clock

6.    _____ : _____

   half past _____

Show each time on the two clocks.

7. half past 6

8. 11 o'clock

Draw lines to match the clocks.

1.  2. 3. 4.

| 4:30 | 1:00 | 9:00 | 2:30 |

5. On what day of the week is January 8?

_____

6. What is the date of the third Thursday?

_____

January

Sun.	Mon.	Tues.	Wed.	Thurs.	Fri.	Sat.
			1	2	3	4
5	6	7	8	9	10	11
12	13	14	15	16	17	18
19	20	21	22	23	24	25
26	27	28	29	30	31	

Write how long the activity lasts.

7. Start   End

____ hours

8. Start   End

| 7:00 | 10:00 |

____ hours

Use the schedule.

9. Dance class is for one hour. When does it end? ____:____

10. Holly plays for 1 hour before bed. What time does she start playing?

____:____

Holly's Afternoon	
Activity	**Time**
Dance	4:00
Homework	6:30
Bedtime	8:30

Name_____

Chapter Test

1. Write **1, 2,** and **3** to show the correct order.

---

2. Circle the time it takes.

about a minute

about an hour

3. Write how long the activity lasts.

Start	End
6:00	8:00

_____ hours

Write each time.

4.  _____ o'clock

5.  half past _____

Show each time two ways.

6. half past 6

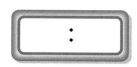 

7. 1 o'clock

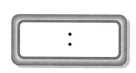 

Use the calendar.

8. What day of the week is November 12?

   _____

9. What date is the fourth Thursday?

   _____

November						
Sun.	Mon.	Tues.	Wed.	Thurs.	Fri.	Sat.
		1	2	3	4	5
6	7	8	9	10	11	12
13	14	15	16	17	18	19
20	21	22	23	24	25	26
27	28	29	30			

Use the schedule.

10. Reading lasts 3 hours.
    When does it end?

    _____ : _____

Class Schedule	
Class	Time
Reading	8:30
Lunch	12:00
Math	1:00

Write About It

The ball game started at 2:00.
It ended at 6:00.
Austin said that it lasted 3 hours.

Is Austin right or wrong? **Explain**.

_____

_____

_____

Name _____

Spinning Time

What You Need

counters ● ○

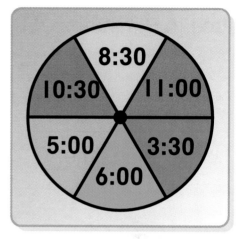

How to Play

① Choose ● or ○ .

② Spin one of the spinners.

③ Find that time in a box on the game board below.

④ Place one of your counters on that box. If the box is taken, lose a turn.

⑤ The player with the most boxes wins.

Name _____

Standards
MG **1.2**, NS **2.4**

Enrichment

Time to Five Minutes

Use what you know about counting by fives to tell time to 5 minutes.

2:20

20 minutes after 2

Write each time.

1.

___ : ___

2.

___ : ___

3.

___ : ___

4.

___ : ___

5.

___ : ___

6.

___ : ___

7.

___ : ___

8.

___ : ___

9.

___ : ___

Two-digit Addition and Subtraction

Assessing Prior Knowledge

This Story Will Help You Review
- Counting by tens
- Tens and ones

Squirrel's Store

A Read-Aloud Story

written by Laura Black

illustrated by Cardona Studio

A Math Storybook for

_____

Good day, Mr. Elephant.
What will you buy?
That's a lot of peanuts
For just one guy!

How many peanuts will Mr. Elephant buy? _____

Good day, Mrs. Pig.
What's in your cart?
Stocking up on corn,
That's pretty smart!

How many ears of corn will Mrs. Pig buy? _____

Good day, little birds.
How is your mother?
You can hold one bag,
And your sister the other!

How many seeds will the little birds buy? _____

Good day, Mr. Dog.
What will it be?
When you buy that many bones,
You get one for free!

How many bones will Mr. Dog take home? _____

Good day, little rabbit.
What a tricky way to shop!
With so many carrots,
It must be hard to hop!

How many carrots will the little rabbit buy? _____

It's been a very good day
At my little store.
Now it's time to get my things
And head out the door!

How many acorns will Squirrel take home? _____

Family Letter

Vocabulary

addend Each of the numbers added in an addition problem.

sum The answer to an addition problem.

difference The answer to a subtraction problem.

Dear Family,

During the next few weeks, our math class will be learning and practicing addition and subtraction of two-digit numbers.

You can expect to see work that provides practice with addition and subtraction of numbers through 99.

As we learn how to add and subtract two-digit numbers, you may wish to use the following sample as a guide.

Adding Two-Digit Numbers

Tens	Ones
1	4
+ 1	2
2	6

$$\begin{array}{r} 1\ 4 \\ +\ 1\ 2 \\ \hline 2\ 6 \end{array}$$

Subtracting Two-Digit Numbers

Tens	Ones
1	4
− 1	2
	2

$$\begin{array}{r} 1\ 4 \\ -\ 1\ 2 \\ \hline 2 \end{array}$$

Knowing how to add and subtract two-digit numbers can help children learn how to solve more complex problems.

Sincerely,

Your child's teacher

LESSON 1
Mental Math: Add Tens

Learn About It

When you add **tens,** you can think of an addition fact.

3 tens + 5 tens = __8__ tens

_30_ + _50_ = _80_

3 + 5 = 8, so
30 + 50 = 80.

Guided Practice

Write the numbers.
Find each sum.

1.

Think:
4 + 4 = 8

4 tens + 4 tens = __8__ tens

_40_ + _40_ = _80_

2.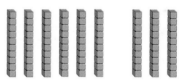

6 tens + 3 tens = ____ tens

___ + ___ = ___

3.

7 tens + 2 tens = ____ tens

____ + ___ = ____

4.

4 tens + 5 tens = ____ tens

____ + ___ = ____

Explain Your Thinking How does knowing 4 + 5 = 9
help you solve 40 + 50?

Independent Practice

Write the numbers. Add.

1.

   3 tens + 6 tens = __9__ tens

   __30__ + __60__ = __90__

2.

   5 tens + 1 ten = ____ tens

   ___ + ___ = ___

3. 3 tens + 4 tens = ____ tens

   ___ + ___ = ___

4. 2 tens + 7 tens = ____ tens

   ___ + ___ = ___

5. 5 tens + 4 tens = ____ tens

   ___ + ___ = ___

6. 2 tens + 6 tens = ____ tens

   ___ + ___ = ___

7. 5 tens + 3 tens = ____ tens

   ___ + ___ = ___

8. 1 ten + 8 tens = ____ tens

   ___ + ___ = ___

Problem Solving • Reasoning

Algebra Readiness • Missing Addends

9. Patty had 30 buttons. She buys some more. Now she has 60 buttons. How many buttons did she buy?

   _____ buttons

Draw or write to explain.

At Home Ask your child to explain how to find 30 + 50.

Name _____

Standards
NS **2.6** MG **2.1,**
MR **1.2**

Add One-Digit Numbers

Learn About It

When one **addend** is a two-digit number, you need to add the ones first.

Find 45 + 3.

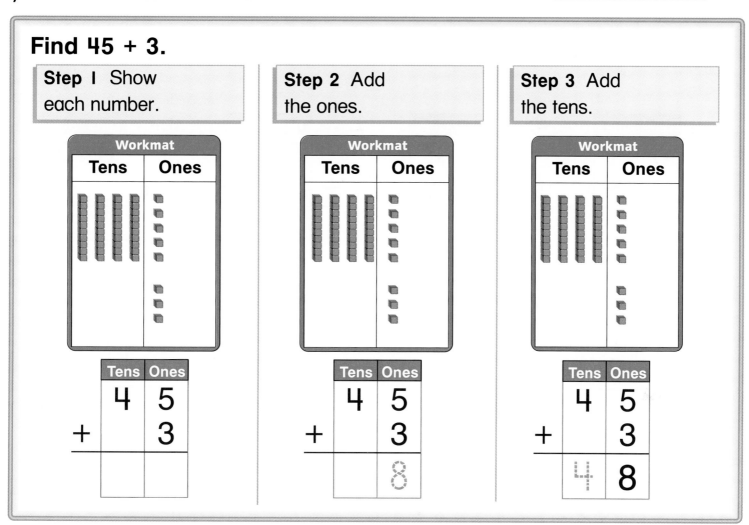

Step 1 Show each number.

Step 2 Add the ones.

Step 3 Add the tens.

Guided Practice

Use Workmat 4 with ▭▭▭▭ and ▪. Add.

1.
Tens	Ones
3	5
+	4
3	9

Think: First, I add 5 + 4.

2.
Tens	Ones
6	7
+	2

Think: First. I add 7 + 2.

Explain Your Thinking How can you count on to find 65 + 2?

Independent Practice

Use Workmat 4 with and .
Write each sum.

1.
Tens	Ones
4	2
+	6
4	8

2.
Tens	Ones
5	4
+	3

3.
Tens	Ones
2	0
+	8

4.
Tens	Ones
3	8
+	1

5.
Tens	Ones
6	4
+	5

6.
Tens	Ones
4	3
+	6

7.
Tens	Ones
7	2
+	7

8.
Tens	Ones
8	3
+	4

9.
Tens	Ones
9	1
+	8

10.
Tens	Ones
7	2
+	6

11.
Tens	Ones
5	6
+	3

12.
Tens	Ones
9	4
+	4

Problem Solving • Reasoning

Visual Thinking

13. Circle the shapes used to make this picture.

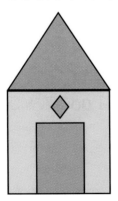

At Home Have your child pick a number less than 8.
Then have your child add that number to 52.

Hands-On Activity

LESSON 3

Name _____

Standards
NS **2.6**
MR **1.2, 2.0**

Add Two-Digit Numbers

Learn About It

You can add two-digit numbers.

Find 35 + 12.

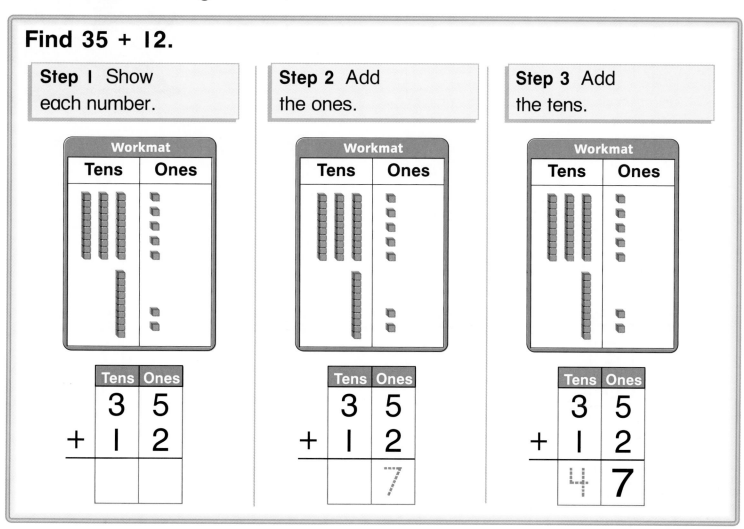

Step 1 Show each number.

Step 2 Add the ones.

Step 3 Add the tens.

Guided Practice

Use Workmat 4 with ▭▭▭ and ▪. Add.

1.
Tens	Ones
2	4
+ 7	5
9	9

Think: First, I add 4 + 5.

2.
Tens	Ones
6	5
+ 3	2

Think: First, I add 5 + 2.

Explain Your Thinking How does knowing addition facts help you add two-digit numbers?

Independent Practice

Use Workmat 4 with 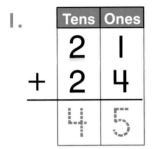 and ▪.
Write each sum.

Remember to start with the ones.

1.
Tens	Ones
2	1
+ 2	4
4	5

2.
Tens	Ones
4	2
+ 3	7

3.
Tens	Ones
3	2
+ 1	3

4.
Tens	Ones
1	8
+ 2	1

5.
Tens	Ones
7	5
+ 1	0

6.
Tens	Ones
3	4
+ 4	5

7.
Tens	Ones
5	5
+ 3	3

8.
Tens	Ones
4	2
+ 1	6

9.
Tens	Ones
2	3
+ 4	2

10.
Tens	Ones
6	1
+ 2	6

11.
Tens	Ones
7	2
+ 1	4

Problem Solving·Reasoning

Number Sense

Circle the one with the greatest sum.

12. 32 + 25

    32 + 15

    32 + 45

13. 44 + 11

    44 + 31

    44 + 21

14. 53 + 14

    53 + 44

    53 + 34

 15. **Write About It** How do you know which sum is greatest?

At Home Have your child add two-digit numbers in which the tens and ones are both less than 5.

Standards
NS **2.6**, MR **1.1**

LESSON 4 Different Ways to Add

Learn About It

There are different ways to add.

$$\begin{array}{r} 50 \\ +40 \\ \hline 90 \end{array}$$

I used mental math. 5 + 4

$$\begin{array}{r} 35 \\ +14 \\ \hline 49 \end{array}$$

I used paper and pencil.

$$\begin{array}{r} 56 \\ +30 \\ \hline 86 \end{array}$$

I used tens and ones blocks.

Guided Practice

Choose a way to add.
Write each sum.

1.

Tens	Ones
5	0
+ 2	0
7	0

2.

Tens	Ones
3	4
+	3

3.

Tens	Ones
2	0
+ 6	3

4.

Tens	Ones
3	3
+ 4	6

5.
$$\begin{array}{r} 67 \\ + 2 \\ \hline \end{array}$$

6.
$$\begin{array}{r} 16 \\ +52 \\ \hline \end{array}$$

7.
$$\begin{array}{r} 40 \\ +30 \\ \hline \end{array}$$

8.
$$\begin{array}{r} 80 \\ + 3 \\ \hline \end{array}$$

9.
$$\begin{array}{r} 50 \\ +20 \\ \hline \end{array}$$

Explain Your Thinking Which way did you choose to add for Exercise 9? Why?

Independent Practice

Choose a way to add.
Write each sum.

1.

Tens	Ones
1	8
+ 4	1
5	9

2.

Tens	Ones
5	3
+ 4	4

3. 58
   +10

4. 14
   +83

5. 72
   + 7

6. 36
   + 0

7. 45
   + 2

8. 10
   +50

9. 43
   +35

10. 40
    +46

11. 24
    +55

12. 85
    + 4

13. $85 + 3 =$ _____

14. $67 + 2 =$ _____

15. $40 + 50 =$ _____

16. $58 + 1 =$ _____

17. $10 + 40 =$ _____

18. $20 + 60 =$ _____

Problem Solving • Reasoning

19. Maria has 35 stickers in one book. She has 54 stickers in another book. How many stickers does she have in all?

_____ stickers

Draw or write to explain.

At Home Ask your child to solve 83 + 2 and explain how she or he got the answer.

LESSON 5

Practice Two-Digit Addition

Learn About It

When you add two digit-numbers,
begin with the ones.

Find 53 + 26.

Step 1 Add the ones.	**Step 2** Add the tens.
53 +26 9	53 +26 79

First I do
3 + 6.

Guided Practice

Write each sum.

1. 80
   +12
   92

2. 40
   +50

3. 56
   + 2

4. 70
   + 4

5. 41
   +35

6. 65
   + 3

7. 20
   + 5

8. 84
   +13

9. 50
   +27

10. 30
   +60

11. 17 + 2 = ___

12. 85 + 3 = ___

13. 40 + 10 = ___

14. 10 + 80 = ___

15. 64 + 3 = ___

16. 20 + 20 = ___

Explain Your Thinking How can you find the
answer to Exercise 16 by using mental math?

Independent Practice

Add. Color sums less than 50 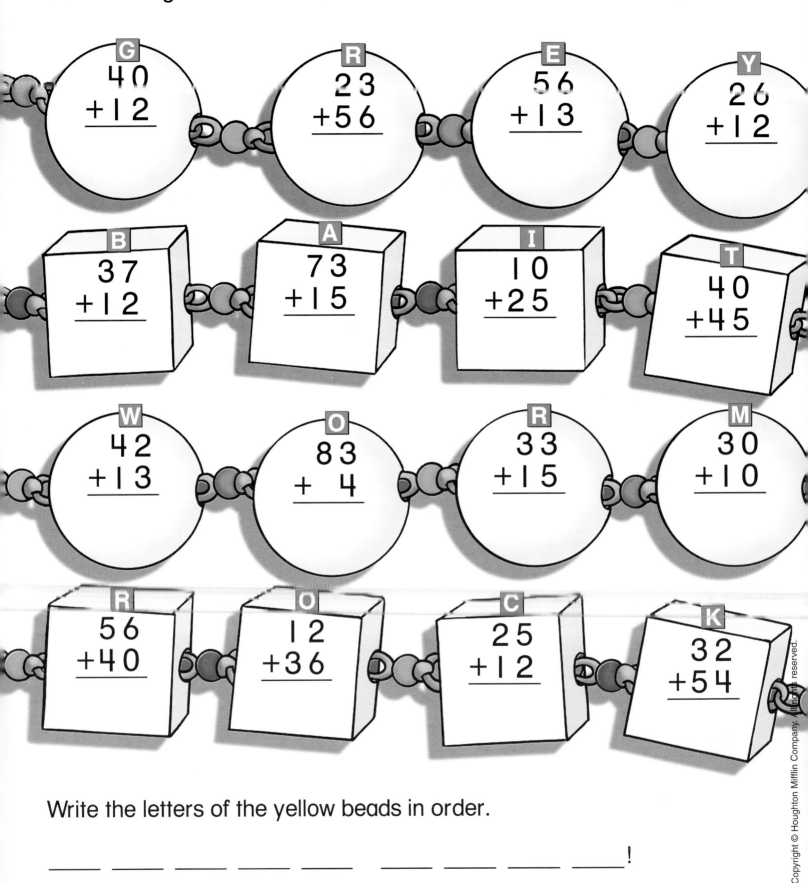.
Color sums greater than 50 ( ).

G
40
+12

R
23
+56

E
56
+13

Y
26
+12

B
37
+12

A
73
+15

I
10
+25

T
40
+45

W
42
+13

O
83
+ 4

R
33
+15

M
30
+10

R
56
+40

O
12
+36

C
25
+12

K
32
+54

Write the letters of the yellow beads in order.

____ ____ ____ ____ ____ ____ ____ ____ ____ !

At Home Ask your child to write a two-digit addition problem that has an answer less than 50.

Name _____

Problem Solving: Make a Table

Standards
NS 2.6, SDP 1.0, 1.2
MR 1.0, 1.1, 2.2

You can make a table to help you solve problems. Trevor collects seashells. Write the numbers in the table. How many shells in all did he find in the water and the grass?

Trevor's Shell Collection	
Place Found	**Number**
Water	
Grass	
Beach	

Understand

What do you already know?

_____ found in water

_____ found in grass

Plan

Circle how you would solve this problem.

add   subtract

Solve

Use the table.

_____ ◯ _____ = _____ in all

Look Back

Did you answer the question? How do you know?

Guided Practice

Solve. Use the answers to complete
the table.

Sandy Beach	
Date	Number of Shells Trevor Found
June 20	21
June 24	41
July 3	
July 7	

1 Trevor found 12 more shells on July 7 than June 24. How many shells did he find on July 7?

_____ shells

Think: How many were found on June 24?

Draw or write to explain.

2 Trevor found 13 more shells on July 3 than June 20. How many shells did he find on July 3?

_____ shells

Think: How many were found on June 20?

3 How many shells did Trevor find on June 24 and July 7 altogether?

_____ shells

Think: Do I add or subtract?

At Home Help your child make a table showing a collection of toys, books, or other items.

Name_____

Choose a Strategy

Solve.
Complete the table.

Items At The Beach	
Items	**Number**
Fins	
Beach balls	16
Umbrellas	31
Sunglasses	

1 Vic saw 8 fewer fins than beach balls. How many fins does he see?

_____ fins

Draw or write to explain.

fins

2 Each beach ball is big or small. There are 4 more big than small. How many of each size are there?

_____ big   _____ small

beach ball

3 People bring 25 more beach umbrellas. How many umbrellas are there now?

_____ beach umbrellas

beach umbrella

4 There are 41 more sunglasses than fins. How many sunglasses are there?

_____ sunglasses

sunglasses

Mixed Practice

Find each sum or difference.

1. $\begin{array}{r} 1\,0 \\ +4\,0 \\ \hline \end{array}$

2. $\begin{array}{r} 1\,8 \\ -\ 8 \\ \hline \end{array}$

3. $\begin{array}{r} 1\,6 \\ -\ 9 \\ \hline \end{array}$

4. $\begin{array}{r} 3\,2 \\ +\ 6 \\ \hline \end{array}$

5. $\begin{array}{r} 1\,3 \\ +5\,4 \\ \hline \end{array}$

6. $\begin{array}{r} 2\,0 \\ -1\,0 \\ \hline \end{array}$

7. $\begin{array}{r} 1\,3 \\ -\ 5 \\ \hline \end{array}$

8. $\begin{array}{r} 5\,1 \\ +\ 8 \\ \hline \end{array}$

9. $\begin{array}{r} 1\,4 \\ -\ 8 \\ \hline \end{array}$

10. $\begin{array}{r} 6\,7 \\ +3\,1 \\ \hline \end{array}$

11. $\begin{array}{r} 1\,7 \\ -\ 8 \\ \hline \end{array}$

12. $\begin{array}{r} 4\,5 \\ +1\,3 \\ \hline \end{array}$

13. $\begin{array}{r} 1\,5 \\ -\ 6 \\ \hline \end{array}$

14. $\begin{array}{r} 1\,3 \\ -\ 7 \\ \hline \end{array}$

15. $\begin{array}{r} 3\,6 \\ +5\,3 \\ \hline \end{array}$

16. $\begin{array}{r} 5\,4 \\ +\ 3 \\ \hline \end{array}$

17. $\begin{array}{r} 1\,9 \\ -\ 9 \\ \hline \end{array}$

18. $\begin{array}{r} 6\,4 \\ +1\,3 \\ \hline \end{array}$

19. $\begin{array}{r} 2\,5 \\ +3\,4 \\ \hline \end{array}$

20. $\begin{array}{r} 1\,5 \\ -\ 8 \\ \hline \end{array}$

Brain Teaser Secret Code

$10 + \bigcirc = 40$

$\star + \bigcirc = 50$

How much is $\bigcirc$? ____

How much is $\star$? ____

Safe Site

Internet Brain Teasers
Visit www.eduplace.com/kids/mhm
for more *Brain Teasers*.

Name_____

Check Your Understanding of Lessons 1–6

Write the numbers. Add.

1. 6 tens + 3 tens = _____ tens

   _____ + _____ = _____

2. 3 tens + 5 tens = _____ tens

   _____ + _____ = _____

Add.

3.
```
  50
+  5
----
```

4.
```
  31
+  6
----
```

5.
```
  85
+  2
----
```

6.
```
  42
+  7
----
```

7.
```
  26
+  3
----
```

8.
```
  30
+ 50
----
```

9.
```
  40
+ 30
----
```

10.
```
  58
+ 20
----
```

11.
```
  74
+ 14
----
```

12.
```
  36
+ 21
----
```

13.
```
  65
+ 12
----
```

14.
```
  83
+ 15
----
```

15.
```
  22
+ 46
----
```

16.
```
  63
+ 15
----
```

17.
```
  71
+ 14
----
```

Use the answer to complete the table.

18. Brittany has the same number of yellow stamps as she has red and blue stamps altogether. How many yellow stamps does she have?

_____ yellow stamps

Stamps	
Color	**Number**
Red	45
Blue	52
Yellow	

Test Prep • Cumulative Review

Maintaining the Standards

Fill in the ○ for the correct answer.

Use the table for Exercises 1–2.

Books on Shelf	
Type	**Number**
Science	28
Joke	5
Story	11

1 How many more story books are there than joke books?

16   8   7   6
○   ○   ○   ○

2 How many science books and story books are there in all?

39   33   16   6
○   ○   ○   ○

3 Add.

$$\begin{array}{r} 53 \\ +26 \\ \hline \end{array}$$

33   39   79   89
○   ○   ○   ○

4 Zach's game is before 5:00. It is after 3:00. Which could be the time when Zach's game starts?

○ 2:30

○ 3:00

○ 4:00

○ 6:00

5 Kris has 1 quarter, 2 dimes, and 4 pennies. Does she have enough money to buy a kite for 50¢?

Explain how you know.

_____

_____

_____

_____

_____

Safe Site

Internet Test Prep
Visit **www.eduplace.com/kids/mhm**
for more *Test Prep Practice*.

Mental Math: Subtract Tens

Review Vocabulary

difference

Learn About It

When you subtract tens, you can think of a subtraction fact.

   6 tens − 4 tens = __2__ tens

60 − 40 = 20

6 − 4 = 2, so 60 − 40 = 20

Guided Practice

Write the numbers.
Find each difference.

1.    **Think:** 8 − 3 = 5

8 tens − 3 tens = __5__ tens

80 − 30 = 50

2.

7 tens − 4 tens = ____ tens

___ − ___ = ___

3.

9 tens − 5 tens = ____ tens

___ − ___ = ___

4.

9 tens − 3 tens = ____ tens

___ − ___ = ___

Explain Your Thinking How does knowing 9 − 3 = 6 help you solve 90 − 30?

Independent Practice

Write the numbers. Subtract.

1. 9 tens − 6 tens = __3__ tens

   _90_ − _60_ = _30_

2. 7 tens − 5 tens = ____ tens

   ____ − ____ = ____

3. 6 tens − 2 tens = ____ tens

   ____ − ____ = ____

4. 8 tens − 2 tens = ____ tens

   ____ − ____ = ____

5. 9 tens − 4 tens = ____ tens

   ____ − ____ = ____

6. 5 tens − 4 tens = ____ ten

   ____ − ____ = ____

7. 8 tens − 5 tens = ____ tens

   ____ − ____ = ____

8. 7 tens − 3 tens = ____ tens

   ____ − ____ = ____

Problem Solving • Reasoning

Using Data

Use the bar graph.

9. How many more cards than rocks does Jill have?

   ____ more cards

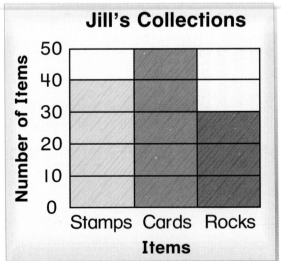

Jill's Collections

564 five hundred sixty-four

At Home Ask your child to use the bar graph to tell how many more stamps than rocks Jill has.

Standards
NS 2.6, MG 1.2
MR 1.2, 2.0

Subtract One-Digit Numbers

Learn About It

When subtracting with a two-digit number,
you need to subtract the ones first.

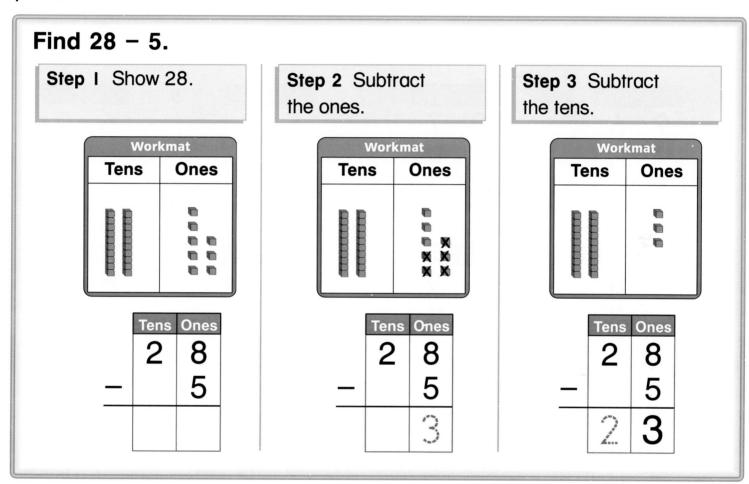

Find 28 − 5.

Guided Practice

Use Workmat 4 with ▬▬▬▬ and ▪. Subtract.

1.
Tens	Ones
9	8
−	6
9	2

Think: First, I subtract 8 − 6.

2.
Tens	Ones
5	9
−	2

Think: First, I subtract 9 − 2.

Explain Your Thinking How can you count back to find 59 − 2?

Independent Practice

Use Workmat 4 with ▭▭▭▭▭▭▭ and ▪.
Write each difference.

1.

Tens	Ones
3	8
−	6
3	*2*

2.

Tens	Ones
2	8
−	2

3.

Tens	Ones
6	9
−	5

4.

Tens	Ones
7	6
−	4

5.

Tens	Ones
9	6
−	5

6.

Tens	Ones
8	7
−	4

7.

Tens	Ones
5	8
−	3

8.

Tens	Ones
6	9
−	3

9.

Tens	Ones
4	5
−	3

10.

Tens	Ones
3	9
−	4

11.

Tens	Ones
8	7
−	1

12.

Tens	Ones
8	7
−	5

13.

Tens	Ones
2	6
−	3

14.

Tens	Ones
5	8
−	5

15.

Tens	Ones
5	6
−	2

16.

Tens	Ones
2	9
−	5

Problem Solving • Reasoning

Write About It

17. Class started at this time.
It lasted 2 hours.
What time did it end? Explain.

At Home Ask your child to pick a number between 1 and 8. Have him or her subtract it from 59.

Name _____

Subtract Two-Digit Numbers

Learn About It

You can subtract two-digit numbers.

Find 36 – 14.

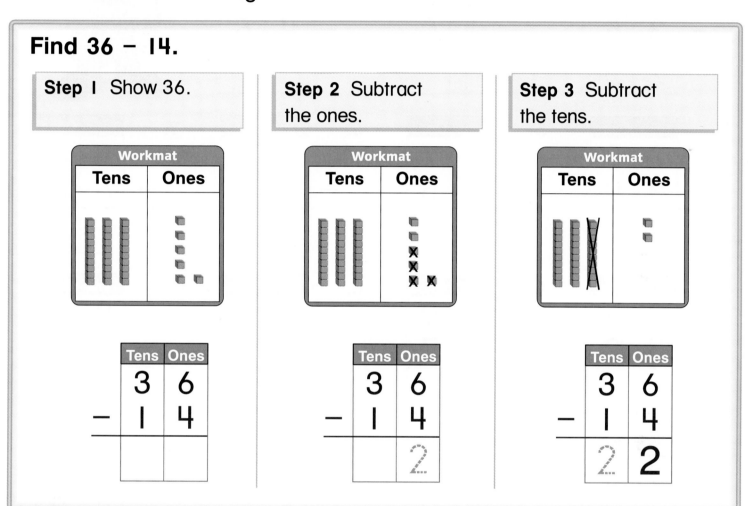

Step 1 Show 36.

Step 2 Subtract the ones.

Step 3 Subtract the tens.

Guided Practice

Use Workmat 4 with ⬛⬛⬛⬛⬛ and ▪. Subtract.

1.
Tens	Ones
8	9
− 5	6
3	3

Think: First, I subtract 9 – 6.

2.
Tens	Ones
7	8
− 3	6

Think: First, I subtract 8 – 6.

Explain Your Thinking How does knowing subtraction facts help you subtract two-digit numbers?

Independent Practice

Use Workmat 4 with ▭▭▭▭ and ▪.
Write each difference.

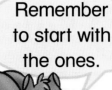

1.

Tens	Ones
5	8
− 3	5
2	3

2.

Tens	Ones
4	6
− 1	0

3.

Tens	Ones
8	9
− 4	6

4.

Tens	Ones
7	0
− 2	0

5.

Tens	Ones
6	7
− 2	5

6.

Tens	Ones
3	8
− 1	6

7.

Tens	Ones
9	5
− 6	3

8.

Tens	Ones
8	4
− 3	2

9.

Tens	Ones
5	9
− 4	7

10.

Tens	Ones
9	6
− 5	5

11.

Tens	Ones
8	7
− 3	0

12.

Tens	Ones
8	5
− 1	4

13.

Tens	Ones
9	7
− 4	2

14.

Tens	Ones
7	4
− 6	3

15.

Tens	Ones
6	8
− 4	2

Problem Solving•Reasoning

Using Vocabulary

16. Write a number sentence that shows two numbers with a difference of thirty.

_____ ◯ _____ = _____

At Home Ask your child to find 59 − 26 and explain the steps he or she used to solve it.

Different Ways to Subtract

Learn About It

There are different ways to subtract.

$$\begin{array}{r} 80 \\ -30 \\ \hline 50 \end{array}$$

I used mental math.
8 – 3

$$\begin{array}{r} 57 \\ -25 \\ \hline 32 \end{array}$$

I used paper and pencil.

$$\begin{array}{r} 65 \\ -20 \\ \hline 45 \end{array}$$

I used tens and ones blocks.

Guided Practice

Choose a way to subtract. Write each difference.

1.
Tens	Ones
5	6
–	2
5	4

2.
Tens	Ones
9	8
– 6	4

3.
Tens	Ones
9	0
– 6	0

4.
Tens	Ones
8	5
– 4	2

5.
$$\begin{array}{r} 96 \\ -23 \\ \hline \end{array}$$

6.
$$\begin{array}{r} 60 \\ -40 \\ \hline \end{array}$$

7.
$$\begin{array}{r} 78 \\ -3 \\ \hline \end{array}$$

8.
$$\begin{array}{r} 87 \\ -20 \\ \hline \end{array}$$

9.
$$\begin{array}{r} 56 \\ -5 \\ \hline \end{array}$$

Explain Your Thinking Which way did you choose to add for Exercise 9? Why?

Independent Practice

Choose a way to subtract.
Write each difference.

Ways to Subtract

Use tens and ones blocks.

Use mental math.

Use paper and pencil.

1.
Tens	Ones
5	6
– 2	5
3	

2.
Tens	Ones
7	0
– 4	0

3.
$$98 - 3$$

4.
$$76 - 24$$

5.
$$59 - 9$$

6.
$$67 - 35$$

7.
$$46 - 20$$

8.
$$80 - 30$$

9.
$$45 - 13$$

10.
$$97 - 63$$

11.
$$75 - 2$$

12.
$$50 - 10$$

13. $86 - 3 =$ _____

14. $58 - 2 =$ _____

15. $90 - 20 =$ _____

16. $50 - 10 =$ _____

17. $75 - 1 =$ _____

18. $60 - 40 =$ _____

Problem Solving • Reasoning

19. Peter had 30 marbles in one box and 40 in another. He gave 10 marbles to Max. How many marbles does he have now?

_____ marbles

Draw or write to explain.

At Home Ask your child to find 80 – 50 and explain how he or she got the answer.

Practice Two-Digit Subtraction

Learn About It

When you subtract two-digit numbers,
begin with the ones.

First I think
6 − 5.

Find 86 − 25.

Step 1 Subtract the ones.	**Step 2** Subtract the tens.
86 −25 ‾‾ 1	86 −25 ‾‾ 61

Guided Practice

Write each difference.

1. 47
   −35
   ‾‾‾
   12

2. 70
   −40
   ‾‾‾

3. 68
   − 5
   ‾‾‾

4. 89
   −45
   ‾‾‾

5. 35
   − 4
   ‾‾‾

6. 56
   − 3
   ‾‾‾

7. 87
   −13
   ‾‾‾

8. 94
   −52
   ‾‾‾

9. 75
   − 2
   ‾‾‾

10. 90
   −50
   ‾‾‾

11. 67 − 3 = ____

12. 80 − 50 = ____

13. 59 − 2 = ____

14. 50 − 40 = ____

15. 80 − 20 = ____

16. 73 − 3 = ____

Explain Your Thinking How did you get the answer
for Exercise 16?

Independent Practice

Use a paper clip and a pencil.
Spin the spinner.
Write the number in the box. Subtract.

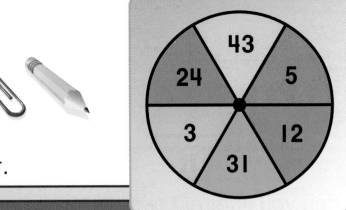

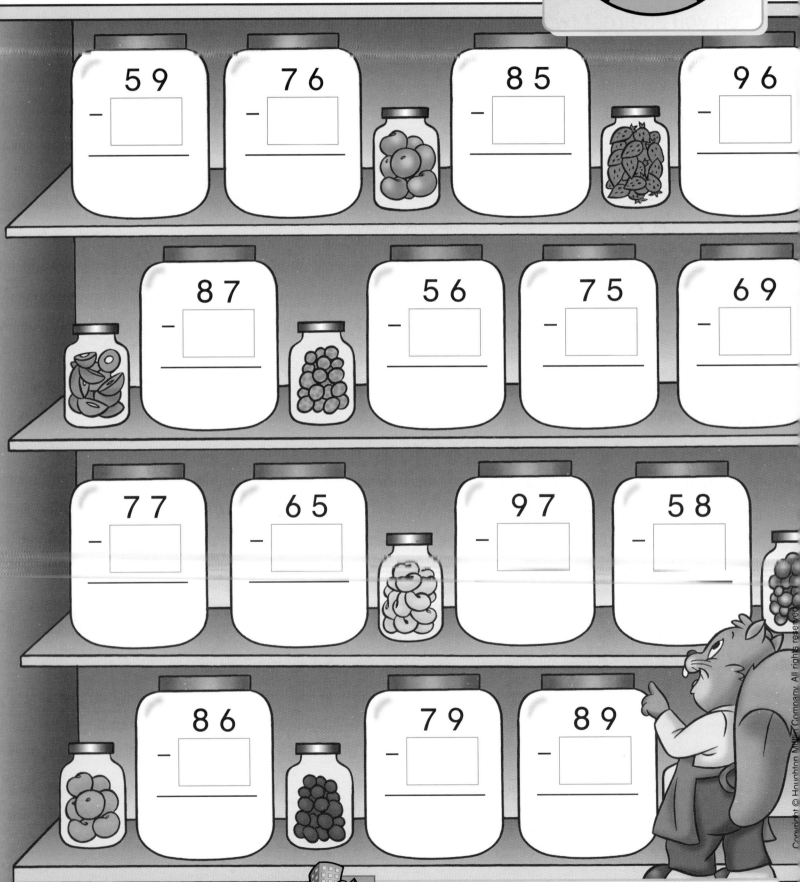

```
  59        76        85        96
-[    ]    -[    ]    -[    ]    -[    ]
_____    _____    _____    _____

  87        56        75        69
-[    ]    -[    ]    -[    ]    -[    ]
_____    _____    _____    _____

  77        65        97        58
-[    ]    -[    ]    -[    ]    -[    ]
_____    _____    _____    _____

  86        79        89
-[    ]    -[    ]    -[    ]
_____    _____    _____
```

At Home Write two-digit numbers with both digits 5 or greater. Have your child use the spinner to subtract the numbers spun from these numbers.

Quick ✓ Check

Check Your Understanding of Lessons 7–11

Write the numbers. Subtract.

1. 9 tens $- 4$ tens $= \underline{\quad}$ tens

$$\underline{\quad} - \underline{\quad} = \underline{\quad}$$

2. 8 tens $- 6$ tens $= \underline{\quad}$ tens

$$\underline{\quad} - \underline{\quad} = \underline{\quad}$$

Subtract.

3.
$$\begin{array}{r} 46 \\ -5 \\ \hline \end{array}$$

4.
$$\begin{array}{r} 23 \\ -2 \\ \hline \end{array}$$

5.
$$\begin{array}{r} 96 \\ -4 \\ \hline \end{array}$$

6.
$$\begin{array}{r} 53 \\ -3 \\ \hline \end{array}$$

7.
$$\begin{array}{r} 27 \\ -5 \\ \hline \end{array}$$

8.
$$\begin{array}{r} 90 \\ -70 \\ \hline \end{array}$$

9.
$$\begin{array}{r} 40 \\ -10 \\ \hline \end{array}$$

10.
$$\begin{array}{r} 75 \\ -60 \\ \hline \end{array}$$

11.
$$\begin{array}{r} 95 \\ -41 \\ \hline \end{array}$$

12.
$$\begin{array}{r} 69 \\ -40 \\ \hline \end{array}$$

13.
$$\begin{array}{r} 98 \\ -82 \\ \hline \end{array}$$

14.
$$\begin{array}{r} 79 \\ -67 \\ \hline \end{array}$$

15.
$$\begin{array}{r} 35 \\ -13 \\ \hline \end{array}$$

16.
$$\begin{array}{r} 48 \\ -28 \\ \hline \end{array}$$

17.
$$\begin{array}{r} 86 \\ -35 \\ \hline \end{array}$$

Complete the table.
Then use the table to solve.

18. Lance has 42 more red cars than blue cars. How many red and green cars does he have in all?

_____ in all

Cars	
Color	Number
Red	
Green	24
Blue	13

Name _____

Test Prep • Cumulative Review

Maintaining the Standards

Fill in the ○ for the correct answer. NH means Not Here.

1 What number comes between?

26, ___, 28

25   27   36   37
○   ○   ○   ○

2 What is the value of these coins?

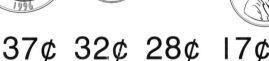

37¢   32¢   28¢   17¢
○   ○   ○   ○

3 Choose a sign to make the sentence true.

74 ○ 57

<   >   =   ¢
○   ○   ○   ○

4 Subtract.

$$\begin{array}{r} 98 \\ -65 \\ \hline \end{array}$$

23   33   34   NH
○   ○   ○   ○

5 Add.

$$\begin{array}{r} 56¢ \\ +23¢ \\ \hline \end{array}$$

33¢   69¢   78¢   NH
○   ○   ○   ○

6 Will wants to measure how long his dog is. Which tools can he use?

| centimeter ruler | scale | inch ruler |

Explain how you know.

_____

_____

_____

Safe Site

Internet Test Prep
Visit **www.eduplace.com/kids/mhm**
for more *Test Prep Practice*.

Standards
NS **2.2, 2.6,** AF **1.3**
SDP **1.0, 1.2**

LESSON 12 Algebra Readiness: Check Subtraction

Learn About It

You can add to check subtraction.

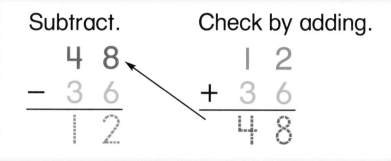

Subtract.

$$
\begin{array}{r}
4\ 8 \\
-\ 3\ 6 \\
\hline
1\ 2
\end{array}
$$

Check by adding.

$$
\begin{array}{r}
1\ 2 \\
+\ 3\ 6 \\
\hline
4\ 8
\end{array}
$$

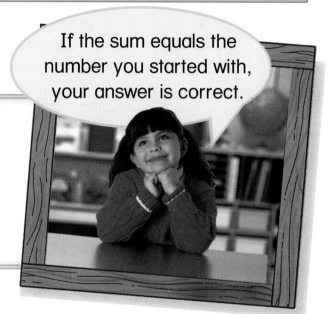

If the sum equals the number you started with, your answer is correct.

Guided Practice

Subtract. Check by adding.

1.
$$
\begin{array}{r}
5\ 7 \\
-2\ 4 \\
\hline
3\ 3
\end{array}
$$

$$
\begin{array}{r}
3\ 3 \\
+\ 2\ 4 \\
\hline
5\ 7
\end{array}
$$

Think: Which two numbers do I add to check?

2.
$$
\begin{array}{r}
9\ 8 \\
-6\ 4 \\
\hline
\end{array}
$$
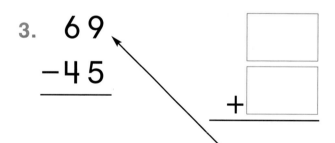

3.
$$
\begin{array}{r}
6\ 9 \\
-4\ 5 \\
\hline
\end{array}
$$

4.
$$
\begin{array}{r}
7\ 6 \\
-\ \ 3 \\
\hline
\end{array}
$$
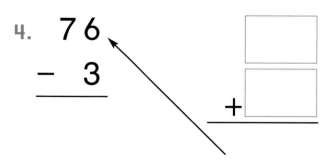

5.
$$
\begin{array}{r}
8\ 0 \\
-6\ 0 \\
\hline
\end{array}
$$
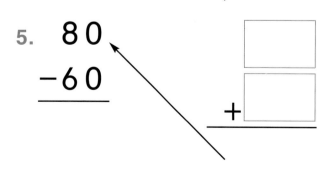

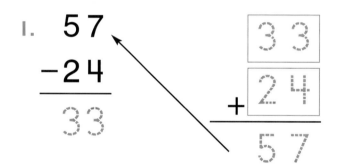

Explain Your Thinking How would you use addition to help you check 28 − 17 = 11?

Independent Practice

Subtract. Check by adding.

1.
```
  64
-  2
  62
```
```
  62
+  2
  64
```

2.
```
  40
- 10
```
```
  ☐
+ ☐
```

3.
```
  87
- 53
```
```
  ☐
+ ☐
```

4.
```
  59
- 26
```
```
  ☐
+ ☐
```

5.
```
  68
-  5
```
```
  ☐
+ ☐
```

6.
```
  97
- 51
```
```
  ☐
+ ☐
```

Problem Solving • Reasoning

Using Data

7. How many less red cars are there than green cars?

_____ less red cars

Model Cars	
Color	**Number**
Red	14
Blue	23
Green	35

8. **Write Your Own** Write a question about this table.

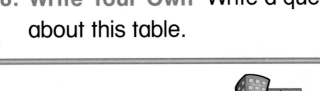

At Home Ask your child to find 75 − 23. Then have him or her check by adding.

LESSON 13 Add and Subtract Money

Learn About It

You add and subtract money the same
way you add and subtract two-digit numbers.

Read **58¢**
as **58 cents.**

Blueberries
58¢

Add.		Subtract.	
4 1 +5 6 *9 7*	4 1¢ +5 6¢ *9 7 ¢*	5 8 −2 3 *3 5*	5 8¢ −2 3¢ *3 5 ¢*

Guided Practice

Add or subtract.

1. 67¢
    −43¢
    24 ¢

2. 32¢
    +57¢
    _____ ¢

3. 47¢
    − 5¢
    _____ ¢

4. 68¢
    −21¢
    _____ ¢

5. 32¢
    + 6¢
    _____ ¢

6. 70¢
    +10¢
    _____ ¢

7. 89¢
    − 7¢
    _____ ¢

8. 40¢
    −10¢
    _____ ¢

9. 52¢
    +15¢
    _____ ¢

10. 67¢
    −34¢
    _____ ¢

11. 86¢
    −52¢
    _____ ¢

12. 30¢
    +50¢
    _____ ¢

13. 25¢
    + 4¢
    _____ ¢

14. 78¢
    −23¢
    _____ ¢

15. 43¢
    + 6¢
    _____ ¢

Explain Your Thinking How is adding dimes and
pennies the same as adding tens and ones?

Independent Practice

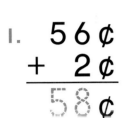

Remember to look at the signs.

Add or subtract.

1. 56¢
   + 2¢
   ——
   58¢

2. 94¢
   −20¢
   ——
   ¢

3. 85¢
   +13¢
   ——
   ¢

4. 76¢
   +10¢
   ——
   ¢

5. 65¢
   −23¢
   ——
   ¢

6. 78¢
   −45¢
   ——
   ¢

7. 30¢
   +30¢
   ——
   ¢

8. 58¢
   + 1¢
   ——
   ¢

9. 69¢
   −57¢
   ——
   ¢

10. 95¢
   −64¢
   ——
   ¢

11. 50¢
   +40¢
   ——
   ¢

12. 65¢
   + 3¢
   ——
   ¢

13. 65¢
   −21¢
   ——
   ¢

14. 59¢
   − 3¢
   ——
   ¢

15. 19¢
   +10¢
   ——
   ¢

16. 97¢
   −54¢
   ——
   ¢

17. 86¢
   +12¢
   ——
   ¢

18. 54¢
   + 4¢
   ——
   ¢

19. 68¢
   − 5¢
   ——
   ¢

20. 80¢
   −30¢
   ——
   ¢

Problem Solving • Reasoning

Write About It

21. Hassan has these coins.
    He wants to buy a card for 40¢.
    Does he have enough money?
    Explain.

At Home Ask your child to solve 58¢ − 3¢ and 25¢ + 63¢.

Count On, Count Back

Learn About It

You can count on to add or count back
to subtract on a hundred chart.

Find 28 + 4.

Start at 28.

Count on 4.

29, 30, 31, 32

$28 + 4 = \underline{32}$

Find 83 − 5.

Start at 83.

Count back 5.

82, 81, 80, 79, 78

$83 − 5 = \underline{78}$

1	2	3	4	5	6	7	8	9	10
11	12	13	14	15	16	17	18	19	20
21	22	23	24	25	26	27	28	29	30
31	32	33	34	35	36	37	38	39	40
41	42	43	44	45	46	47	48	49	50
51	52	53	54	55	56	57	58	59	60
61	62	63	64	65	66	67	68	69	70
71	72	73	74	75	76	77	78	79	80
81	82	83	84	85	86	87	88	89	90
91	92	93	94	95	96	97	98	99	100

Guided Practice

Use Workmat 5. Count on or count back.

1. $45 + 6 = \underline{51}$ 2. $71 − 4 = \underline{}$ 3. $57 + 5 = \underline{}$

Explain Your Thinking How can you use the
hundred chart to find 92 − 4?

Independent Practice

Remember to watch the signs.

Count on or count back.

1. $18 + 3 = \underline{21}$

2. $42 - 4 = \underline{}$

3. $59 + 2 = \underline{}$

4. $28 + 5 = \underline{}$

5. $39 - 3 = \underline{}$

6. $78 + 4 = \underline{}$

7. $81 - 1 = \underline{}$

8. $66 + 5 = \underline{}$ 9. $94 - 5 = \underline{}$ 10. $52 - 3 = \underline{}$

11. $52 - 4 = \underline{}$ 12. $75 + 6 = \underline{}$ 13. $83 - 4 = \underline{}$

Problem Solving • Reasoning

Number Sense

Do you add or subtract? Write **+** or **−**.

14. $28 \bigcirc 4 = 32$ 15. $54 \bigcirc 5 = 49$

16. $19 \bigcirc 2 = 21$ 17. $49 \bigcirc 3 = 52$

580 five hundred eighty

At Home Ask your child to use the hundred chart to find $81 - 3$.

Name

Problem Solving:
Multistep Problems

Standards
NS 2.6, MR 1.0, 1.1

Vicky collects leaves. She puts them in a scrapbook to share with her friends.

Vicky finds 4 green leaves and 6 red leaves. She pastes 5 leaves in her scrapbook. How many leaves are left?

First, you need to find the total.

☐ green

○ ☐ red
_____
☐ leaves in all

> **Think:**
> Add to find
> the total.

Next, you need to find the difference.

☐ leaves in all

○ ☐ leaves in scrapbook
_____
☐ leaves left

> **Think:**
> Subtract to find
> the difference.

Guided Practice

Solve. Decide which operation to use first.
Decide which operation to use next.

1 Mom finds 12 photos upstairs and 13 downstairs. 10 photos are of her. The rest are not. How many photos are not of her?

Think: How many photos are there in all?

15 are not of her

Draw or write to explain.

2 Les finds 18 photos. He gives 6 to his brother. Then he finds 7 more. How many photos does Les have now?

Think: Do I add or subtract first?

_____ photos now

3 Dad puts 41 photos in one album and 35 photos in another. 55 are old. The rest are new. How many photos are new?

Think: How many photos are in the albums?

_____ photos are new

At Home Create a multistep problem about something outdoors for your child to solve.

Name_____

Choose a Strategy

Strategies

Draw a Picture
Write a Number Sentence
Use Models to Act It Out

Solve.

① Leo has 17 large ash leaves and 12 small ash leaves. He puts 10 leaves in his scrapbook. How many leaves are left?

_____ leaves

Draw or write to explain.

ash

② Jo has 12 leaves. She has twice as many birch leaves as oak leaves. How many of each does she have?

_____ birch   _____ oak

birch

③ Ty finds 12 oak leaves. He throws 4 away. Then he finds 10 more. How many leaves does Ty have now?

_____ oak leaves

oak

④ Liz collects 26 maple leaves in spring and 31 in fall. She puts 42 in a bag. The rest she puts on a poster. How many leaves are on the poster?

_____ leaves

maple

Mixed Practice

Find each sum or difference.

1. $\begin{array}{r} 32 \\ +\ 7 \\ \hline \end{array}$
2. $\begin{array}{r} 40 \\ -20 \\ \hline \end{array}$
3. $\begin{array}{r} 28 \\ -\ 5 \\ \hline \end{array}$
4. $\begin{array}{r} 53 \\ +21 \\ \hline \end{array}$
5. $\begin{array}{r} 34 \\ +15 \\ \hline \end{array}$

6. $\begin{array}{r} 76 \\ -53 \\ \hline \end{array}$
7. $\begin{array}{r} 67 \\ -\ 6 \\ \hline \end{array}$
8. $\begin{array}{r} 45 \\ +33 \\ \hline \end{array}$
9. $\begin{array}{r} 97 \\ -25 \\ \hline \end{array}$
10. $\begin{array}{r} 52 \\ +34 \\ \hline \end{array}$

11. $\begin{array}{r} 59¢ \\ -\ 5¢ \\ \hline ¢ \end{array}$
12. $\begin{array}{r} 43¢ \\ +23¢ \\ \hline ¢ \end{array}$
13. $\begin{array}{r} 80¢ \\ -20¢ \\ \hline ¢ \end{array}$
14. $\begin{array}{r} 98¢ \\ -55¢ \\ \hline ¢ \end{array}$
15. $\begin{array}{r} 10¢ \\ +80¢ \\ \hline ¢ \end{array}$

16. $\begin{array}{r} 62¢ \\ +14¢ \\ \hline ¢ \end{array}$
17. $\begin{array}{r} 86¢ \\ -51¢ \\ \hline ¢ \end{array}$
18. $\begin{array}{r} 43¢ \\ +42¢ \\ \hline ¢ \end{array}$
19. $\begin{array}{r} 58¢ \\ -\ 5¢ \\ \hline ¢ \end{array}$
20. $\begin{array}{r} 31¢ \\ +\ 7¢ \\ \hline ¢ \end{array}$

Brain Teaser Missing Numbers

Find the missing numbers.

$\begin{array}{r} 3\square \\ +\ \square 5 \\ \hline 57 \end{array}$
$\begin{array}{r} 4\square \\ +\ \square 1 \\ \hline 84 \end{array}$
$\begin{array}{r} \square 9 \\ -\ 6\square \\ \hline 14 \end{array}$
$\begin{array}{r} \square 8 \\ -\ 5\square \\ \hline 27 \end{array}$

Safe Site

Internet Brain Teasers
Visit **www.eduplace.com/kids/mhm**
for more *Brain Teasers*.

Quick ✓ Check

Check Your Understanding of Lessons 12–15

Subtract. Check by adding.

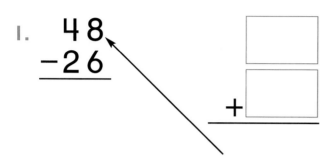

1. 48
   −26
   +☐ ☐

2. 99
   −35
   +☐ ☐

Add or subtract.

3. 52¢
   +35¢
   ____¢

4. 28¢
   −15¢
   ____¢

5. 96¢
   −30¢
   ____¢

6. 75¢
   − 3¢
   ____¢

7. 30¢
   +20¢
   ____¢

8. 45¢
   + 4¢
   ____¢

9. 82¢
   +17¢
   ____¢

10. 39¢
   −25¢
   ____¢

11. 67¢
   − 5¢
   ____¢

12. 78¢
   −67¢
   ____¢

Count on or count back. Use Workmat 5 if you want.

13. $46 + 5 =$ _____

14. $81 − 4 =$ _____

15. $58 + 3 =$ _____

---

16. Bo gets 6 baseball cards from his mom and 8 from his dad. He gives 5 of them to Ed. Now how many cards does Bo have?

   Draw or write to explain.

   _____ baseball cards

Name _____

Test Prep • Cumulative Review

Maintaining the Standards

Fill in the ○ for the correct answer.

1 Count by tens. What number comes next?

20, 30, 40, 50, ___

51   55   60   65
○   ○   ○   ○

2 What time is it?

- ○ 3:00
- ○ 3:30
- ○ 4:30
- ○ 6:30

3 What shape is this face?

- ○ circle
- ○ square
- ○ triangle
- ○ cube

4 Which sign will make this sentence true?

$5 + 4$ ○ $3 + 6$

>   <   =   ¢
○   ○   ○   ○

5 Count by twos. What number comes next?

58, 60, 62, 64, ___

65   66   67   74
○   ○   ○   ○

6 Liza had 52 stickers. She bought 27 more. Then she gave her friend 34. How many does she have now? **Explain** how you found out.

_____

_____

_____

Safe Site

Internet Test Prep
Visit **www.eduplace.com/kids/mhm**
for more *Test Prep Practice.*

Chapter Review

1. Write the **addends** for 6 + 4 = 10. ____ and ____

2. Find the **sum** of 40 + 50. ____

Write the numbers. Add or subtract.

3. 5 tens + 4 tens = ____ tens

____ + ____ = ____

4. 9 tens − 7 tens = ____ tens

____ − ____ = ____

Add or subtract.

5. $\begin{array}{r} 16 \\ +\ 2 \\ \hline \end{array}$

6. $\begin{array}{r} 84 \\ +\ 4 \\ \hline \end{array}$

7. $\begin{array}{r} 47 \\ -\ 7 \\ \hline \end{array}$

8. $\begin{array}{r} 55 \\ -\ 3 \\ \hline \end{array}$

9. $\begin{array}{r} 68 \\ -\ 6 \\ \hline \end{array}$

10. $\begin{array}{r} 79 \\ -26 \\ \hline \end{array}$

11. $\begin{array}{r} 23 \\ +52 \\ \hline \end{array}$

12. $\begin{array}{r} 84 \\ +14 \\ \hline \end{array}$

13. $\begin{array}{r} 56 \\ -24 \\ \hline \end{array}$

14. $\begin{array}{r} 47 \\ +20 \\ \hline \end{array}$

Subtract. Check by adding.

15. $\begin{array}{r} 85 \\ -21 \\ \hline \end{array}$

16. $\begin{array}{r} 56 \\ -43 \\ \hline \end{array}$

Add or subtract.

1. 40¢
   +40¢
   ____
    ¢

2. 56¢
   + 1¢
   ____
    ¢

3. 86¢
   −20¢
   ____
    ¢

4. 73¢
   +14¢
   ____
    ¢

5. 65¢
   −45¢
   ____
    ¢

6. 85¢
   − 3¢
   ____
    ¢

7. 32¢
   +35¢
   ____
    ¢

8. 95¢
   −72¢
   ____
    ¢

9. 58¢
   +30¢
   ____
    ¢

10. 43¢
   +50¢
   ____
    ¢

Count on or count back. Use Workmat 5 if you want.

11. 56 + 5 = ___   12. 72 − 3 = ___   13. 80 − 2 = ___

14. Jenna had 25¢. She found 13¢.
    She bought a ring for 15¢.
    How much money does
    she have now?

    ____ ¢

Draw or write to explain.

Complete the table.
Then use the table to solve.

15. There are 10 more children in
    Room 2 than in Room 1. Which of
    the 4 rooms has the most children?

    room ____

Children in Class	
Room	Number
1	27
2	
3	15
4	30

Chapter Test

Write the numbers. Add or subtract.

1. 3 tens $+ 6$ tens $=$ ____ tens

   ___ $+$ ___ $=$ ___

2. 8 tens $- 4$ tens $=$ ___ tens

   ___ $-$ ___ $=$ ___

3. 9 tens $- 5$ tens $=$ ____ tens

   ___ $-$ ___ $=$ ___

4. 5 tens $+ 3$ tens $=$ ___ tens

   ___ $+$ ___ $=$ ___

Add or subtract.

5.
$$\begin{array}{r} 23 \\ + 2 \\ \hline \end{array}$$

6.
$$\begin{array}{r} 58 \\ - 8 \\ \hline \end{array}$$

7.
$$\begin{array}{r} 46 \\ - 4 \\ \hline \end{array}$$

8.
$$\begin{array}{r} 74 \\ + 5 \\ \hline \end{array}$$

9.
$$\begin{array}{r} 63 \\ - 2 \\ \hline \end{array}$$

10.
$$\begin{array}{r} 68 \\ -35 \\ \hline \end{array}$$

11.
$$\begin{array}{r} 96 \\ -34 \\ \hline \end{array}$$

12.
$$\begin{array}{r} 41 \\ +38 \\ \hline \end{array}$$

13.
$$\begin{array}{r} 25 \\ +61 \\ \hline \end{array}$$

14.
$$\begin{array}{r} 60 \\ -50 \\ \hline \end{array}$$

15.
$$\begin{array}{r} 94¢ \\ + 5¢ \\ \hline ¢ \end{array}$$

16.
$$\begin{array}{r} 30¢ \\ +30¢ \\ \hline ¢ \end{array}$$

17.
$$\begin{array}{r} 87¢ \\ -75¢ \\ \hline ¢ \end{array}$$

18.
$$\begin{array}{r} 35¢ \\ +24¢ \\ \hline ¢ \end{array}$$

19.
$$\begin{array}{r} 68¢ \\ - 6¢ \\ \hline ¢ \end{array}$$

Count on or count back. Use Workmat 5 if you want.

20. $67 + 4 =$ ___

21. $52 - 5 =$ ___

22. $79 + 3 =$ ___

Subtract. Check by adding.

23.
```
   7 6
 - 4 5
```
$+\boxed{}\ \boxed{}$

24.
```
   8 7
 - 2 6
```
$+\boxed{}\ \boxed{}$

Complete the table.
Then use the table to solve.

25. There are 12 fewer tigers than lions.
How many tigers and bears are
there in all?

_____ in all

Zoo Animals	
Animal	**Number**
Tiger	
Lion	37
Bear	10

Write About It

1. Find the difference for 63 − 5.
Explain how you found your answer.

_____

_____

2. Find the sum for 48 + 3.
Explain how you found your answer.

_____

_____

_____

Name _____

Two-Digit Takedown

What You Need

counters

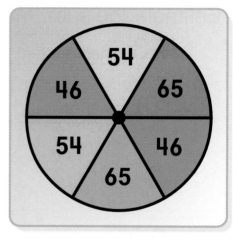

How to Play

1 Choose ● or ○ .

2 Spin both spinners. Then add or subtract.

3 If the answer is on one of the boxes below, place your counter on it.

4 Take turns until the game board below is filled. The player with the most counters on the board wins.

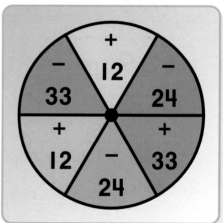

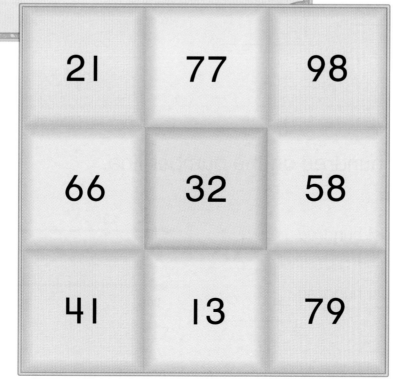

21	77	98
66	32	58
41	13	79

Name _____

Enrichment

Estimate Sums

Find the nearest ten on the number line.

Estimate the sum.

```
  4 3   nearest ten →      4 0
+ 3 1   nearest ten →   +  3 0
_____                   ____
                           7 0
```

1.
```
  2 2   nearest ten →
+ 3 9   nearest ten →   +
_____
```

2.
```
  4 4   nearest ten →
+ 5 1   nearest ten →   +
_____
```

Super Challenge

Find the nearest hundred on the number line.

Estimate the sum.

3.
```
  2 3 5   nearest hundred →
+ 3 8 6   nearest hundred →   +
_____
```

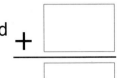

Picture Glossary

above

← above the boat

bar graph
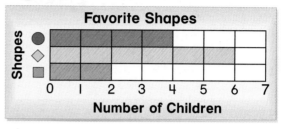

add

2 + 1 = 3

before
41, 42
41 is before 42.

addend
5 + 3 = 8
↑ ↑
addends

behind
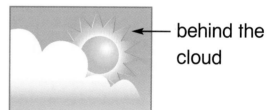
← behind the cloud

addition sentence
4 + 2 = 6

below
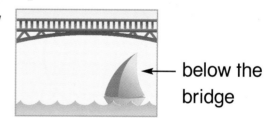
← below the bridge

after
37, **38**
38 is after 37.

between
54, **55**, 56
55 is between 54 and 56.

calendar

February						
S	M	T	W	T	F	S
1	2	3	4	5	6	7
8	9	10	11	12	13	14
15	16	17	18	19	20	21
22	23	24	25	26	27	28

cent

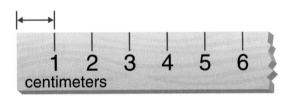

A penny is one cent or 1¢.

centimeter

circle

cone

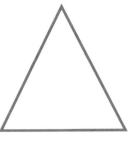

corner

where the sides meet

cube

cup

1 cup

cylinder

difference

$$7 - 2 = 5$$

difference

$$\begin{array}{r} 7 \\ -2 \\ \hline 5 \end{array}$$

dime

 or

10 cents or 10¢

down

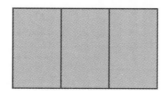

down the slide

equal parts

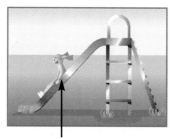

3 equal parts

equals sign

2 + 3 = 5

equals sign

estimate

about 10 fish

face

fact family

$6 + 4 = 10$ $10 - 4 = 6$

$4 + 6 = 10$ $10 - 6 = 4$

fraction

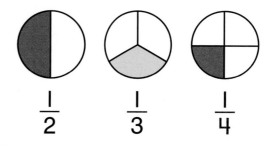

$\dfrac{1}{2}$ $\dfrac{1}{3}$ $\dfrac{1}{4}$

greater than

   32 > 24

32 is greater than 24

half-hour

30 minutes = one half-hour

heavier

heavier

hour

60 minutes = 1 hour

hour hand

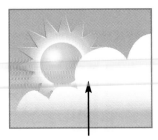

hour hand

in front

in front of the Sun

inch

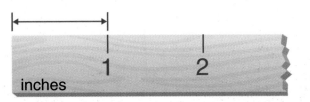

inches

kilogram

about 1 kilogram

left

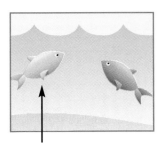

to the left of the orange fish

less than

26 < 37

26 is less than 37

lighter

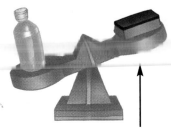

lighter

liter

1 liter

longer, longest

long

longer

longest

nickel

or

5 cents or 5¢

minus sign

$$6 - 3 = 3$$

↑

minus sign

number line

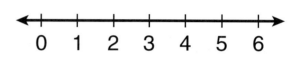

0 1 2 3 4 5 6

minute

about 1 minute

o'clock

 5:00

5 o'clock

minute hand

 — minute hand

one fourth

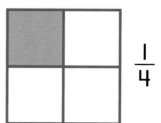

$\dfrac{1}{4}$

next to

next to the house

one half

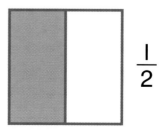

$\dfrac{1}{2}$

one hundred

100

one third

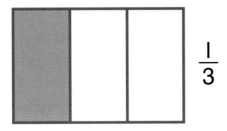

$\frac{1}{3}$

ones

3 ones

penny

 or

1 cent or 1¢

picture graph

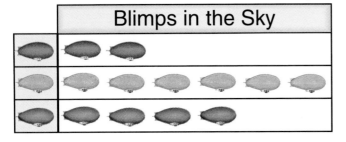

pint

1 pint = 2 cups

plus sign

2 + 2 = 4

plus sign

pound

about 1 pound

pyramid

quart

1 quart = 2 pint = 4 cups

quarter

 or

25 cents or 25¢

right

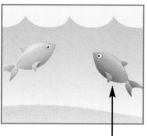

to the right of the yellow fish

rectangle

shorter, shortest

short

shorter

shortest

rectangular prism

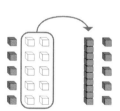

side

Sides are straight. This rectangle has 4 sides.

regroup

regroup 15 ones as 1 ten 5 ones

sphere

related fact

$$6 + 3 = 9$$

$$9 - 3 = 6$$

square

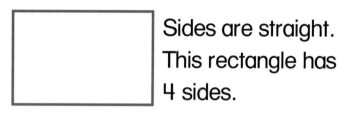

subtract

$$5 - 2 = 3$$

subtraction sentence

$$6 - 4 = 2$$

sum

$$4 + 1 = 5$$

$$\begin{array}{r} 4 \\ +1 \\ \hline 5 \end{array}$$

sum ⟶ 5

symmetry

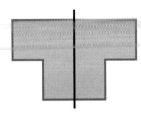

Shapes with symmetry have matching parts.

taller, tallest

tall   taller   tallest

tally marks

tens

3 tens

triangle

up

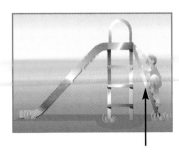

up the ladder

zero

6 flowers   **0** flowers

Whole

Part

Part

Tens	Ones

1	2	3	4	5	6	7	8	9	10
11	12	13	14	15	16	17	18	19	20
21	22	23	24	25	26	27	28	29	30
31	32	33	34	35	36	37	38	39	40
41	42	43	44	45	46	47	48	49	50
51	52	53	54	55	56	57	58	59	60
61	62	63	64	65	66	67	68	69	70
71	72	73	74	75	76	77	78	79	80
81	82	83	84	85	86	87	88	89	90
91	92	93	94	95	96	97	98	99	100

Hundred Chart

Credits

Excerpts from MATHEMATICS CONTENT STANDARDS FOR CALIFORNIA PUBLIC SCHOOLS, Copyright © December 1997 are reprinted by permission of the California Department of Education.

PHOTOGRAPHY

All photographs by Houghton Mifflin Company (HMCo.) unless otherwise noted.

All coin photography by Mike Tesi for HMCo. 21: *t.* Stan Osolinski/FPG International; *m.t.* The Image Bank; *m.b.* Third Coast Stock Source Inc./Index Stock Imagery; *b.* © Carolyn A. McKeone/Photo Researchers, Inc. 33–34: Carl Baker for HMCo. 35: Michael Fogden/Bruce Coleman Inc. 37: *t.* Index Stock Imagery; *m.t.* Gary Conner/PhotoEdit; *m.b.* Michael Newman/PhotoEdit; *b.* Michael Gaffney for HMCo. 38: Richard Hutchings for HMCo. 65: Joseph Schuyler/Stock Boston. 67: *t.* Siede Preis/PhotoDisc, Inc.; *m.t.* Corbis. 70: *l.* Carl Baker for HMCo. 71: *l.* Carl Baker for HMCo. 73: *l.* Carl Baker for HMCo. 77: *l.* Dwight R. Kuhn; *r.* Index Stock Imagery. 79: *t.* Dave Rusk/Index Stock Imagery; *m.t.* George McCarthy/Corbis; *m.b.* © Joyce Photographics/Photo Researchers, Inc.; *b.* Richard T. Nowitz/Corbis. 87: *t.* Carl Baker for HMCo. 103: *l.* Carl Baker for HMCo. 117: Richard Hutchings for HMCo. 119: Phillip James Corwin/Corbis. 121: *t.* Bob Jensen/Bruce Coleman Inc.; *m.t.* E.R. Degginger/Color-Pic, Inc.; *m.b.* Rod Planck/Dembinsky Photo Associates; *b.* Index Stock Imagery. 125: *t.* Carl Baker for HMCo.; *b.* Richard Hutchings for HMCo. 126: Carl Baker for HMCo. 127: Carl Baker for HMCo. 131: *l.* Larry West/FPG International; *r.* © Anthony Mercieca/Photo Researchers, Inc. 133: *t.* Index Stock Imagery; *m.t.* Jan Taylor/Bruce Coleman Inc.; *m.b.* Lynn M. Stone/Index Stock Imagery; *b.* Gary Meszaros/Dembinsky Photo Associates. 153: Mike Tesi for HMCo. 159: *t.l.* Lee Foster/Bruce Coleman Inc.; *t.m.* © Eunice Harris/Photo Researchers, Inc.; *t.r.* Bob Burch/Bruce Coleman Inc.; *b.l.* Lee Foster/Bruce Coleman Inc.; *b.m.* © Eunice Harris/Photo Researchers, Inc.; *b.r.* Bob Burch/Bruce Coleman Inc. 161: *t.* Richard Cummins/Corbis; *m.t.* NASA/Media Services; *m.b.* Patrick Ward/Corbis; *b.* Tony Stone Images. 171: *t.* Joe Sroka/Dembinsky Photo Associates; *b.* Douglas Peebles/Corbis. 173: *t.* Index Stock Imagery; *m.* Lawrence Migdale/Pix; *b.* C.C. Lockwood/Animals Animals/Earth Scenes. 178: Mike Tesi for HMCo. 181: Parker/Boon Productions for HMCo. 202: Alex Kerstitch/Bruce Coleman Inc. 211: *t.* Index Stock Imagery; *m.* Index Stock Imagery; *b.* Fred Bavendam/Peter Arnold, Inc. 217: © Andrew J. Martinez/Photo Researchers, Inc. 219: *t.* © Stephen J. Krasemann/Photo Researchers, Inc.; *m.t.* Marilyn Kazmers/Dembinsky Photo Associates; *m.b.* Eastcott/Momatiuk/Tony Stone Images; *b.* Susan Blanchet/Dembinsky Photo Associates. 231: *l.* Zig Leszczynski/Animals Animals/Earth Scenes; *r.* Tony Arruza/Corbis. 233: *t.* Michael Simpson/FPG International; *m.t.* E.R. Degginger/Color-Pic, Inc.; *m.b.* Alex Kerstitch/Bruce Coleman Inc.; *b.* Mark J. Thomas/Dembinsky Photo Associates. 252: Don Lowe/Tony Stone Images. 253: *t.* Richard Hutchings for HMCo.; *b.* Carl Baker for HMCo. 254: Carl Baker for HMCo. 255: Richard Hutchings for HMCo. 256: *l.* Lee Rentz/Bruce Coleman Inc.; *r.* Ernest Janes/Bruce Coleman Inc. 259: *l.* Carl Baker for HMCo.; *r.* Richard Hutchings for HMCo. 260: Carl Baker for HMCo. 263: *t.* Gunter Marx/Corbis; *m.* Robert Maier/Animals Animals/Earth Scenes; *b.* Frank Siteman/Color-Pic, Inc. 269: Carl Baker for HMCo. 271: *t.* Index Stock Imagery; *b.* Barry Runk/Grant Heilman Photography, Inc. 275: Richard Hutchings for HMCo. 279: Richard Hutchings for HMCo. 281: Richard Hutchings for HMCo. 283: *t.* Bill Lea/Dembinsky Photo Associates; *b.* Richard Nowitz/FPG International. 285: *t.* Grant Heilman/Index Stock Imagery; *m.t.* Index Stock Imagery; *m.b.* © Jean Claude Carton/Bruce Coleman Inc.; *b.* Frank Siteman/Stock Boston. 303: *r.* Parker/Boon Productions for HMCo.

304: Mike Tesi for HMCo. 311: *t.* Parker/Boon Productions for HMCo. 312: Mike Tesi for HMCo. 323: Mike Tesi for HMCo. 331: *m.t.* Michael Gaffney for HMCo. 333: Mike Tesi for HMCo. 335–336: Mike Tesi for HMCo. 359: Mike Tesi for HMCo. 365: *t.* Richard Cummins/Corbis; *b.* © NASA/Science Photo Library/Photo Researchers, Inc. 371: *r.* Dave Clegg for HMCo. 389: Parker/Boon Productions for HMCo. 399: *t.l.* C Squared Studios/PhotoDisc, Inc.; *t.m.* C Squared Studios/PhotoDisc, Inc. 401: *b.l.* PhotoDisc, Inc. 402: *bkgd.* PhotoLink/PhotoDisc, Inc. 419: Lawrence Migdale/Pix. 421: Michael Gaffney for HMCo. 431: *t.* Brenda Jorgens/Omni Photo Communications, Inc.; *b.* David A. Lee/Greenwood Creek Photos. 451: *t.l.* Michael Gaffney for HMCo. 465: *b.l.* Carl Baker for HMCo. 466: *t.m.l.* PhotoDisc, Inc. 469: *b.r.* PhotoDisc, Inc. 475: Richard Hutchings for HMCo. 490: *l. to r., t. to b.* Michael Gaffney for HMCo.; Michael Gaffney for HMCo.; PhotoDisc, Inc.; Michael Gaffney for HMCo.; PhotoDisc, Inc. 558: Myrleen Ferguson Cate/PhotoEdit/Picture Quest Network International/PNI. 559: *t.* Tony Freeman/PhotoEdit/PNI; *m.t.* Terry Why/Index Stock Imagery/Picture Quest Network International/PNI; *m.b.* Catherine Karnow/Corbis; *b.* Nicola Sutton/Life File/PhotoDisc, Inc. 575: Richard Hutchings for HMCo. 577: Richard Hutchings for HMCo. 583: *t.* Randall B. Henne/Dembinsky Photo Associates; *m.t.* Michael P. Gadomski/Dembinsky Photo Associates; *m.b.* Larry West/Bruce Coleman Inc.; *b.* Index Stock Imagery.

ILLUSTRATORS

vi-viii: Chuck Primeau. 1–10, 15, 17, 18, 20, 23, 25, 29–31, 33, 38: Karen Stormer Brooks. 47–56, 58, 60–61, 63–64, 66, 68, 72, 74, 75, 83–86: Martin Lemelman. 89–102, 104, 106–108, 111–112: Kathy Couri. 114: *frame* Kathy Couri, *puzzle* Robert Roper. 117–119, 123, 127–130, 132: Kathy Couri. 143–151, 154–158, 160: Doris Barrette. 164: Kathy Couri. 165–170, 175, 178, 180: Doris Barrette. 183–190, 194–195, 201–203: Janet Skiles. 204: *frame* Janet Skiles, *dot-to-dot* Robert Roper. 205–216, 218, 221, 223–224, 226–228, 230, 235–236, 238–240, 242: Janet Skiles. 243–253, 255–259, 261, 264, 267, 269, 271, 275–280, 283, 294: C.D. Hullinger. *clay toys* 297–303, 305–311, 313, 315, 318, 320, 326–327: Jack Graham. 330: Patrick Gnan. 334: *t.* Janet Skiles, *b.* Kathy Couri. 335–337: Jack Graham. 341–352, 354, 357: Russell Benfanti. 358: Kathy Couri. 361–362: Patrick Gnan. 364: Russell Benfanti. 367: Patrick Gnan. 380: Russell Benfanti. 385: Patrick Gnan. 387: Russell Benfanti. 390: Patrick Gnan. 391–398, 400, 407, 411, 418, 420, 422, 425–426, 435: Rusty Fletcher. 443–453, Terry Kovalcik. 455, 457: Batelman Illustration. 458: Terry Kovalcik. 460: *t.* Terry Kovalcik; *bracelets* Scott Fray. 462–463, 465–471: Terry Kovalcik. 472, 474 Terry Kovalcik. 475: Bryan Ballinger. 476: *t.* Margo De Paulis; *m.* Bryan Ballinger. 477: *t.* Bryan Ballinger; *b.* Terry Kovalcik. 478, 482: Terry Kovalcik. 483: *t.* Bryan Ballinger; *b.* Terry Kovalcik. 485: *m.l.* Terry Kovalcik; *m.r.* Bryan Ballinger. 486: *m.t.* Bryan Ballinger; *b.* Terry Kovalcik. 488: *t., m.t.* Bryan Ballinger; *m.* Terry Kovalcik; *b.* Batelman Illustration. 489: Batelman Illustration. 491–500, 502, 505–507, 511, 516, 518, 523–524: Michele Noiset. 532: C.D. Hullinger. 533, 535: Michele Noiset. 539–547, 552, 554, 556, 563, 568, 570, 572, 575–576, 578–580: Cardona Studio. 593: Russell Benfanti. 594: *m.l.* Batelman Illustration; *b.l., t.r.* Patrick Gnan; *m.r.* Bryan Ballinger; *b.r.* Patrick Gnan. 595: *t.l.* Russell Benfanti; *b.l.* Janet Skiles; *t.r.* Patrick Gnan. 596: *t.r.* Terry Kovalcik; *m.r.* Russell Benfanti; *b.r.* Batelman Illustration; *t.l.* Terry Kovalcik; *m.t.r.* Russel Benfanti; *b.r.* Bryan Ballinger. 597: *t.l.* Terry Kovalcik; *m.l.* Michele Noiset; *b.l.* Terry Kovalcik. 598: *t.l.* Janet Skiles; *b.l.* Doris Barrette; *t.r.* Bryan Ballinger; *m.r.* Terry Kovalcik; *m.b.r.* Patrick Gnan; *b.r.* Bryan Ballinger. 599: *m.l.* Patrick Gnan; *t.r.* Russell Benfanti; *m.b.r.* Patrick Gnan. 600: *t.l.* Martin Lemelman; *b.l., m.b.r.* Russell Benfanti; *b.r.* Karen Stormer Brooks.